MICAH AND ISAIAH:
A FORM AND TRADITION HISTORICAL COMPARISON

SOCIETY
OF BIBLICAL
LITERATURE

DISSERTATION SERIES

J. J. M. Roberts, Old Testament Editor
Charles Talbert, New Testament Editor

Number 85

MICAH AND ISAIAH:
A FORM AND TRADITION HISTORICAL COMPARISON

by
Gary Stansell

Gary Stansell

MICAH AND ISAIAH:
A Form and Tradition
Historical Comparison

Scholars Press
Atlanta, Georgia

BS
1615.2
.S73
1988

MICAH AND ISAIAH:
A Form and Tradition Historical Comparison

Gary Stansell

Dr.theol., 1981
Ruprecht-Karl-Universität

Advisor:
Hans Walter Wolff

Library of Congress Cataloging-in-Publication Data

Stansell, Gary.
Micah and Isaiah: a form and tradition historical comparison.

(Dissertation series / Society of Biblical
Literature ; no. 85)
Thesis (Dr.theol.)–Ruprecht-Karl-Universität, 1981.
Bibliography: p.
1. Bible. O.T. Micah–Criticism, interpretation.
etc. 2. Bible. O.T. Isaiah–Criticism, interpre-
tation, etc. I. title. II. Series: Dissertation
series (Society of Biblical Literature); no. 85.
BS1615.2.S73 1988   224'.106   86-1936
ISBN 0-89130-962-4
ISBN 0-89130-963-2 (pbk.)

Printed in the United States of America

Contents

Acknowledgments

This study of Micah and Isaiah was originally a dissertation presented to the Theological Faculty of Ruprecht-Karl-Universität, Heidelberg, Germany, in 1981. I am deeply indebted to a number of people and institutions for their interest in and support of this research project. The Lutheran World Federation and the Deutscher Akademischer Austauschdienst provided generous financial help for my studies in Heidelberg. To Professor Dr. Jörg Jeremias I owe much thanks for general advice and friendship; to Professor Rolf Rendtorff I am indebted for serving as the Korreferent of the dissertation. Above all, I express my deepest appreciation and respect to my *Doktorvater*, Professor D. Hans Walter Wolff, D.D., who proposed the book of Micah for my dissertation, and who accompanied my work with constant interest, encouragement, and friendship.

To the former editor of the SBL Dissertation Series, Professor Robert R. Wilson, and to the anonymous readers who evaluated the manuscript for publication, I express my sincere gratitude.

Finally, I dedicate this book to my wife Ginny, and to our daughter Amanda, whose patience and constancy flagged never.

Introduction

A. THE PROBLEM

What is the relationship between the prophecy of Micah of Moresheth and his contemporary Isaiah? At least since the appearance of B. Stade's[1] series of now classic articles on Micah, Old Testament critics have noted, in one connection or another, that there is some kind of theological kinship between Micah and Isaiah. Thus, for example, H. Schmidt[2] regarded Micah as a "Schüler" of Isaiah, while others have suggested that they were "personally acquainted" in view of the "kinship" of their message.[3] The words left to us in their name have been characterized as being in "fundamental agreement"[4] and "complete harmony."[5] O. Procksch[6] thought of Micah as Isaiah's "successor," one who stood in the shadow of his great theological predecessor. Indeed, Micah is said to have been "influenced"[7] by Isaiah and very likely knew of the words Isaiah spoke or

---

[1] B. Stade, "Bemerkungen über das Buch Micha," *ZAW* 1 (1881) 161–72; cf. especially 164, where Stade argues that only Micah 1–3 are authentic and calls attention to comparable passages in Isaiah to support his case. Stade's other articles on Micah are "Weitere Bemerkungen zu Micha 4 und 5," *ZAW* 3 (1883) 1–16; "Micha 2,4," *ZAW* 8 (1888) 122f.; "Micha 1,2–4 und 7:7–20, ein Psalm," *ZAW* 23 (1903) 163–71.

[2] H. Schmidt, *Die grossen Propheten,* SAT 2, 2 (²1923) 131; W. Caspari, *Die israelitischen Propheten* (1914) 74, supposed that Micah was included among those disciples of Isaiah referred to in Isa 8:16; further, see the more recent comments of J. T. Willis, "The Meaning and Authenticity of Mic 5:9–14," *ZAW* 81 (1969) 367.

[3] Cf. H. Ewald, *Die Propheten des Alten Bundes* 1 (²1867) 324: "Mikha gibt sich ganz als ein jungerer zeit- und landesgenossen Jesajas . . . der inhalt ist sehr ähnlich, auch in den einzelnen vorstellungen, gedanken, redensarten und vortragsweise ist bedeutende verwandtschaft. . . ." Cf. also A. Weiser, *Einleitung in das AT* (⁵1963) 157; A. Weiser, *Das Buch der zwölf Kleinen Propheten* 1, ATD 24 (⁵1967) 230; G. W. Anderson, *A Critical Introduction to the OT* (1959) 157: ". . . close similarities make it not altogether fanciful that there was some link between Micah and Isaiah or the Isaianic circle."

[4] G. B. Gray, *The Book of Isaiah 1–27,* ICC (1912) lxix.

[5] R. Wolfe, "Micah," IB 6 (1956) 898. Cf. J. Smith, *A Critical and Exegetical Commentary on the Books of Micah, Zephaniah, and Nahum,* ICC (1911) 10.

[6] O. Procksch, *Theologie des Alten Testaments* (1950) 207.

[7] O. Eissfeldt, *The Old Testament: An Introduction* (1965) 407. Cf. O. Procksch, *Jesaia* 1, KAT 9 (1930) 17. Procksch also saw an influence of Northern Israelite thinking upon Micah, especially as it is found in the Elohist source of the Pentateuch (*Theologie des AT,* 210; also his *Geschichtsbetrachtung und geschichtliche Überlieferung bei den vorexilischen*

wrote.[8] On the other hand, in a recent monograph on Micah, W. Beyerlin[9] suggests that any relationship between Micah and Isaiah would stem not from any dependence of one upon the other, but rather from their dependence upon the same *cultic* tradition.

Scholars have also called attention to remarkable similarities in specific texts in the respective books. C. F. Keil thought that the two prophets agree in their portrayal of the nation's leaders and the social corruption of their time; that the messianic hope found in each book is very similar. He listed several texts which are supposed to provide evidence for this, although he offers no discussion or comparison of them.[10] Stade[11] too, listed passages in each book which he considered representative of the similarities in the prophecy of Micah and Isaiah. More recently, A. Weiser[12] has also pointed to similar texts in each book: Mic 1:10–16 and Isa 10:27bff.; Mic 2:1–5 and Isa 5:8ff.; Mic 5:9–14 and Isa 2:6ff., but no comparison of these texts is undertaken to demonstrate what he means by "Verwandtschaft."[13] In addition to these texts, it is generally recognized that Mic 5:1–5 and Isa 7:14; 9:1ff. and 11:1ff. exhibit certain similarities,[14] although a number of scholars deny their authenticity.[15] G. Fohrer thinks the similarities between Mic 1:10–16 and Isa 10:27b–32; Mic 2:1–3 and Isa 5:8–10 sufficient to conclude that Isaiah directly influenced Micah.[16]

Propheten [1902], 158ff.). This hypothesis is questionable, however, and has not found a positive echo in more recent studies. Moreover, it is based primarily on Mic 6:1ff., whose authenticity is very problematic. Cf. J. Hempel, *Althebräische Literatur* (1930) 137; C. F. Keil, *Biblischer Commentar über die zwölf kleinen Propheten* (³1888) 305, concludes that each influenced the other. On the other hand, some critics consider Micah's proclamation more closely related to Amos or Hosea. W. Nowack, *Die kleinen Propheten,* HK (³1922) 189, supposed that there is an especially close affinity between the prophecy of Amos and Micah. In addition, see K. Marti, *Das Dodekapropheton,* KHC (1904) 261, who thought Micah was most like Amos; also J. Lindblom, *Micha literarisch untersucht* (1929) 37, 138, 146; and Th. H. Robinson, *Die Zwölf Kleinen Propheten,* HAT 1, 12 (³1964) 128. P. J. King, in his article on Micah in the *Jerome Bible Commentary* (1968) 283, calls Micah "Amos redivivus."

[8] G. Fohrer, *Introduction to the Old Testament* (1968) 444.

[9] W. Beyerlin, *Die Kulttraditionen Israels in der Verkündigung des Propheten Micha,* FRLANT 72 (1959) 9f.

[10] C. F. Keil, *Die zwölf kleinen Propheten,* 305: Mic 2:11 and Isa 28:7; 3:5–7 and 29:9–12; 3:12 and 32:13f.; 4:1–5 and 2:2–5; 5:2–4 and 7:14 and 9:5; see also 308.

[11] Cf. his more extensive listing in "Bemerkungen," 164.

[13] Weiser, *Einleitung,* 223; ATD 1, 24 (⁵1967) 230.

[13] Also cf. the lists of passages in J. Lippl, J. Theiss, H. Junker, *Die Zwölf Kleinen Propheten,* HS VIII, 1 (1937) 118, and J. Fichtner, *Obadja, Jona, Micha* (1957) 37.

[14] Cf. the commentaries.

[15] Concerning the Micah texts in chaps. 4–7, see below, p. 7.

[16] Fohrer, *Introduction,* 444.

Significant contrasts between Micah and Isaiah have not been overlooked. In the first place, Micah is hardly directly concerned with the court and with politics, whereas Isaiah frequently speaks out against Israel's political dealings with foreign nations and directly addresses the king. Micah was from Moresheth, a town in the Shephelah, while Isaiah apparently stemmed from aristocratic, courtly circles in Jerusalem![17] The sayings of Micah which have been preserved are few in number in comparison with the numerous, rich, and varied prophecies of Isaiah.

It is hardly surprising that similarities between Micah and Isaiah occur, for they were of course contemporaries![18] both preached in Judah and Jerusalem![19] witnessing many of the same events of the last part of the 8th century B.C., and reacting to the same problems of the people of their day. But no thorough comparison of Micah and Isaiah has attempted to critically examine the relationship between their proclamation as found in their prophetic utterances. This suggests that a study of Micah in comparison with Isaiah could serve more sharply to define the points of similarity and difference between these two 8th century prophets.[20]

---

[17] E.g., B. Duhm, *Das Buch Jesaia* (⁵1968) 15, and G. von Rad, *Old Testament Theology* 2 (1965) 147.

[18] Although the date Isaiah began his prophetic activity is disputed (it is yet debated whether Isa 6:1 refers to the beginning of his ministry, during "the year King Uzziah died," or whether this refers to a second phase of his activity; see the bibliography cited below, chap. 1, notes 92 and 94), he was obviously active before Micah, whose earliest words (1:2ff.) are to be dated just before Samaria's fall (722/21 thus e.g., B. Duhm, *Israels Propheten* [²1922], 101f.; Robinson; Eissfeldt, *Introduction,* 407). The superscription in Mic 1:1 locates the prophet in the time span of the reigns of Jotham, Ahaz, and Hezekiah, but there is no evidence that he was at work during the time of Jotham (thus Weiser). If in fact Hezekiah ascended the throne in the year 725 (cf. 2 Kgs 18:1 and A. Jepsen, R. Hanhart, *Untersuchungen zur israelitisch-jüdischen Chronologie,* BZAW 88 [1964] 42), Micah probably would have been active only during his reign (cf. Jer 26:18, which quotes Mic 3:12 and assigns these words to the time of Hezekiah). On the other hand, 2 Kgs 18:13 appears to date the beginning of Hezekiah's reign in 715 (cf. W. F. Albright, "The Chronology of the Divided Monarchy of Israel," *BASOR* 100 [1945] 22); Ahaz would have been king when Micah first became active. In any case, it seems possible that Micah was active until around 701, if for example 3:9-12 belongs to the events of this time. Some scholars think his prophetic work covered a much shorter span of time: Marti, 705-701; Smith, around 701; J. Marsh (*Amos and Micah,* Torch Bible Commentaries [⁴1967]) 712-701; Rudolph (*Micha-Nahum-Habakuk-Zephanja,* KAT 13, 3 [1975] 21), before 722-701; Mays (*Micah: A Commentary,* OTL [1976] 15), the months preceding Sennacherib's invasion in 701.

[19] Micah, too, prophesied in Jerusalem, as is apparent from the addressees named in some of his sayings (cf. 3:1, 9).

[20] The validity of such an investigation was noted by Lindblom in his commentary of 1929 (*Micha literarisch untersucht,* 166): "Lohnend wäre es, sein [Michas] Verhältnis zu dem grossen Zeitgenossen Jesaja zu untersuchen.").

To be sure, the nature of the relationship of one prophet to another has not gone without attention. In 1930, K. Gross'[21] dissertation investigated the connection of Jeremiah's prophecy with that of Hosea. Deutero-Isaiah has been compared with Trito-Isaiah by K. Elliger,[22] and the linguistic and theological relationship of Jeremiah and Ezekiel has been investigated in the Baseler dissertation of J. W. Miller.[23] R. Fey's[24] study of Amos and Isaiah tests K. Budde's hypothesis which claimed that Isaiah not only knew Amos' prophetic sayings, but consciously used them, adapted them, and applied them in his proclamation. The most recent endeavor to examine the relationship of one prophet to another, D. Baltzer's *Ezekiel und Deuterojesaja: Berührungen in der Heilserwartungen der beiden grossen Exilspropheten,* has shown that, although certain differences are to be noted, there are nevertheless substantial points of agreement in the prophecies of salvation in Ezekiel and Deutero-Isaiah.[25]

B. METHODOLOGICAL CONSIDERATIONS

Did Micah know Isaiah? Was he influenced by his great contemporary? As interesting as such questions are, they are inadequate as the starting point of any investigation which proposes to compare one with the other. Such categories as "teacher-disciple," "predecessor-successor," "agreement," "kinship," "influence" do not take us far in describing the way their individual proclamation is related.[26] These catchwords are much too imprecise and in the end serve only to confuse the issues in need of detailed analysis. Moreover, they tend to lay stress upon agreement and similarity at the exclusion of difference and contrast.

---

[21] K. Gross, *Die literarische Verwandtschaft Jeremias mit Hosea* (Diss. Berlin, 1930) 33: "Jeremia hat die Schrift Hoseas mit Eifer und Andacht gelesen . . ., das seine Sprache und Ausdrucksweise besonders in der ersten Zeit seines Wirkens, unter ihren Einfluss stand, und sich von ihr reich hat befruchten lassen."

[22] K. Elliger, *Deuterojesaja in seinem Verhältnis zu Tritojesaja,* BWANT 4, 11 (1933).

[23] J. W. Miller, *Das Verhältnis Jeremia und Ezekiel sprachlich und theologisch Untersucht* (1955). Miller asserts that Ezekiel read Baruch's scroll; that it is very likely that Ezekiel knew and studied a copy of the salvation oracles in Jer 30;31 (cf. 118f.). He considers the similarity in their preaching not due to coincidence, for Ezekiel consciously continued the work of his predecessor. Cf. also W. Zimmerli, *Ezekiel,* BK XIII/1, in his introduction, par. 6, no. 3, concerning Ezekiel's relationship to Israelite traditions and earlier prophecy. In 1879 F. Kostlin undertook a comparison of Jeremiah's prophecy with Isaiah's (*Jesaia und Jeremia*), but his work is most superficial. He characterizes Isaiah as one who, in all he did, went from success to success, whereas Jeremiah was unsuccessful from start to finish; see 173ff.

[24] R. Fey, *Amos und Jesaja,* WMANT 12 (1963). Fey concludes (147): Isaiah knew at least a third of the Amos material that has come down to us, although he never takes over Amos' words without making his own changes. For a critique of Fey's conclusions, see H. W. Wolff, *Amos' geistige Heimat,* WMANT 18 (1964) 22, note 1, and esp. 55–58.

[25] BZAW 121 (1971) 179. See the critical statement regarding Baltzer's conclusions in relation to the interpretation of individual texts made by J. M. Schmidt, "Probleme der Prophetenforschung," *VuF* 17 (1972) 69.

[26] Cf. Fey, *Amos und Jesaja,* 19.

The question of the relationship of Micah's prophecy to Isaiah's needs to be set in a much broader context, one which allows the largest possible selection of texts. But how should a selection of texts be ordered, and what organization-principle might best provide the over-arching scheme to guide a meaningful comparison? The word "comparison" implies that attention is to be focused upon similarities *and* differences. Yet these are broad categories which, in terms of this discussion, must in the course of the investigation be carefully defined. Precisely how might one claim that Micah is in "close agreement with" or "quite unlike Isaiah"? One possibility would be to arrange the sayings of Micah in chronological order, so that his reaction to the historical events of his time would be apparent, and then proceed to Isaiah and compare the ways in which each addressed a particular historical hour in the history of his people. Yet this would be a manifestly questionable procedure,[27] even if it were possible to date accurately Micah's sayings. Or, one might compare Micah's linguistic usage and style with that of Isaiah in order to establish what, if any, characteristic expressions they shared or borrowed from each other in proclaiming their message.[28] This, too, would be a limited methodology, for it would leave too many important issues uninvestigated and its end result would be unsatisfactory. Moreover, since Micah and Isaiah were contemporaries, the question of *literary* dependence of one upon the other does not bear any significance.[29]

Recent Old Testament scholarship has clearly demonstrated that the Israelite prophets were rooted deeply in the ancient traditions of their people, and that their messages were informed by their use, adaptation and reinterpretation of tradition.[30] It would seem eminently clear, then, that any critical comparison of Micah with Isaiah would need to take into account the question of their roots in tradition. It has been established, for example, that Isaiah "moves within a

[27] Cf. G. von Rad, *Old Testament Theology* 2 (1965) 145.

[28] As does J. W. Miller, *Das Verhältnis Jeremia und Ezekiel,* part II.

[29] Cf. the studies of Gross (see note 21, above) and Fey (see note 24, above) who proceed in this way.

[30] Von Rad, *OTT* 2, 328. The importance and legitimacy of the inquiry into the prophets' relationship to tradition has been repeatedly emphasized by Old Testament scholars. See, for example, H. W. Wolff's formulation: ". . . so muss notwendig weitergefragt werden nach der früheren Bezeugung Jahwes in Israel und den Verhältnis der Propheten zu diesen altisraelitischen Traditionen," in "Hauptprobleme alttestamentlicher Prophetie," *Ges. St.,* ThB 22 (²1973) 217. To be sure, there are voices which caution against the concern for the role played by tradition in the prophets (e.g., G. Fohrer, "Remarks on Modern Interpretation of the Prophets," *JBL* 80 [1961] 313ff.). As regards Isaiah, J. Vollmer (*Geschichtliche Rückbliche und Motive in der Prophetie des Amos, Hosea und Jesaja,* BZAW 119 [1971] 196), concludes that Isaiah makes no significant or functional use of Israel's ancient traditions. But see W. Zimmerli, "Prophetic Proclamation and Reinterpretation," in *Tradition and Theology in the Old Testament,* ed. Douglas Knight (1977) 82ff., who emphasizes that Isaiah appropriates but also *transforms* them. For a review and assessment of prophecy's relation to tradition, see also R. E. Clements, *Prophecy and Tradition* (1975).

different sphere of tradition than does Hosea."[31] But what can be said about
Micah in comparison with Isaiah? Are there spheres of tradition which they both
share? If so, does their appropriation of certain traditions function in similar or
in different ways? How might the traditions common to both be used, adapted,
and reinterpreted in their respective messages? Or, does Micah make use of a
tradition which has no counterpart at all in Isaiah? Such questions as these
suggest that an analysis of the traditional material in these two 8th century
contemporaries would provide a sound basis for drawing lines of comparison
between them.

But it is obvious that a comparison of traditions does not exhaust all the
possibilities of such a comparative study. There are also broader topics which we
may simply designate as "themes" and within those themes, smaller "motifs"
which could afford further critical access to a comparison and contrast of Micah
with Isaiah. To briefly illustrate what is meant by the terms "tradition," "theme,"
and "motif," we may with respect to Micah point to the presence of the
theophany *tradition* (1:2ff.), the *theme* of social critique (e.g., 3:1ff.), or the
recurrent *motif* "my people" (2:8, 9; 3:2, 5).

But in order to give attention to the traditions, themes, and motifs in Micah
and Isaiah in an appropriately critical manner, it will also be necessary to ask
form critical questions of all texts that are to be analyzed. Are there prophetic
forms and form-elements which are shared by Micah and Isaiah, but which
function in different ways? Where there are significant similarities, is there
dependence upon each other, or rather upon a pre-existing form? Is there a
speech form or forms which, say, are unique to Micah? It should be emphasized
here, however, that form critical questions are to be executed within the framework of the broader pursuit of issues relating to tradition and theme; that is, no
separate chapter or unit deals only with form critical questions. This procedure
will lend a unity to the work and help avoid treating the same texts twice, once
under form critical aspects and then again under tradition historical and
thematic concerns.

The foregoing considerations suggest that a form and tradition historical
comparison of Micah and Isaiah would best enable us to address the question
of the relationship between the two. Here it should be made clear that our
interest focuses primarily on Micah, and that the purpose of drawing on the
Isaian material is to help answer the comparative questions of form, tradition,
and theme. Ultimately, it is the goal of the study to clarify the following
questions: which elements in the Micah tradition are commonly shared with
Isaiah, and which are to be understood as unique or characteristic? Was he
nothing more than a follower of Isaiah, one who stood in his shadow, bringing
essentially the same message to Jerusalem and Judah as did his greater contemporary? Or, does he rather stand to some degree alone, perhaps even saying, at
points, precisely the opposite of Isaiah?

[31] Zimmerli, "Prophetic Proclamation," 82.

C. THE TEXTS TO BE STUDIED

Which texts in Micah should constitute the basis for our study? The question is not so simple, for considerable disagreement continues to be found concerning the authenticity of chaps. 4–7. There is no debate over the late psalm in 7:8–20, nor is there much question regarding 4:1–5, 6–8, 11–13; 5:6–8,[32] but the remaining passages are occasionally defended as possibly from Micah himself. An indication of the continued lack of consensus may be seen in two recent commentaries by W. Rudolph and J. Mays. Rudolph considers only the following texts in the book to be from a later hand: 1:5bβ 7aβ; 4:1–4; 4:5; 5:4b, 5a; 5:6–8; 6:9aβ; 7:8–20.[33] Mays informs his readers that he began his study on the assumption (following A. Weiser, ATD 1, 24 ⁵1967) that only 2:12f.; 4:1–5, the final form of 4:6–5:1 (containing some reworked fragments); 5:7–9; 7:8–20 were later material.[34] Mays notes, however, that his work led him to the conclusion that B. Stade's position, voiced in 1881,[35] is correct: only chaps. 1–3 (less several glosses or additions) contain prophetic sayings from Micah.

For the purposes of this present study, it seems best to have as the textual basis in Micah a critically assured minimum and therefore to limit our investigation to Micah 1–3, following Stade and Mays. This will enable us to proceed from texts whose authenticity remains unquestioned and permit us to place beyond the scope of this investigation matters relating to the authenticity of texts and the various criteria for making adequate judgments about authenticity.[36] Obviously, the texts from Isaiah will be drawn from "first Isaiah" (chaps. 1–39), with critical discussion of authenticity questions of this material only where it is pertinent to this investigation.

[32] Cf. e.g., the commentaries by Wellhausen; Marti; Nowack; Smith; Robinson; Mays.

[33] Rudolph, 136.

[34] Mays, 13.

[35] Stade, "Bemerkungen," *ZAW* 1 (1881) 161ff.

[36] Mays, 13, suggests several criteria for determining the authenticity of the various sayings in the book: (1) time of the reign of Hezekiah; (2) consistency with the purpose of Micah's activity as stated in 3:8; (3) continuity and consistency of style, setting, and message; (4) later material appears to belong to the late seventh century as suggested by language, setting, and message.

1
The Theophany Tradition in Micah and Isaiah

"The descriptions of theophanies are undoubtedly the most central subject of an Old Testament aesthetic, for they reveal more clearly than all else how the special experience of God undergone by Israel also became normative for the special features in the experience of beauty." Thus wrote Gerhard von Rad (*Old Testament Theology* 1, 366) in his discussion of Israel's perception of beauty in relation to Yahweh's actions in the world. These theophany descriptions, he continues, "in which Israel took delight from her earliest times right down to the latest writings of the Psalms," found an important place particularly in the sayings of Israel's prophets, who could picture Yahweh's coming to judge and to save in the vivid colors of a theophany. In the subsequent paragraphs of this chapter we shall focus upon the use and function of the theophany description first in the book of Micah and then in Isaiah. Our task involves posing both form critical and tradition historical questions of the theophany texts in Micah and Isaiah. Our purpose is to compare and contrast the manner in which Micah and Isaiah draw upon older, *traditional theophany material* and put it to use in their respective messages, and also to compare the *forms* in which this material is found, and their precise function and goal. Thus we begin in Part A with a study of Mic 1:2ff., a text which announces divine judgment upon Samaria. In Part B we turn to the Isaian texts which are thought to contain a theophany description or elements thereof (30:27-33; 29:5f.; 31:4; 6:1ff.; 3:13-15), and then conclude with a brief excursus on the theme of judgment on Samaria and the Northern Kingdom in Micah and Isaiah.

A. THE THEOPHANY TRADITION IN MICAH (MIC 1:2-7)

v. 2   Hear, O peoples, all of them,[a]
        hearken, O earth, and all that fills it.
       And let the [Lord][b] Yahweh be a witness against you,
        the Lord from his holy temple.
v. 3   For behold,[c] Yahweh comes forth from his place
        and comes down and treads[d] upon the high places of the
       earth.

9

v. 4 And the mountains will melt under him and the valleys
will be cleft
like wax before fire,
like water poured down a steep place.[e]

v. 5 All this is for the transgression of Jacob,
and for 'the sin'[f] of the house of Israel.[g]
What is the transgression of Jacob?
Is it not Samaria?
What is the 'sin'[h] of Judah?
Is it not Jerusalem?

v. 6 Therefore I will make Samaria
into ' '[i] an open field,
into a planted vineyard.
And I will pour down her stones into a valley,
and I will lay bare her foundations.

v. 7 All her images shall be smashed,
all her hires shall be burned with fire.
For from the hire of a harlot she gathered[j] them,
and to the hire of a harlot they shall return.

Textual notes:

a $G = $ Ἀκούσατε λαοί λόγους, reading λόγους for Aramaic מלם instead of
כלם. כ and מ could be easily confused in the old script (cf. Smith).
Instead of כלם Sellin and Robinson read כלכם which could be expected
after the vocative; but the 3rd per. plur. often follows the vocative (cf.
Ges.-K. 144p). 1 Kgs 22:28 (absent in G apparently is borrowed from Mic
1:2 and confirms M (cf. Wellhausen).

b G has only κύριος as in v. 2bβ. Qere inverts the subject and verb יהוה אדני
יהיה. Omit אדני with 2 Mss, Duhm, "Anmerkungen," 81; Marti; Smith;
et al., for it is superfluous to the meter, and is likely a gloss on אדני in
v 2bβ (cf. Smith).

c   BHS proposes changing to הנהו to improve the meter (also Duhm, in
reference to Jer 18:3). But if v. 2 is secondary (see below) then the 3rd
per. suffix would have no antecedent. For metrical reasons כי which
connects v. 3 with v. 2 may be deleted. (cf. Jeremias, *Theophanie,* 11, note
3).

d G and V omit the verb ודרך; however, the phrase ודרך על במותי ארץ
occurs elsewhere (Am 4:13; Job 9:8); on the phrase in these passages and
other variations, cf. J. Crenshaw, "Wedōrēk 'al-bāmŏtê 'āreṣ," *CBQ* 34
(1972) 37–53. Commentators are divided: Duhm ("Anmerkungen," 81)
suggests eliminating either ויֹרד or ודרך. Smith omits the latter, following
G; Sellins' translation of the verse indicates that he views ויֹרד as part of
v. 2b and thus secondary. Jeremias, *Theophanie,* 11, note 4, deletes ודרך,

seeing here the redactor's understanding of the mountains' melting as a
result of Yahweh's treading upon them.

e   מוֹרָד "descent, slope" (BDB, 434; cf. Jos 7:5; Jer 48:5); according to R.
    Köbert, *Biblica* 39 (1958) 82f., the noun, since it occurs with the words
    "wax" and "water," which belong to the sphere of one's daily life, must
    mean "drinking trough" (Tränkkufe).

f   *GT* presuppose the sing., which the parallel noun פֶּשַׁע would also
    require. Read חַטַּאת with Duhm ("Anmerkungen," 81); Ehrlich, *Rand-
    glossen;* Smith, et al.

g   Wellhausen suggested changing בֵּית יִשְׂרָאֵל to בֵּית יְהוּדָה in the light of
    v. 5bβ which understands v. 5aα as referring to the Southern Kingdom.
    Thus also Nowack; Smith; and recently Fohrer, "Micah 1," 70; also BHS.
    But v. 5b is certainly secondary (see below, p. 13) and should not be used
    as a basis for changing "Israel" to "Judah"; cf. Budde, "Das Rätsel," 80.

h   Read חַטַּאת instead of בָּמוֹת with *GST* (*G* reads "sin of the house"),
    Smith; Sellin; Robinson.

i   *G* reads εἰς ὀπωροφυλάκιον; omit לְעִי with Marti and Smith, who take the
    ל with the following word (לְשָׂדֶה). Nowack suggests the reading לִיַּעַר (cf.
    Ezek 21:2, also Wellhausen). Perhaps עִי is a gloss taken from 3:12 (cf.
    Donner, *Israel,* 94).

j   Read קֻבָּצוּ (pu.) to correspond with יְכַתּוּ, cf. Marti, BHS.

1. The length of the first saying in the book of Micah, as well as its unity
and authenticity, is a matter which has no general agreement among scholars.
Nowack divides the chapter into two parts: vv. 2–7, 8–16;[1] Smith[2] includes
vv. 8–9 with the foregoing verses, while Sellin[3] sees the major break after v. 8
(vv. 2–8, 9–16). The structure of the chapter depends, however, upon the authenticity of certain verses in 1:2–7, and one's conclusions as to its form. To these
matters we now turn.

Micah's prophecy begins, following the redactor's superscription in v. 1,
with a "summons to hear"[4] addressed not specifically to Israel (cf. vv. 5a, 6) but

---

[1] W. Nowack, cf. also B. Duhm, "Anmerkungen zu den zwölf Propheten," *ZAW* 31
(1911) 82f.; J. Lindblom; A. Weiser; H. Donner, *Israel unter den Völkern: Die Stellung der
klassischen Propheten des 8. Jahrhunderts v. Chr. zur Aussenpolitik der Könige von Israel
und Juda,* Suppl VT 11 (1964) 95, sees three parts in chap. 1: vv. 2–7, 8–9, 10–16, and notes
that these three sections are closely related according to both form and content. However,
the present (literary) shape appears rather to be the work of the redactor; see below.

[2] Smith; also G. Fohrer, "Micha 1," *Das ferne und nahe Wort,* BZAW 105 (1967) 70ff.

[3] Sellin; also K. Budde, "Das Rätsel von Micha 1," *ZAW* 37 (1917/18) 91.

[4] The "summons to hear" or "proclamation formula" in v. 2a employs a double
imperative, as also in Mic 6:2a (שִׁמְעוּ; read וְהַאֲזִינוּ instead of וְהַאֲזִינִים; cf. BHS and most
commentaries), which is addressed not to "the peoples-earth" but to the "mountains" and
"foundations of the earth." Mic 3:1, 9 use only one imperative to summon the "heads of

to the whole world (עמים/ארץ).⁵ Whereas some commentators take v. 2, together with vv. 3-4, as non-genuine,⁶ others, most recently for example Willis,⁷ take the entire verse as original to the passage. Some scholars delete only v. 2b,⁸ for the language of v. 2b suggests that it is later than the 8th century. But the entire verse is to be regarded as suspect, for the connection between v. 2 and vv. 3-4 is problematic since: (a) the "summons to hear" does not fit vv. 3-4, where a description of Yahweh's appearance, not his (or the prophet's) words, are found (hence the rearrangement of the verses 3, 4, 2, 6 by Budde, which has rightly found little acceptance); (b) "Yahweh," the subject of 2b, is repeated in v. 3; (c) Yahweh comes from "his holy temple" in v. 2b, but "from his place" (heaven) in v. 3a. The language of v. 2b is drawn from the legal proceeding (בכם לעד),⁹ while vv. 3f. are couched in the language of theophany; (d) the phrase עמים כלם,

---

(the house of) Jacob, rulers of the house of Israel." On the formula "summons to receive instruction" (*Lehreröffnungsformel*) and the main catchwords connected with it, cf. H. W. Wolff, *Hosea*, BK XIV/1, 122f.

⁵ Here the "peoples . . . and earth and all who fill it" are summoned, not "heavens" (Deut 32:1; Jer 2:12) or "heavens and earth" (Isa 1:2; Ps 50:4). A. Ehrlich, *Randglossen zur hebräischen Bibel* 5, and Bruno, *Micha und der Herrscher aus der Vorzeit* (1923), read עמי instead of עמם, which would make the addressee in v. 2a correspond to vv. 5f. In the above mentioned texts, "heaven and earth" have been understood as the summoned witnesses to a previously made covenant or treaty, which presumably has its background in ancient Oriental treaty concepts (cf. H. Huffmon, "The Covenant Lawsuit in the Prophets," *JBL* 78 (1959) 285ff.; J. Harvey, "Le 'Rib-Pattern'," *Bib* 43 (1962) 172ff.; G. E. Wright, "The Lawsuit of God," in *Israel's Prophetic Heritage: Essays in honor of J. Muilenburg,* 26ff. Weighty arguments against a covenantal background for the prophetic use of the formula are offered by J. Jeremias, *Kultprophetie und Gerichtsverkündigung in der späten Königszeit Israels,* WMANT 35 (1970) 154ff.; W. Whedbee, *Isaiah and Wisdom* (1971) 30ff.

⁶ B. Stade, "Streiflichter auf die Entstehung des jetzigen Gestalt der alt. Propheten-schriften," *ZAW* 23 (1903) 163, reasons that Micah would have no judgment against the heathen; that the idea of Yahweh's dwelling in heaven (v. 3) is late in origin; that only in later times was a connection made between Israel's impending doom and judgment upon the world. Accordingly, he considers v. 5a a redactional seam, with the prophet's speech beginning first in v. 5b. Nowack followed Stade here; more recently, also R. E. Wolfe, "Micah," IB 6. Smith formulates objections to Stade's view. See also Budde's disagreement with Stade ("Rätsel," 82ff.). The question of the authenticity of v. 2 should be kept separate from vv. 3-4, which, with most recent commentators, should not be taken as later material (see below) (otherwise V. Fritz, "Das Wort gegen Samaria Mic 1:2-7," *ZAW* 86 [1974] 328).

⁷ J. T. Willis, "Some Suggestions on the Interpretation of Micah 1:2," *VT* 18 (1968) 372ff.; cf. also Smith; Th. Robinson and F. Horst, *Die Zwölf Kleinen Propheten,* HAT 1, 14 (³1964); Fohrer, "Micha 1," 70ff.

⁸ Sellin; Lindblom; Jepsen, "Beiträge," 96; Jeremias, "Deutung," 331, note 9.

⁹ Cf. D. McKenzie, "Judicial Procedure at the Town Gate," *VT* 14 (1964) 102; H.-J. Boecker, *Redeformen des Rechtslebens im Alten Testament* (1964) 32.

in addition to Mic 1:2, occurs only in texts later than Micah![10] Finally, it is not unimportant that the "summons to hear" followed immediately by a theophany description is not found in any other prophetic judgment speeches, which further suggests that we have here a secondary connection. Indeed, the redactor no doubt intentionally introduces Micah's entire prophecy (not just vv. 3ff.) with a summons to the world, which is to take note that Yahweh's judgment of his people has world-wide implications. It is therefore quite probable, as Lescow[11] suggests, that v. 2 is part of a liturgical framework provided by a postexilic redactor.

The redactor's hand is also apparent in v. 5b, as has long been recognized, and recently emphasized by Jeremias,[12] who finds here a later attempt to apply to the Southern Kingdom words originally concerning only the Northern Kingdom (v. 5a).

If the prophetic saying begins, then, with the theophany description in vv. 3f., which seems to be a kind of prelude to the accusation (v. 5a) and announcement of judgment (vv. 6f.), where does the saying conclude? Did the original rhetorical unit reach a climax in v. 6 or continue on with v. 7, or with vv. 8–9? The central question as to the chapter's division is whether vv. 8–9 conclude the previous verses or begin the following passage.

Recently Fohrer[13] once again defended the view that the personal lament in

---

[10] In addition to Mic 1:2b, the expression עַמִּים כֻּלָּם occurs only 5 times in the OT (Lam 1:18; Ps 67:4, 6; 1 Kgs 22:28; 2 Chr 18:27; cf. Lescow, "Micha 1–5," 60.

[11] Lescow, ibid., 60f.; Weiser suggests that, since v. 2 places Yahweh's judgment against Samaria into a "cosmic universal framework," perhaps Micah is here dependent upon Isaiah. But this is hardly possible, not only in view of the secondary character of v. 2 but also because nowhere else in Micah is there evidence for such a concept. Although Micah 1:2 is similar to Isa 1:2 (which is addressed not to "nations/peoples" but to "heaven/earth"), there is, form critically speaking, little similarity between the two passages. Isa 1:2f. is a "Gerichtsrede" (rib-pattern; cf. Wildberger, BK X/1) in which the "summons to hear" introduces not a theophany but Yahweh's "Anklage" (vv. 2bf.). What appears quite likely, however, is that the redactor of Mic 1:2, by introducing Micah's prophetic work with the universal summons in v. 2, has the similar formula in Isa 1:2 in mind.

[12] Jeremias, "Deutung," 332 (cf. 347). This secondary addition in v. 5b is an "actualizing interpretation," probably suggested by v. 9. Cf. also Budde, "Rätsel," 79f.; Nowack; Jepsen, "Beiträge," 98; Robinson.

[13] Fohrer ("Micha 1," 69ff.) identifies three strophes: vv. 2–5a, 5b–7, 8–9, and suggests this arrangement on the basis of meter and style. The resulting genre he designates a "prophetische Gerichtsrede" whose structure exhibits five parts: summons of audience (v. 2); Yahweh's appearance and motivation (vv. 3–5a); accusation (v. 5b); judgment (v. 6); lament (vv. 8–9). Aside from Fohrer's arguments on the basis of meter, which are tenuous at best, the "stylistic similarities" he finds between v. 9 and v. 5b (Judah/Jerusalem appear in both verses) are of little significance, since v. 5b is clearly secondary, as has just been noted. Furthermore, Fohrer is unable to present any analogous form in which a *prophetic lament* follows a theophany description plus motivation and threat. He skirts this issue in

vv. 8f. concludes the pericope of vv. 2ff. However, several arguments speak against this. In the first place, the prophet would hardly lament (v. 8) the destruction of the images in v. 7; nor would vv. 8f. seem to refer back as far as the doom against Samaria announced in v. 6. The expression על זאת (v. 8), if it does not stem from the redactor's hand, thus secondarily joining vv. 8ff. with the foregoing, could point forward to v. 9, which gives the reason (כי) for the prophet's lament.[14] Secondly, if one emends "her wound" מכותיה to read "Yahweh's wounds" (see note 31, p. 44), one need not find the antecedent for the fem. suffix in Samaria. Finally, the tone, vocabulary, as well as the genre of vv. 8f. strongly suggest that these verses belong with vv. 10-16;[15] compare, for example, the lament theme in vv. 8, 10, 11, 16; the "self-summons" in v. 8 (cohortative verbs) with the imperative summons in vv. 10, 13a, 16. Vv. 9b and 12b are strikingly similar; both are motive clauses introduced by כי; both speak of calamity, indeed Yahweh's calamity, that has *Jerusalem* as its ultimate goal; the phrase "gate of my people" (v. 9b) is picked up in v. 12b with the words "gates of Jerusalem."

If vv. 8f. belong with vv. 10ff., the question remains whether v. 7 is the conclusion of the passage. All or part of the verse has been questioned as secondary. Lindblom,[16] following Duhm, Budde, Nowack, and Mowinckel, deletes only v. 7aα₂ ("and all her hires shall be burned with fire"; cf. also BHS) as a later addition. But Jepsen, Smith and Lescow remove the entire verse,[17] including v. 6. Jeremias, following in part earlier conclusions of Procksch and Elliger, has attempted — unsuccessfully in our opinion — to show that only v. 7b is genuine and is the original continuation of v. 6.[18] The arguments against the

---

maintaining that vv. 8f. are not a "genuine lament" but rather a lament used as a *threat* to further underline the threat in v. 6. This distinction between form and function is appropriate and applicable here; however, vv. 8-9 as a threat belong with vv. 10-16.

[14] Thus see K. Elliger, "Die Heimat des Propheten Micha," *Kleine Schriften zum Alten Testament,* ThB 32 (1966) 59 and cf. Jos 14:14; 2 Sam 7:22; Isa 9:16 and Lindblom.

[15] Cf. Jeremias, "Deutung," 331, note 8.

[16] Lindblom (29) thinks v. 7aα₂ disturbs the meter, anticipates the thought of v. 7c [= 7bαβ?] and seems to presuppose destruction caused by an earthquake.

[17] Jepsen, "Beiträge"; Smith; Lescow, "Micha 1-5." Whereas Jepsen finds the language of v. 7 to be Hosean, Lescow's examination of the vocabulary leads him to conclude that v. 7 is more probably from postexilic times.

[18] Jeremias, "Deutung," 335ff., separates v. 7a from v. 7b, beginning with the observation that אתנן is used differently in each part of the verse. He suggests that מאתנן in v. 7b refers either to the products Israel has gathered from her commercial dealings and treaties with foreign countries (cf. Procksch, *Die kleinen prophetischen Schriften vor dem Exil,* 102, and Elliger, "Heimat" 59, note 184) or — what he considers more probable — to the city's splendor achieved from oppressing the poor (and notes Isa 1:21 as a comparison). But Jeremias' reconstruction seems a bit too complex and hypothetical to be entirely convincing. His interpretation does not meet the chief *problems* posed by understanding v. 7b as a continuation of v. 6: (1) form critically (on the form of vv. 3-5a, 6 see below) the prophetic speech seems to reach its climax in v. 6; a further motivation (כי) in v. 7b after the motivation (v. 5a) and threat (v. 6) is unnecessary and there is no analogy in Micah

authenticity of the entire verse, however, are weighty (see notes 18 and 19). Not
v. 7 but v. 6 is the climax and conclusion of the passage, as a form critical analysis
will show.

2. We turn now to a form critical analysis of Mic 1:3f., 5a, 6. This passage,
introduced by הנה, begins with a *theophany description*[19] which is an example
of the oldest, two-part form with two-part content as isolated by Jeremias.[20] The
first part (v. 3) portrays the coming of the deity: Yahweh is the subject, followed
by two verbs (on ודרך see textual note "d" on 1:3) denoting his coming: יצא//ירד.
Both יצא (cf. Jgs 5:4; Zech 14:3; Isa 26:1; 42:13; Hab 3:13; Ps 68:8 [7]) and ירד
(cf. Exod 19:18; 34:5; 2 Sam 22:10 = Ps 18:10 [9]; Isa 31:4; 63:19b) are verbs

---

for such a pattern. (2) A syntactic connection of v. 7b with v. 6 is difficult, at best; if one
reads קָבָּצה (pi. perf., 3rd fem. sing., *M*) then Samaria would be the subject, and thus, since
Yahweh is the subject in v. 6, the change in subject indicates a break here. If one reads קֻבָּצוּ
(pu. pl., cf. *S T* and BHS), the syntactic connection with v. 6 remains just as difficult, for
then v. 7b has a passive construction. (3) Furthermore, the verb קבץ occurs elsewhere in
Mic only in secondary passages (2:12; 4:6; 4:12;) nor is it found in genuine Isaiah texts
(11:12; 13:14; 34:15; 34:16). Amos does not have the verb at all; Hosea only twice: 8:10 refers
to a gathering together for judgment, while 9:6 speaks of Egypt's gathering of Israel for
death (cf. Wolff BK XIV/1; Eng. p. 156). The motif of "gathering from the nations" is
frequent later, e.g., in Jeremiah (29:14; 31:8, 10; 32:37) and Ezekiel (11:17; 20:34; 28:25; etc.).
(4) Finally, it remains unclear how the harlotry motif in v. 7b elucidates the accusation in
v. 5a (פשע/חטאת). In spite of Jeremias' reference to Isa 1:21, אתנן זונן does not appear
to refer to commercial-political policies or to oppression of poor; on meaning and usage
of this phrase, see J. Kühlewein, "זונה" *THAT* 1, 518ff.

[19] The terminology that has developed to speak of theophany in the OT is not uniform.
Here I use J. Jeremias' (*Theophanie*, WMANT 10 [1965] 3) term "Theophanieschilde-
rung," which he interprets as a Gattung, under stood in the sense of Alt's classic definition:
". . . each individual form, as long as it remains in use in its own context, the ideas it
contains are always connected with certain *fixed* forms of expression. This characteristic
connection is not imposed arbitrarily on the material by the literary redactors of a later
period. The inseparable connection between form and content goes back behind the
written records to the period of popular oral composition and tradition, where each form
of expression was appropriate to some particular circumstance among the regularly
recurring events and necessities of life." (A. Alt, "The Origins of Israelite Law" in *Essays
on OT History and Religion*, tr. R. A. Wilson [Oxford, 1966] 87 [*Kleine Schriften* 1,
München, 1959, 284]). A. Weiser uses the term "theophany tradition" in a broad sense. C.
Westermann seeks to make the terminology more precise by suggesting that "theophany"
be used for the divinity's appearance to a mediator who in turn speaks to the people, while
"epiphany" designates a divine coming to bring help (*The Praise of God in the Psalms*,
tr. K. Crim [Richmond, 1965] 99. Further, cf. F. Schnutenhaus. "Das Kommen und
Erscheinen Gottes im AT," *ZAW* 76 (1964) 1–21.

[20] Jeremias, *Theophanie*, 7ff., names as the oldest *forms* of the theophany description
Jgs 5:4f.; Mic 1:3f.; Ps 46:7; 68:8f.; Isa 63:19b. His thesis is that all other theophany
descriptions have developed from these forms (p. 15 and passim).

common to theophanies,[21] but they stand parallel only in Mic 1:3. It is typical of the form that the place from which Yahweh comes is preceded by the preposition מ. In v. 3 Yahweh comes from "his place" (ממקומו), which apparently means "heaven"[22] (cf. Isa 26:21; 63:19; Jer 25:30; Ps 10:13; etc.), although in the form, the reference to place can be omitted (cf. Pss 46:7; 68:8). The second part of the form (v. 4), which stands in a cause-effect relationship to the first part, describes the tumult in nature in reaction to Yahweh's coming. The mountains (cf. Jgs 5:5; Isa 63:19b; Ps 97:5; 104:32; etc.) melt and the valleys split open (בקע; cf. Hab 3:9) before the divinity's awful presence. Two similes in v. 4b, introduced by כי, further describe the tumult in nature;[23] v. 4b probably is a later expansion of the original two-part form with corresponding content of two parts.[24] Vv. 3f. are not a creation of the prophet, but—as Jeremias' form critical analysis has made clear—the appropriation of an originally pre-formed, self-contained unit which, however, is not to be isolated from its present context.[25]

Immediately following the theophany description the prophetic accusation is made (v. 5a), which gives the motivation for the announcement of judgment in v. 6. The phrase כל זאת, whether a later addition or not, refers back to vv. 3f. and grammatically connects the theophany with the accusation.[26] The guilt is referred to only in general terms (פשע//חטאת); cf. Mic 2:1f., 8f.; 3:1-3, 5, 9b-11, where the accusations are specific as to the nature of the transgression. The language of v. 5a is quite similar to 3:8b: "I will declare to Jacob his transgression and to Israel his sin." V. 5a should be understood as prophetic speech (cf. the

---

[21] For a study of the verbs common to theophanies, see Schnutenhaus, "Das Kommen," 1ff. He limits to the sphere of theophanies these verbs צרה, נגה, הופיע, קום, ירד, יצא and בא (p. 19).

[22] According to Jeremias, *Theophanie,* 12 "his place" refers to heaven, as the verb ירד would indicate. On the other hand Schnutenhaus, "Das Kommen," 5, thinks this refers to the Jerusalem temple; but this is impossible, since for Micah, Jerusalem is not the place where Yahweh dwells but rather the object of his wrath; cf. 3:12. Theophanies also describe other places as the origin of Yahweh's coming: Sinai (Jgs 5:4f.), Zion (Am 1:2), the North (Ezek 1:4), Temen/Mt. Haran (Hab 3:3), or "from afar" (Isa 30:27); cf. on this Jeremias' excursus "Die Ausgangsorte Jahwes," 115ff.

[23] The first of the two similes "like wax before a fire" does not fit v. 4aβ but v. 4aα, which speaks of "melting." Nowack suggests that the first simile originally stood after תחתיו. This is unlikely in view of the secondary character of v. 4b, which this stylistic unevenness would further support.

[24] Jeremias, *Theophanie,* 11f.

[25] Ibid., 130.

[26] Budde ("Das Rätsel," 82); Lescow ("Mic. 1-5," 54) suggest deleting כל זאת; cf. על זאת in v. 8 and זאת in 3:1. Lindblom views the phrase as a grammatical connective with vv. 3-4. If it is genuine, v. 5a would be a nominal clause closely connected with vv. 3f.: "All this is because of the transgression of Jacob. . . ." But if it is to be deleted, v. 5a would be a dependent clause, subordinate to v. 6: "because of the transgression of Jacob . . . therefore I will. . . ." Lescow, on the other hand, sees v. 5a as the motivation for the theophany and the connection between vv. 3f. and vv. 8f.

accusations in 2:1f; 3:1–3, 9b–11) rather than divine speech (Sellin).

The announcement of judgment in v. 6 is formulated as a 1st person Yahweh speech (cf. the narrative, 3rd per. form in v. 3) like 2:3f. (cf. 3:5); unlike 2:3f. (cf. 3:5) the messenger formula כה אמר יהוה is not found here, nor is there a לכן (cf. 2:3; 3:6, 12) to introduce the announcement, but rather a ו[27] followed by three parallel verb clauses, the first two in the perfect and the last in the imperfect. Whereas the accused party in v. 5a is the Northern Kingdom (on this see the excursus below, pp. 34ff.), v. 6 names the capital city, Samaria, as the object of the impending doom.

What is the precise genre or Gattung to which this passage might belong? Lindblom[28] speaks of a "Form einer Predigtrevelation" of two parts, a "Prophetenrede" (v. 2–5) and a "Gottsrede" (v. 6). Elliger[29] finds here a "threat with the motifs of a lawsuit speech" (Gerichtsrede). Weiser[30] identifies four parts (vv. 2–7), a summons to the nations and theophany followed by *Scheltwort* and *Drohwort*. Fohrer,[31] who defines the unit so as to include vv. 8–9 (vv. 2–9) speaks of a *prophetic lawsuit speech* ("prophetische Gerichtsrede,") which he understands as a loose designation of a large complex of speech forms. Fritz,[32] concluding that vv. 2–7 date from a circle of postexilic cultic prophets, thinks that "eine Bestimmung der Gattung des gesamten Abschnitt" is not possible.

But if we look first at the kernel of the passage, namely, vv. 5a, 6, it is clear that here we have simply a two part prophetic speech composed of accusation and announcement of divine punishment, a "Gerichtswort," which has a multitude of parallels in the prophetic literature, and which has been explicated especially by Wolff and Westermann. Other examples in Micah are found in

---

[27] On the connection of a prophetic announcement with the accusation by a *waw* followed by the perf., cf. for example Hos 9:4b, 10, etc., and Wolff, *ThB* 22 (²1973) 10f.; also Westermann, *Basic Forms,* 149. Duhm ("Anmerkungen," 45, cited by Jepsen, 97, note 1), Jepsen, and more recently Lescow find the Yahweh speech in v. 6 non-genuine because there is no introductory formula for it, as in 2:3; 3:5; 6:2, 9. But form critically considered, this is hardly reason to contest the genuineness of the verse. Westermann notes that "in the legal procedure, God speaks as the judge directly and without any introduction (by a messenger formula)," ibid., 199.

[28] Lindblom, 17.

[29] Elliger, "Die Heimat," 58, note 182. The term "lawsuit speech" ("Gerichtsrede") should carefully be distinguished from "judgment speech" ("Gerichtswort") for the sake of precise form critical terminology. The former should be reserved for passages in which the "image of legal proceedings" does occur (cf. Hos 2:4ff.; 4:1ff.; Isa 1:2f. and K. Koch, *The Growth of the Biblical Tradition,* 193). With the deletion of v. 2 as secondary, "lawsuit" is not a proper form critical designation of our passage (see above, note 5).

[30] Weiser, ATD 1, 24.

[31] Fohrer ("Micha 1," 72f.), although he accepts v. 2 as original, correctly rejects any connection with covenant concepts or the influence of international treaties; rather, he finds the background in Israel's "profane legal institutions" (*Rechtsleben*).

[32] V. Fritz, "Das Wort gegen Samaria Mi 1,2–7," *ZAW* 86 (1974) 329.

2:1ff.; 3:1ff.; 3:5ff.; 3:9ff. What is of special interest here is that Micah has introduced his Gerichtswort with old, pre-formed material, which exhibits the characteristics of the ancient theophany description. The passage thus has a three part structure:

I. vv. 3–4   Theophany description
II. v. 5a   Prophetic speech: accusation
III. v. 6   Yahweh speech: announcement of disaster

As Jeremias'[33] study of the history of the theophany Gattung has shown, there are a number of prophetic texts, in addition to Mic 1:3ff., which make use of a theophany, or elements of it. In this group of texts he includes the following: Am 1:2; Isa 66:15f.; 59:15bff.; Jer 25:30b-31; Mal 3:1ff.; Isa 26:21; Ps 50 (texts in which divine judgment is against Israel and/or the nations); the second group is comprised of Isa 19:1ff.; 30:27ff.; 31:4; 40:10; 42:13ff.; Hag 2:6ff.; Zech 9:11ff. 14:3f. (texts in which Yahweh intervenes for Israel against her enemies). Although it is beyond the scope of our investigation here to compare in detail Mic 1:3ff. with these two groups of texts—we shall turn to the Isaian texts below—a few form critical observations will prove helpful in our understanding of Mic 1:3ff. Above it was noted that Mic 1:3ff. has a three part structure of theophany, accusation, and announcement. (1) Like Mic 1:3ff., in each passage in both groups, Yahweh's coming or arrival is in some sense mentioned or described. But only in Mic 1:3ff. and Am 1:2 does one find the second part of the old theophany form, the tumult in nature. Unlike Mic 1:3ff., however, the Amos passage has neither an accusation or a separate threat of disaster; rather the tumult in nature (Am 1:2b) is the threat itself. (2) In most of these texts, there is no specific accusation as in Mic 1:5a; only Isa 59:15b–19 (v. 15b "no justice") and Isa 26:21 ("their iniquity," "bloodshed") speak of wrongdoing as a motivation for Yahweh's coming. (3) Only in Mic 1:3ff. does a Yahweh speech (v. 6) follow a description of his coming; Yahweh does not speak in the other prophetic theophany descriptions (Ps 50 is one exception, but to what *extent* it is prophetic material is unclear). (4) Only the complex structured and form critically difficult Ps 50 mentions the summons of an audience (v. 1) immediately before the theophany (v. 2f.). But here the verb is קְרָא, not the double verb summons (with שִׁמְעוּ plus other verbs) typical of the prophetic call to listen. Thus of these above mentioned groups of prophetic texts employing elements of theophany, Micah's appropriation of this ancient form is apparently not only one of the oldest, but the *only* text which has combined the complete, two part theophany form with the typical prophetic judgment speech.[34] It represents therefore one link in the chain of development of simple, brief, two part prophetic judgment speeches into expanded forms.[35]

[33] Jeremias, *Theophanie,* 130ff.
[34] Ibid., 138.
[35] On the development of the two-part form to more complex forms, cf. Westermann, *Basic Forms,* 181ff.

3. A form critical analysis of Mic 1:3ff. has shown that the prophet, in proclaiming Yahweh's impending punishment of Samaria, has made use of a theophany description which derives from an ancient two-part Gattung describing Yahweh's coming and nature's reaction. We must now proceed to the question of the *background* and *roots* of this theophanic material in vv. 3-4. From what kind of tradition has Micah appropriated the theophany which introduces his judgment speech?[36]

In his book *Die Kulttraditionen Israels in der Verkündigung des Propheten Michas,* W. Beyerlin argues that our text recalls in numerous ways the ancient Sinai Theophany.[37] The verb ירד, which denotes Yahweh's descent in Mic 1:3, is also used in connection with Yahweh's appearance upon Mount Sinai in the J and E narrative in Exod 19:18, 20.[38] In Mic 1:4 the mountains are said to melt in response to the divinity's fearful appearance and in Exod 19:18 "the whole *mountain* quaked" (RSV) at Yahweh's descent. Mic 1:4b reports that the mountains became "like wax before the *fire,*" while in Exod 19:18 (cf. Deut 4:11, 12) Yahweh comes down in *fire* to Sinai. How might one account for this remarkable similarity?

---

[36] A complete bibliogaphical listing of material relating to theophany is not necessary here. In addition to the recent monographs by J. Jeremias, *Theophanie,* and K. Kuntz, *The Self-Revelation of God,* both of which contain complete bibliogaphies, the following may be noted: H. Gunkel, "Theophanie," *RGG*[2] 5, 1130-1132; G. B. Gray, "Theophany," *Encyclopaedia Biblica* 4, 5033-5036; J. Morgenstern, "Biblical Theophanies," *ZA* 25 (1911) 139-193; *ZA* 28 (1913) 15-16; E. Wurthwein, "Elijah at Horeb," *Proclamation and Presence* (1970) 152ff.; J. Hempel, "Theophanie," *RGG*[3] 6, 842; A. Weiser, "Zur Frage nach den Beziehungen der Psalmen zum Kult: Die Darstellung der Theophanie in den Psalmen und im Festkult," *Bertholet-Festschrift* (Tübingen: 1950) 513-531; W. Beyerlin, *Herkunft und Geschichte der ältesten Sinaitraditionen;* J. Lindblom, "Theophanies in Holy Places in Hebrew Religion," *HUCA* 32 (1961) 91-106; James Barr, "Theophany and Anthropomorphism in the Old Testament," *Congress Volume,* Suppl VT 7 (1962) 31-38; G. H. Davies, "Theophany," *IDB* 4 (1962) 619-620 [cf. also Davies art. for bibliography]; J. Muilenburg, "The Speech of Theophany," *Harvard Divinity Bulletin* 28 (1964) 34-47; F. Schnutenhaus, "Das Kommen und Erscheinen Gottes in AT," *ZAW* 76 (1964) 1-21; H. P. Müller, "Die kultische Darstellung der Theophanie," *VT* 14 (1964) 183-191; C. Westermann, *The Praise of God in the Psalms,* tr. K. Crim (Richmond: John Knox Press, 1965) 93-101; J. Crenshaw, "Amos and the Theophany Tradition," *ZAW* 80 (1968) 203-215; E. von Waldow, "Theophanie," *VuF* 14 (1969) 69-76; W. Rast, *Tradition History and the Old Testament* (Philadelphia: Fortress Press, 1972) 47-54; cf. also the work of F. M. Cross concerning the "Theophany of Ba'l" and the "Storm Theophany in the Bible" in his *Canaanite Myth and Hebrew Epic,* 147ff.; on the influence of Mic 1:4 on Enoch 1:3bff., cf. J. vander Kam , "The Theophany of Enoch 1:3b-7,9," *VT* 23 (1973) 145.

[37] W. Beyerlin, *Kulttraditionen,* 30ff.

[38] Wellhausen (*Composition des Hexateuchs,* 1876; [2]1899) assigned 19:20-25 to J., 19:10-19 to E (cf. B. Childs, *The Book of Exodus*). S. R. Driver, *An Introduction to the Literature of the OT,* 31f., takes 19:18 as E, 19:20 as J. Noth, *Exodus,* takes both v. 18 and v. 20 as Yahwistic.

Following the work of Mowinckel,[39] von Rad[40] and especially Weiser,[41] Beyerlin[42] contends that in the Jerusalem cult, the *Sinai theophany tradition* was actualized in a regular covenant festival ceremony. This would therefore account for the continued vitality of the theophany descriptions which are now found in different Gattungen in the narrative, prophetic, and poetic literature of the Old Testament. The cultic celebration kept the Sinai tradition alive. According to Beyerlin, this suggests that Micah's theophany description has a close connection with the cultic theophany, for, he says, the Sinai theophany was still given cultic actualization in Micah's time, as the report of Isaiah's call (chap. 6) would make evident. Furthermore, there is presumed to be evidence in the Psalms (e.g., 97, 50) of a theophany in the Jerusalem covenant festival. Beyerlin[43] concludes that Micah's vision of the theophany is influenced by the cultic celebration of the covenant in Jerusalem, where the Sinai theophany tradition is actualized. He also finds the announcement of judgment in Mic 1:6, the reference to "images" in v. 7, and the universal dimension of the "summons to hear" in v. 2, to be shaped by and rooted in the tradition of the Sinai theophany.[44]

Beyerlin's interpretation of this passage thus makes two closely related conclusions: (1) that Mic 1:(2)3ff. exhibits a "Verwandtschaft" with the Sinai theophany; (2) that Micah came to know the theophany tradition, whose prototype is in the Sinai tradition, in the dramatic actualization of it in the Jerusalem cult's covenant festival. Both of these items must be analyzed to see if Beyerlin's interpretation is correct. We begin with the second item first.

For the present, we shall leave aside the question of Micah's contact with the Jerusalem cult and focus upon the relation of *theophany* to the *cult*.

a. Concerning the problem of theophany in relation to the cult.

Weiser,[45] followed by Beyerlin, thinks of the Yahweh theophany in terms of a *tradition* composed of heterogeneous elements, which "as far as the history of tradition is concerned . . . has its model in the Sinai theophany," and remained alive and vital to Israel's worship life through regular cultic "actualization." Both C. Westermann and J. Jeremias have brought weighty criticism against this interpretation. Westermann,[46] distinguishing between an "epiphany" (God appears to aid his people) and a "theophany" (God appears in order to reveal himself

---

[39] Mowinckel, *Le Décalogue, Études d'Histoire et de Philosophie Religieuses* (1927), 119f. and passim.

[40] Von Rad, *Das formgeschichtliche Problem des Hexateuchs*, BWANT 4, 26 (1938) 18ff.

[41] Weiser, "Zur Frage nach den Beziehungen der Psalmen zum Kult: Die Darstellung der Theophanie in der Psalmen und im Festkult," in *Bertholet-Festschrift*, 513–531.

[42] *Kulttraditionen*, 31ff.

[43] Ibid., 35.

[44] Beyerlin includes Mic 3:11 as a further example of a reference to the theophany tradition in Jerusalem. On this text, see the discussion below, chap. 2, pp. 50ff.

[45] "Darstellung," 515.

[46] Westermann, *Praise*, 99ff.

and communicate through a mediator to his people) points out that Exodus 19 and 34 are theophanies which display the cultic features of locality, time and personnel (Moses as mediator). The epiphanies, however, which include Mic 1:3f. (also Jgs 5:4f.; Ps 18:7ff.; Hab 3:3ff.; Ps 68:7f.; etc.), are totally lacking in these cultic features. Moreover, Westermann notes of the three features most frequently encountered in almost all epiphanies (God's coming forth; cosmic disturbances; God's wrathful intervention for or against) the last one is completely lacking in Exodus 19 and 34. He therefore concludes that the epiphanies (and thus Mic 1:3f.) do not have their prototype in the Sinai tradition in Exodus 19, and casts doubt on Weiser's thesis "that the theophany tradition had its origin in the cult of the festivals and that it went back to the Sinai theophany."

Jeremias[47] has criticized Weiser's thesis from a different point of view. His criticism may be briefly summarized as follows. Weiser, who with the term "theophany tradition" denotes several different kinds of theophanies, takes as his point of departure the "theophany descriptions" (Theophanieschilderungen) such as are found in the Psalms (e.g., 18; 50; 68; etc.), but uses the evidence from these texts only at the beginning of his study. According to Jeremias, Weiser's methodological mistake lies in not strictly separating the "theophany description," the two-part Gattung, from theophanies in which a person engaged in prayer encounters Yahweh's *Panim*. The latter, of course, has its *Sitz im Leben* in the cult; the former does not. Furthermore, Jeremias argues that a connection between ark in the Jerusalem temple and theophany is impossible, for the ark tradition had no influence upon the *theophany descriptions*. He further reasons that cultic events are characterized by that which is static, permanent, and regularly occurring, while Yahweh's theophany has the attributes of the sudden, incalculable, and dynamic. The thesis that the theophany stems from the Jerusalem cultic festival as described by Weiser, remaining unsupported by textual evidence, is a "pure hypothetical reconstruction."[48]

In the light of the far-reaching criticism of Weiser's thesis (and thus also of Mowinckel and Beyerlin) by Westermann and Jeremias, the form of the theophany in Mic 1:3f. could hardly have any tradition historical connection with the theophany in the cult.

b. Concerning the relation of Mic 1:3f. to the Sinai narrative in Exodus 19.

We noted above (pp. 19f.) that Beyerlin sees a close connection between Exodus 19 and Mic 1:3f. A closer examination of the two texts, however, will demonstrate that the differences far outweigh the similarities.

(1) The verb ירד, which occurs in both Exod 19:18, 20 and in Mic 1:3, does not indicate that there is either a literary or a tradition-historical influence of the Sinai pericope upon Micah's theophany description, for this verb is merely a terminus technicus for the divinity's "descent," as its occurrence in other theophanic contexts shows (cf. Ps 18:10; Isa 31:4; 63:19b; etc.).[49]

(2) In both Mic 1:4 and Exod 19:18 there is reference to mountain(s), but the Exodus text speaks of *the* mountain, Sinai, while Mic 1:4 refers not to a

---

[47] Jeremias, *Theophanie*, 119ff.; cf. 1f.

[48] Ibid., 122.

[49] Ibid., 106.

specific mountain but to *mountains* in the plural, as is typical of other theophany descriptions (cf. Jgs 5:5; Isa 63:19b; Ps 97:5; etc.).[50]

(3) Whereas the fire mentioned in Exodus 19 (cf. Exod 24:17; Deut 4:12) is a phenomenon which *accompanies* Yahweh's appearance, in Mic 1:4b and in texts to which it stands form critically related (Isa 64:1; Ps 18:9) the fire motif is expressed as the *result* of Yahweh's coming. In addition to these important differences, the following remarks also show the significant contrasts between the Sinai pericope and the Micah text.

(4) Yahweh comes to Sinai to speak to a mediator and bring salvation and a covenant relationship to his chosen people; the theophany in Micah is a horrifying, terrible appearance which brings judgment upon his people.

(5) Finally, and of special importance, is the form critical observation that the second member of the two-part theophany description — the report of nature's tumult — is completely missing in the formation of the Sinai theophany.[51] Moreover, the Sinai narrative reports an event in the past, while the prophet announces future, impending doom.

We may conclude, therefore, that the passage Mic 1:3ff. does not in fact exhibit a close relationship with Exodus 19 and the Sinai tradition. The evidence for this offered by Beyerlin is not compelling. One must then ask from which sphere of tradition Micah has borrowed the theophany description in 1:3f.

The results of the studies of theophany by both Westermann and Jeremias show conclusively that the "epiphanies" (Westermann) or "theophany descriptions" (Jeremias) cannot have their original *Sitz im Leben* in the cultic actualization of the Sinai theophany.

Westermann locates the epiphanies in the context of Israel's declarative praises of Yahweh who intervenes to save his people from their enemies.[52] Jeremias' conclusion is in reality quite similar (although he approaches the issue from a somewhat different point of view), for he also speaks of songs which attend to Yahweh's saving activity.[53] Westermann emphasizes the Red Sea experience as constitutive here, whereas Jeremias emphasizes victory celebrations of the Israelite army.[54] But the positions stand together to a large degree and both

---

[50] In Exodus 19 Yahweh comes *to* a specific place but in Mic 1:3f. he comes *from* a specific place, "heaven"; cf. Westermann, *Praise*, 100; the oldest form of the theophany descriptions mentions the particular place *from which* Yahweh comes (Sinai: Jgs 5:4f.; Hab 3:3; etc.; Zion: Am 1:2; Ps 50:2) etc., but in Exodus 19 this element of the form finds absolutely no place. In the Sinai tradition Yahweh comes *to* Sinai but in some of the theophany descriptions, Yahweh can be said to come *from* Sinai.

[51] Cf. Westermann, *Praise*, 98f.; Jeremias, *Theophanie*, 109.

[52] Ibid., 101.

[53] *Theophanie*, 136ff.

[54] Jeremias, 148, finds in Jgs 5:4f. the best and oldest (form critically) text which exhibits the connection between theophanies and "Yahweh war." Jeremias' reconstruction of the possible original setting of the theophany descriptions has not gone unchallenged. See, for example, B. Childs (*Isaiah and the Assyrian Crisis*, 49); cf. also E. von Waldow's review of the book in *VuF* 14 (1969) 74ff.

take us away from the unfounded theory that the cultic actualization of the Sinai theophany is the traditional historical background of the theophany.

How does the theophany tradition *function* in Mic 1:3ff.? We noted above that the theophany description has been made *a part* of a typical *prophetic judgment* speech. This adaptation of the ancient Gattung gives it an entirely new setting and therefore a different function. In its original setting in the hymns or victory songs, the Yahweh theophany described the divinity's coming in order to save his people from their enemies. This is reflected in Jgs 5:4f., and in other examples of the oldest two-part *form* (cf. Ps 46:7; Isa 63:19b; Ps 68:8f.). But Mic 1:3ff. has *radically reversed* the object of the Yahweh theophany: here he comes not to help and protect but to bring disaster upon his own people. The prophet thus takes up an ancient tradition, but he changes it to suit the needs of his message. What is "old" is the appropriated tradition; what is "new" is its setting and function: it proclaims not salvation but doom on God's people.

B. THE THEOPHANY TRADITION IN ISAIAH

In the following paragraphs, we shall consider several passages in Isaiah in which the theophany tradition, or elements of it, has been employed. The texts which provide the basis for our investigation are Isa 30:27-33; 29:5f.; 31:4; 6:1ff.; 3:13-15. These are passages which critical scholarship has viewed as bearing a relationship to the theophany tradition. It of course remains to be discussed whether and to what extent the theophany tradition is reflected in these passages. Our task is to raise the question of the form and tradition history of these texts: What are the roots in tradition of the theophanic material found here? In what kind of form does the theophany tradition function? How do they compare form and tradition critically with Micah's use of the tradition?

1. Isa 30:27-33

Fohrer[55] divides this passage into four strophes: vv. 27-28; 29-30; 31-32; 33. Kissane[56] thinks chap. 30 is composed of eight strophes, with vv. 27-29; 30-33 comprising the seventh and eighth strophe. Regardless of how one may divide the unit, a clear break between vv. 28-29 is evident, for after the description of Yahweh in the 3rd person (vv. 27-28), v. 29 is addressed to the 2nd pers. plural. According to Duhm[57] the passage is "mehr Gedicht als Rede," though he considers it a genuine Isaian word near the time of Sennacherib's invasion. Duhm,[58] Procksch,[59] Kissane[60] and Fohrer[61] maintain the text's authenticity,

---

[55] Fohrer, *Das Buch Jesaja* 1, ZBK (²1966).

[56] Kissane, *The Book of Isaiah I-XXXIX* (1960).

[57] Duhm, *Das Buch Jesaja,* HKAT 3, 1 (⁵1968).

[58] Ibid.

[59] Procksch, *Jesaja* I, KAT IX (1930).

[60] Kissane.

[61] Fohrer.

while Cheyne,[62] Marti,[63] Donner,[64] and Kaiser[65] contest its genuineness. We find no compelling grounds to regard the entire passage as late (see below).

Introduced by הנה (cf. Mic 1:3), v 27aα contains the elements typical of the theophany description form: the perf. verb בא[66] (cf. Deut 33:2; Hab 3:3f.) is common in the form, and the place whence Yahweh comes is mentioned (ממרהק; cf. Jer 31:3). The subject, however, is not simply "Yahweh," but שם־יהוה.[67] The remainder of the verse and also v. 28aα graphically depict the terrifying nature of the divinity's appearance in a series of participial, nominal and verbal clauses which use anthropomorphic language (Yahweh's lips, tongue, breath). But the second element of the two-part ancient theophany form is missing here. Form critically, Jeremias[68] classifies the passage as one in which the first element has become independent of the "reaction in nature." Instead of nature's response, Yahweh's coming is rather elaborately described as intensely wrath-filled, with "fire" being the predominant image ("burning wrath; tongue like a devouring fire").

The *purpose* of Yahweh's coming is indicated by the announcement of judgment which follows in v 28aβb, introduced by ל with the infinitive[69] (נוף hiph; cf. Isa 10:15): Yahweh will "sift the גוים with a sieve of destruction" (שוא[70] cf. 1:13; 5:18 and the related form שואה in 10:3). The second bicolon in this line continues the announcement but with a completely different metaphor: Yahweh will "place[71] on the jaws of the עמים a bridle that leads astray," that is, that leads

[62] Cheyne, *Introduction to the Book of Isaiah* (1895).

[63] Marti, *Das Buch Jesaja*, KHC (1900).

[64] Donner, *Israel*, 164.

[65] Kaiser, *Isaiah 1-12: A Commentary* (1972).

[66] The verb בא is frequently used in the OT to express the approach of divine judgment (cf. Am 4:2; 8:2; 1 Sam 2:31) (cf. H. D. Preuss, *ThWAT* 1, 552). Yahweh is subject of the verb approximately 33 times, most of which are in the context of an "epiphany." According to Schnutenhaus ("Das Kommen," 15) the oldest epiphany texts which speak of Yahweh's coming (בוא) are Deut 33:2 and Hab 3:3f., 16. He emphasizes that the goal of Yahweh's coming in the epiphanies is Israel's enemies. בוא is not used for a cultic theophany in the temple until later texts (Schnutenhaus, 17f.). On this verb see also E. Jenni, "Kommen im theologischen Sprachgebrauch des AT," in *Wort-Gebot-Glaube: W. Eichrodt zum 80. Geburtstag,* AThANT 59 (Zürich, 1970) 251–261; idem, THAT 1, בוא, 264–269.

[67] Duhm thinks the word שם has been added by a later hand; thus also Fohrer.

[68] Jeremias, *Theophanie,* 56ff.

[69] The infinitive construction is apparently dependent upon the verb בוא in v. 27 (contra Kissane).

[70] שוא I means "emptiness, vanity" (BDB), although it is here often translated "destruction" or "devastation" (שואה from שוא II, BDB), as for example in RSV; cf. Childs, *Assyrian Crisis,* 46; Kaiser. The phrase בנפה שוא literally means "sieve of vanity" which makes little sense. Accordingly, Kissane thinks the text is not in order; he reads לשומ instead of שוא, for the following clause needs a verb, such as "to place," before רסן.

[71] See note 70; also Kaiser, who reads לשים instead of שוא.

to destruction (cf. Job 12:23f. and Kissane). Thus it is divine judgment not upon Israel but her enemies, the "nations"//"peoples," which Isaiah here announces, prefacing his threatening words with a theophany description.

The announcement in v 28aβb changes to a *promise* in v. 29, which is now addressed to the 2nd pers. plur.: "You will have a song in the night as when a holy feast (גח) is kept."[72] This juxtaposition of threat and promise appears to raise difficulties, however. B. Childs[73] makes a convincing case when he points out that such a combination of threat to Assyria and promise to Israel is not otherwise found in the genuine Isaian tradition; the threat, however, has the character of independence and originality and is not paralleled in later tradition. He concludes that vv. 29 and 32 are to be taken as later additions to the original saying in vv. 27-28, 30-31, 33.

Vv. 30-31 are closely connected: in v. 30 "Yahweh makes his majestic *voice* heard" and in v. 31 "the Assyrians are terror-stricken at his *voice*." Although the language of v. 30 is not, strictly speaking, theophany language (thus Jeremias),[74] it stands remarkably parallel to v. 27: in v. 30, *Yahweh's voice* comes in judgment and strikes terror; in v. 27 *Yahweh's name* descends and brings disaster. Moreover, the imagery used in both verses to describe Yahweh's wrath is similar: "burning anger" (v. 27), "furious anger" (v. 30), "like a devouring fire" (v. 27), "flame of devouring fire" (v. 30). The close relationship between vv. 27f. and vv. 30ff. suggests that the two parts stand parallel to each other, and therefore are not two different threats, one against the nations, the other against Assyria. Rather, the divine judgment upon

[72] To which circle or group might v. 29 have been addressed (if v. 29 is genuine)? Would Isaiah address such a promise to all of Israel? Duhm suggests that the prophet speaks these words to his close circle of friends, those who "wait in hope" with Isaiah (cf. 8:16ff.).

[73] B. Childs, *Assyrian Crisis,* 47ff.

[74] The language of vv. 30f. is remarkably similar to Canaanite descriptions of the "Ba'l theophany." Cross, *Myth and Hebrew Epic,* 149, cites this text (CTA 4.7. 29-35):

"Ba'l gives forth his holy voice,
Ba'l repeats the utterance of his lips,
His holy voice shatters the earth."

Whereas it is Assyria that is terror-stricken at Yahweh's voice in Isa 30:31, the Ba'l theophany continues:

"[At his roar] the mountains quake,
Afar [   ] before Sea,
The highplaces of the earth shake."

Cross finds two patterns in the Ba'l theophany: 1) The Divine Warrior marches to battle and with him his weapons, the thunderbolt and the winds; nature reflects his wrath: mountains shatter, heavens collapse. 2) The Divine Warrior returns from battle to his temple on his newly won mount.

Isa 30:27ff. is thus reminiscent of the first pattern. Cross finds in v. 27 (v. 29?) an explicit quotation from a war song (p. 176). It is Cross' thesis that the "language of theophany in early Israel was primarily language drawn from the theophany of Ba'l" (p. 157).

the nations (vv. 27f.) has more the function of an introduction to the chief point of the text:[75] Yahweh's punishment of Assyria. Moreover, Isaiah can speak of גוים in a context in which Assyria is the primary object of divine judgment. After the threat to Assyria in 14:25 ("I will break the Assyrian in my land") the prophet with the "summary appraisal form"[76] speaks of this judgment on Assyria as Yahweh's purpose concerning the "whole earth" and "all nations." Punishment of Assyria includes the other heathen nations as well in Isaiah's thought. Or, Isaiah can speak of Assyria as a *"nation* afar off" (5:26). In the light of 29:7f., the "nations" and Assyria would seem to be indistinguishable, for the words "multitude of all the nations that fight against Ariel" can only mean the Assyrians.[77]

Isa 30:27f., 30f., 33 is thus a passage explicitly announcing judgment upon Assyria and therefore belongs together with the other Isaian texts which proclaim Yahweh's wrath against his former "tool" (cf. 10:5-15, a woe-saying against Assyria because of her hybris; 14:24-27; 29:15ff.). It should be noted that there is *no motivation* connected with the announce ments of doom in vv 27f., 30f., 33.

Isa 30:27f., 30f., 33 is an example of Isaiah's use and adaptation of the ancient theophany form. There is no evidence that the background of the theophany is to be found in the Sinai tradition; rather the description of Yahweh's coming in vv 27-28 belongs to the "theophany description" Gattung which was originally connected with Yahweh's appearance as a warrior to help and defend his people and slaughter their enemies. Isaiah has taken the theophany and combined it with an announcement of disaster upon Assyria. Thus, as in Mic 1:3ff., the theophany is a part of a prophetic announcement of divine punishment. Several differences are evident if Mic 1:3ff. is compared with Isa 30:27f., 30f., 33. (1) Form critically, whereas the two-part theophany description is utilized in Micah, only the first part of the form —Yahweh's coming —is found in the Isaian text. (2) Moreover, the theophany-accusation-announcement pattern in Mic 1:3ff. is not found here; instead, Isaiah combines the theophany description only with an announcement. Judgment on Assyria requires, at least here, no specific motivation. (3) Micah's reversal of the tradition as judgment *on Israel* finds no correspondence here: Isaiah understands Yahweh's coming as punishment of Israel's enemies, and thus, perhaps as salvation for Israel.

---

[75] Jeremias, *Theophanie,* 134; cf. Hab 2:12 in relation to vv. 13-15.

[76] On this form in Isaiah, cf. Childs, *Assyrian Crisis,* 128ff.

[77] On the important but complicated issue of Isaiah's attitude toward Assyria, see the older treatments in F. Küchler, *Die Stellung des Propheten Jesaja zur Politik seiner Zeit,* especially 45ff. and in W. Staerk, *Das assyrische Weltreich im Urteil der Propheten,* 46-124, 137-147. A more up-to-date discussion is offered by N. Gottwald, *All the Kingdoms of the Earth,* 175-196. See also H. Donner, *Israel,* 117ff.; Childs, *Assyrian Crisis,* 20-68.

2. Isa 29:5f.

The impressive and rich poem on Ariel in Isa 29:1ff. presents intriguing and in part unsolved problems for Isaiah's views concerning Yahweh and Zion's future. Some of the literary and form critical problems of the unit are touched on below in chap. 2. This permits us to leave these aside here and focus on our main concern, namely the reminiscence of theophany in v. 6.

Vv. 1-3 speak of Yahweh's war-like attack[78] on Ariel.[79] As David once camped at the city (2 Sam 5:6-9), Yahweh himself will now "besiege you with towers" (v. 3). V. 4 apparently expresses the ruin of Zion by means of two different figures, (1) a person "who has been hurled to the ground so that his voice comes from the dust" and (2) a person "who has been slain, and whose voice is that of a disembodied spirit."[80] Whether these verses refer to events of the year 701[81] or 586[82] is disputed; we take the passage as genuine.

The thought changes radically in vv. 5ff.;[83] now Yahweh is no longer Jerusalem's enemy but her defender and protector. The "multitude of her foes" (v. 5) and the "multitude of all the nations" (v. 7) — usually thought of as the Assyrians[84] — will be reduced to nothing, for

> . . . suddenly, in an instant (v. 5) you will be
> visited[85] by Yahweh Sabaoth,
> with thunder and earthquake and great noise,
> with whirlwind and tempest, and
> the flame of a devouring fire (v. 6).

---

[78] V. 2 "I will distress" (I צוק hiph.; usually followed by ל "to constrain, bring into straits" [BDB]; cf. Deut 28:53; Jer 19:9; noun, Isa 8:22; 30:6). V. 3a "I will encamp against you" (הנה + על) with hostile powers, cf. 2 Sam 11:1; 1 Kgs 15:27; 16:17; etc.). V. 3 "I will besiege you" (צור . . . or "enclose with sentries" KBL). The language is that of hostile military attack, but the subject is not an enemy nation but the "I" of Yahweh (vv. 1-3); cf. v. 6, where Yahweh is spoken of in the third person.

[79] "Ariel" refers to Jerusalem (cf. G. Fohrer, "Zion-Jerusalem in the OT," art. Σιών, *TDNT* 7, 300. According to Procksch (KAT), Ariel refers to the oldest part of the city, where the fortress is situated. Gressmann (*Der Messias,* 102) thinks Ariel designates the city as "Todesstadt" and is related to the "Totengeister" of v. 4. Lutz (*Jahwe, Jerusalem und die Völker,* WMANT 27 [1968], 100) translates "Feuerstadt."

[80] Kissane, 314.

[81] Donner, *Israel,* 155. Duhm suggests the time of Sennacherib or the last days of Sargon; Fohrer, 716-711 B.C.

[82] Kissane.

[83] On the problem of the authenticity of these verses and their relationship to the foregoing verses, see chapter 2, p. 56.

[84] Procksch; Gressmann, *Der Messias,* 98; Kissane.

[85] Read תִּפָּקֵדִי with BHS; Kaiser. V. 6 returns to the second person address (cf. v. 3). According to the context (vv. 5, 7) the divine "visitation" is not a threatening but a saving one (cf. Duhm). On this word, see J. Scharbert, "Das Verbum PQD in der Theologie des AT," *BZ* 4 (1960) 209-226.

The language of v. 6 is not explicitly that of the theophany Gattung, for there is no express mention of Yahweh's "coming," "descent," etc. Nevertheless, the natural phenomena enumerated here suggest that the language is dependent upon the theophany motif. As is common in the theophany description form, the thunder, earthquake, and fire are symbols of divine power. These elements of nature are not just accompanying phenomena, as in the Sinai tradition, but are Yahweh's weapons (cf. 30:30; 66:15f.) against which there is no defense.[86] The second element of the two-part theophany form—the reaction of nature—is here incorporated into a promise of Yahweh's salvation for Jerusalem (Ariel), who will defend the city against the "nations" that besiege her. As in 30:27ff., theophanic language belongs to an announcement of disaster for the enemy (Assyria).

As in Mic 1:3ff., Isaiah here makes use of material drawn from the theophany tradition. Both texts picture Yahweh's presence as evoking "fire" (אשׁ), symbolizing the deity's destructive force. But the *differences* in the adaptation of the tradition are again significant: whereas Yahweh comes against Samaria in Mic 1:3ff., Isaiah presents Yahweh's "visitation" as destructive for Jerusalem's enemies; unlike Mic 1:3ff., no guilt is connected with Yahweh's destructive force, for Jerusalem's enemies merely vanish like a dream (Isa 29:6). Thus again we observe how Micah and Isaiah, both drawing on the traditional form and motifs of ancient theophanic conceptions, adapt and use the material differently.

3. Isa 31:4

This passage may be discussed in this context only briefly; see chap. 2 for a fuller treatment of the passage and the difficulties in its interpretation. After the preceding simile in v. 4a, the language of theophany is found in v. 4b:

> So Yahweh Sabaoth will come down (ירד)
>> to fight upon Mount Zion.
>> and upon its hill.

The verb ירד is a typical verb for Yahweh's descent in the theophanies (Mic 1:3; Ps 18:10; Isa 63:19). But none of the other common motifs of the theophany descriptions are present.[87] Nevertheless, Isaiah presents the picture here of Yahweh's coming down, apparently for the purpose of protecting Zion: he comes down "to fight" לצבא,[88] a word which picks up the language of "holy war."[89] V. 4 thus combines the language of theophany with that of the ancient Yahweh wars. As Yahweh once fought for Israel, giving her the victory, so he will protect Zion, the place of his dwelling (8:18), when the Assyrians attack (cf. 31:8). Hence Isa 31:4 is complementary to Isa 30:27ff. and represents a similar view presented

[86] J. Jeremias, *Theophanie,* 108.

[87] Cf. Jeremias, ibid., 61.

[88] Num 31:7, 42; Isa 27:7, 8; Zech 14:12.

[89] Cf. G. von Rad, *Der Heilige Krieg im alten Israel* (⁴1965) 60.

there: Yahweh comes down in a theophany to protect his own by defending them against the advances of the Assyrian enemy. Missing is a portrayal of nature's reaction; instead the *result* of Yahweh's coming is emphasized by v. 5: Yahweh "protects," "delivers," "spares," and "rescues" Jerusalem. As in 29:1ff., Zion is the place of Yahweh's intervention to protect his city from hostile invaders. Isa 31:4 therefore has the character of a promise to Zion, but it does not necessarily imply that divine punishment of Judah has been averted. V. 4, like 30:27ff. and 29:5f., is further evidence of Isaiah's adaptation of the theophany tradition.

In each of these Isaiah texts (30:27ff.; 29:5f.; 31:4), the prophet draws upon the theophany tradition, either to portray Yahweh's coming (30:27; 31:4) or the reaction in nature to his coming (29:6). Yahweh's presence means destruction for the foreign enemy (30:28, 31; 29:7; implied in 31:5) and thus salvation for his own. This remains consistent with the ancient theophany tradition. How different is Micah: the two-part form remains intact (Mic 1:3f. Yahweh's coming; nature's reaction) and becomes part of a typical prophetic announcement of judgment; the purpose of the deity's approach is to bring destruction not on the enemy of his people but on his people themselves, specifically, on Samaria (1:6).

4. Isa 6:1ff.

Chap. 6 in the book of Isaiah is written as an autobiographical account of the prophet's visionary experiences and is prefaced by a historical notation that these events took place "in the year King Uzziah died" (6:1).[90] Chap. 6 is commonly regarded as part of Isaiah's "Denkschrift" or Memoirs (6:1-9:6[7]). The problems of whether this passage reports an "inaugural" vision[91] or a later phase of the prophet's activity;[92] whether chap. 6 originally belonged after 1:1 or 2:1[93] or in its present position before chaps. 7 and 8,[94] need not concern us here. Rather, we wish to focus briefly upon the elements of theophany in chap. 6 and their tradition historical background. First, however, a glance at the problem of the Gattung of chap. 6 will prove instructive.

It is clear that this chapter speaks of a prophetic vision (vv. 6:1, 2, 5, 6) and audition (vv. 3, 4, 7, 8, 9ff.) and that it also reports the prophet's own words of response to what he sees and hears (vv. 5, 8, 11). Since the theme of "call to be

[90] On the problem of the precise date, see the literature cited in note 92 and also I. Engnell, *The Call of Isaiah* (Uppsala, 1949) 25.

[91] Thus J. K. Kuntz, *The Self-Revelation of God* (Philadelphia: Westminster, 1967) 154.

[92] Cf. J. M. Schmidt, "Gedanken zum Verstockungsauftrag Jesajas," *VT* 21 (1971) 68–90; J. Milgrom, "Did Isaiah Prophesy during the Reign of Uzziah," *VT* 14 (1964) 164–182, especially 172ff. and Wildberger's discussion of this view.

[93] Cf. O. Eissfeldt, *Introduction*, 310.

[94] See especially O. H. Steck, "Bemerkungen zu Jesaja 6," *BZ* NF 16 (1972) 198ff., who argues that chap. 6 is not an independent Gattung but belongs to the Denkschrift from the time of the Syro-Ephraimite War; that chap. 6 is continued by chaps. 7 and 8; that the events reported in chap. 6 were given written form in 733, along with chaps. 7 and 8.

a prophet" appears to be a dominant element here, the chapter has come to be
thought of as a "Berufungsbericht"[95] or a "Sendungsbericht,"[96] and the parallels
between Isaiah 6 and 1 Kings 22 and Ezekiel 1-3 are often referred to. N. Habel[97]
speaks of a "call Gattung" and finds in Isaiah 6 a five-part division: (1) divine
confrontation, vv. 1-2; (2) introductory word, vv. 3-7; (3) commission, vv. 8-10;
(4) objection, v 11a; (5) reassurance, vv 11b-13. He discusses the history and
development of the Gattung and concludes that Isaiah, like Jeremiah, Ezekiel and
2 Isaiah, "appropriates and develops the call traditions reflected in the structure
of the calls of Moses and Gideon."[98] In a detailed article on "The Vocation of
Isaiah," Knierim[99] contends that Isaiah 6 is the combination of two different
Gattungen, a vision of judgment which becomes a vision of a call; and that it has
the "purpose of legitimating and justifying the prophetic message. . . ."[100]
Steck's[101] analysis of Isaiah 6 leads him to dispute whether this text is properly
characterized by the term Berufungsgattung (as, for example, in the calls of Moses,
Gideon, Jeremiah, etc.). He notes that these instances of a call from Yahweh have
as a characteristic element Yahweh's address to a certain person at the very outset,
followed by the person's objections to Yahweh's call. But in Isaiah 6, the
framework of which is the events in Yahweh's council, someone is first of all sought
out ("Whom shall I send . . .," v. 8) and then the prophet makes himself available
("Here am I . . .," v. 8) and is commissioned ("Go . . ."). Accordingly, it is Steck's
opinion that Isaiah 6 is *not* an example of a Berufungsgattung. He suggests the
cumbersome phrase "the bestowal of an extraordinary commission in the heavenly
council[102] ("Vergabe eines ausserordentlichen Auftrags in der himmlischen Thron-
versammlung") as an appropriate designation, and understands the Gattung to be
a specific example of the fixed form of a commissioning in the heavenly court
(Zech 1:7ff.; Job 1:6-12). This is not, he continues, an independent Gattung but
rather a fixed part of the report framework which tells of the execution of the
commission.

Regardless of the label one may wish to use in classifying Isaiah 6 as to its
form critical characteristics, it is apparent that *elements of theophany* play a
significant part in the chapter. But what may be appropriately claimed to be
theophany here? In J. K. Kuntz's monograph on theophany in the Old Testament,
he entitles his study of chap. 6 "The Inaugural Theophany to Isaiah of Jerusalem,"
and speaks of three phases of the theophany: vv. 1-4, 5-7, 8-12.[103] Thus Kuntz
places the entire chapter under the rubric "theophany." Such an understanding is
based on an apparently broad definition of what belongs under the category of

[95] Fohrer.
[96] Wildberger.
[97] N. Habel, "The Form and Significance of the Call Narratives," *ZAW* 77 (1965) 310ff.
[98] Ibid., 316.
[99] R. Knierim, "The Vocation of Isaiah," *VT* 18 (1968) 59.
[100] Ibid., 62.
[101] O. H. Steck, "Bemerkungen zu Jesaja 6," *BZ* NF 16 (1972) 189ff.
[102] Ibid., 191.
[103] J. K. Kuntz, *The Self-Revelation of God* (Philadelphia: Westminster, 1967) 162; cf.
Wildberger's designation for chap. 6: "Theophanie und Sendungsauftrag" (theophany:
vv. 1-5; commission: 6-13).

theophany,[104] and is perhaps too undefined and general for a correct form critical understanding of the chapter. Let us now turn to what may be claimed to be theophanic elements here in the narrower sense.

V. 1 reports in first person style that Isaiah "saw Yahweh sitting on his throne."[105] In the strict sense this is not a theophany, which describes Yahweh's coming, descent, etc., but a *vision*. According to v. 2 the prophet's vision includes the heavenly creatures, the שׂרפים[106] who praise Yahweh (v. 3) with the *trishagion;* Yahweh is holy; the earth is full of his כבוד. But here are elements of a "gerichtstheophane Präsenz":[107] the seraphim are a personification of fiery, impending judgment; their song of praise to Yahweh is a "Gerichtsdoxologie."[108] That this scene is one of threatening doom is further illustrated by v. 4, which continues with a *waw consecutive:* וינעו אמות הספים, "And the foundations of the thresholds quaked." This is a motif associated with a divine theophany, as

[104] Here it is helpful to recall Westermann's (*Praise of God in the Psalms,* 98ff.) distinction between epiphany and theophany, and his further distinction between two kinds of theophanies, the Sinai, and the later appearances of God to a prophet (1 Kings 19; Isaiah 6, Ezekiel 1); cf. also Jeremias (*Theophanie,* 1ff.), who distinguishes between Yahweh's coming and the resultant tumult in nature and a theophany which tells of seeing Yahweh, his form, eyes, etc., or perceiving him in a dream, etc. This difference would require that one form critically differentiate strictly between a *vision* and a *theophany*. Accordingly, one must speak of the theophany *elements* in Isaiah 6 rather than the entire chapter as a theophany.

[105] On Yahweh and the divine council, see especially F. M. Cross, "The Council of Yahweh in Second Isaiah," *JNES* 12 (1953) 274ff. and his book, *Canaanite Myth and Hebrew Epic* (Cambridge, 1973) 177-190. Cross argues that whereas Baʻl's characteristic mode of revelation is the storm theophany, El's mode of revelation is his word or decree in the council of the gods. These two modes or patterns he finds well preserved in Canaanite, particularly in Ugaritic, sources. What is important for our purposes here is that, in terms of Isaiah 6, we have material which recalls, not the Baʻl stormy theophany, as in Mic 1:3ff. or Isa 30:27ff., but a picture which, according to Cross, originates ultimately in the judgments of El (cf. 1 Kgs 22:5-28; Psalm 82; Jer 23:18). This would help draw the lines even more sharply between prophetic *vision* in Isaiah 6 and a prophetic theophany description form, as the two belong to completely different patterns and forms.

[106] What are the seraphim? Here they are apparently attendants of Yahweh, super-human beings, having a body of a serpent, wings, and human heads and hands (cf. A. S. Herbert, *Isaiah Chapters 1-39,* The Cambridge Bible Commentary Cambridge: Cambridge University Press, [1973]). The plural is found only here and in v. 6; but cf. Isa 14:29; 30:6; Num 21:6 and Deut 8:15 for the singular. The verbal root שׂרף "to burn" would indicate that the seraphim are fiery creatures; see Karen Jones, "Winged Serpents in Isaiah's Inaugural Vision," *JBL* 76 (1967) 410-415.

[107] Steck, "Jesaja 6," 193, note 17; 195, note 22.

[108] Knierim "Vocation," 57: "This type of doxology of judgment is a known tradition. It confesses to and glorifies the power of Yahweh and mankind before the majesty of God, when he appears to judge sin."

the similar language of Ps 18:8 shows: Yahweh's theophany (ירד v. 10) is connected with "the trembling and quaking of the mountains' foundations" (v. 8). V. 4b continues the description of the reaction to divine presense: "the house was filled with smoke" (עשׁן) again, a typical theophany element (cf. Ps 18:9). Finally, Isaiah's own personal reaction (אוי־לי) is perhaps to be understood as a theophanic element.[109] As Knierim and Steck have underlined, the seraphim, their doxology, the shaking of the foundations, and the smoke are elements of a "theophany of judgment" in the temple.[110]

What is the background of these elements? Where in the tradition do these motifs have their roots? V. Maag suggests that here we have the "entire aura of the Sinai theophany,"[111] while Kuntz finds that the smoke-filled temple has an affinity to the smoke and clouds which are part of the Sinai tradition.[112] But caution is here in order (cf. Wildberger). Indeed, Steck is surely correct in asserting that here we should not simply ask where else in the OT similar motifs occur, but rather, where does one find such motifs in relation to Isaiah's understanding of "Yahweh who dwells on Zion."[113] We agree with Steck that it is *not* the Sinai tradition which is the background for these theophanic elements; instead, the seraphim as fire, quaking of foundations, and smoke, are motifs which belong to the *Jerusalem theophany tradition*, which derives from pre-Israelite origins.[114] This tradition speaks of Yahweh's appearance from Zion for the purpose of coming against his enemies. But as Steck points out, what is extraordinary here is that Yahweh does not come against the "Frevler" wherever they may be, but in the *temple*, which is usually where he appears as *protector* of Israel.

If this is correct, then Isaiah in his vision report in chap. 6, which includes a complex of traditions, has made use of and adapted the Jerusalem cult theology's[115] theophany language so that it becomes a part of his vision of judgment. As in Mic 1:3ff., Isaiah has reversed the theophany concept: Yahweh

---

[109] Cf. Gen 32:31; Exod 3:6; Jgs 6:22 and Wildberger.

[110] Knierim, "Vocation," 50ff.; Steck, "Jesaja 6," 195, note 22.

[111] V. Maag, "Malkût JHWH," VT Suppl. 7 (1960) 143, cited by Wildberger, 251.

[112] Kuntz, *Self-Revelation*, 159.

[113] Steck, "Jesaja 6," 195, note 22.

[114] See Steck, ibid., for a list of passages in support of this. In his book, *Friedensvorstellungen im alten Jerusalem*, Th St 111 (1972) 42, note 112, Steck further described the contours of the Jerusalem theophany tradition: the Sinai tradition has left no positive marks on the Jerusalem cult tradition. According to the latter, Yahweh dwells or thrones permanently in Zion, which would exclude any concept of a cultic festival theophany. In the Jerusalem theophany concept, Yahweh does not appear in the cult in a cultic exercise; rather, he powerfully comes against his enemies wherever they oppose him; cf. Ps 11:6; 18:8ff.; 46:3; etc.; cf. also F. Stolz, *Strukturen und Figuren im Kult von Jerusalem*, BZAW 118, 92f., note 93.

[115] Steck, ibid., 9ff.

comes not to save but to punish his chosen people. But here Isaiah draws upon traditions which are rooted in the Jerusalem theology, whereas Micah's theophany is rooted in a tradition originally at home in the victory hymns of holy war traditions in pre-monarchic Israel. Moreover, in Isaiah 6 the theophany motifs are part of larger vision and audition in which the prophet is commissioned to preach divine judgment and to harden the peoples' hearts; in Micah, on the other hand, the theophany functions as an introduction to a prophetic Gerichtswort. Furthermore, Isaiah employs the tradition to proclaim divine judgment on a broad scale: "this people" (vv. 9f.), their "cities" and "land" (v. 11); in Micah, the disaster of the theophanic appearance has *only* Samaria as its goal (Mic 1:6).

5. Isa 3:13-15

Does this text show evidence of the theophany tradition? In the "coming of Yahweh" (יבוא . . . יהוה) in v. 14 one might find a reminiscence of a theophany motif (cf. Isa 30:27; Deut 33:2; Hab 3:3). Wildberger finds here a reflection of a cultic "Gerichtsrede" employing theophanic elements.[116] But in this text we do not have a cultic judgment speech, as Boecker has demonstrated.[117] Rather, the phrase יהוה במשפט יבוא reflects the language of Israel's prophetic legal procedure; it means therefore not a theophanic "coming" of Yahweh but "to come before the court" (cf. 1 Kgs 3:16; 2 Sam 15:4).[118] Our conclusion is a negative one: 3:13-15 is *not* an example of a cultic Gerichtsrede employing a theophany motif, and is therefore not evidence of Isaiah's use of the theophany tradition.

Summary Conclusion

The foregoing study of theophany texts in Micah and Isaiah leads us to the following conclusions.

1. Both prophets reach back to ancient theophanic tradition and incorporate it into their prophetic sayings.

2. As regards form critical categories, both prophets take up elements of the traditional Gattung and incorporate it into prophetic judgment speeches. In Micah the two-part form (Yahweh's coming, nature's reaction) remains intact and is used as an introduction (1:3f.) to a judgment speech (1:5 accusation; 1:6 announcement of judgment). In Isaiah, by contrast, the first part of the theophany form (Yahweh's coming) is incorporated into either a judgment speech (Isa 30:27f., 30f., 33) or a promise of protection/salvation (31:4f.). Or, the second part (nature's reaction) is used in a threat to Israel's enemies (29:6f.), which implies salvation for Jerusalem. A different formal usage is found in Isaiah 6—no comparable text occurs in Micah—which incorporates theophanic elements into a call narrative.

---

[116] On the "cultic Gerichtsrede," see E. Würthwein, *ZThK* 49 (1952) 1ff.

[117] H.-J. Boecker, *Redeformen des Rechtslebens im AT*, 85.

[118] Ibid., 85f., 91f.; see also E. Jenni, art. בוא, *THAT* 1, 268.

3. The tradition-historical roots of the theophany in Micah and Isaiah lie in the same sphere. Mic 1:3ff. and Isa 30:27ff.; 29:6; 31:4 are to be traced to the theophanic description in the victory hymns of pre-monarchic Israel, in which Yahweh fights for, saves, and defends his people. However, the background of Isaiah 6 is to be assessed differently: here it appears most probable that elements of the Jerusalem cultic theophany (perhaps a complex combination of pre-Israelite and Israelite theophany) are utilized, a stream of tradition to which Micah exhibits no *positive* relationship. (He is critical of the Jerusalem theology, see below, chap. 2.)

4. It is significant that the traditional material is adapted and used in *functionally* different ways by Micah and Isaiah. For Micah Yahweh comes not to help and save his people, as in the ancient tradition, but to destroy, in this case, the capital Samaria (1:6). For Isaiah, Yahweh comes to destroy the enemy, the Assyrian and the nations (30:28, 31; 29:6f.) or explicitly to protect and defend Zion (31:4f.). In each of these Isaian texts, the old function of the tradition is retained: Yahweh comes to save. Thus we see how these two eighth-century prophets can reach back to the same ancient traditional material and yet adapt it in important, contrasting ways. It is also significant that Isaiah's dependence on the Jerusalem cultic theophany finds *no* correspondence in Micah.

EXCURSUS I
SAMARIA AND THE NORTHERN KINGDOM
UNDER PROPHETIC JUDGMENT IN MICAH AND ISAIAH

The superscription in Mic 1:1 indicates that the redactor(s) who was responsible for this verse (or at least the second אשר clause, 1:1b) understood Micah's prophecy to concern not only Jerusalem but also *Samaria*.[119] But the only place Samaria is mentioned in the prophetic sayings is 1:6, where, without any introductory formula, a first person Yahweh speech announces approaching doom for the capital city. "Therefore I will make Samaria into an open field, into a planted vineyard. And I will pour down her stones into a valley, and I will lay bare her foundations." A series of three verbal clauses, which emphasize that Yahweh is the agent of disaster, picture complete devastation of Samaria. The city will be "transformed"[120] into a field and a vineyard, its foundations exposed from the devastation (cf. Ezek 13:14; Ps 137:7; Lam 4:11). The tone and vocabulary are similar to 3:12, which says that Jerusalem will also be destroyed in like manner. Mic 1:6 is not a *vaticinium ex eventu*, but belongs before 722, for Samaria's capitulation to Assyria did not involve destructive events as described here![121] As

---

[119] On the city-state Samaria, see A. Alt, "Der Staatstadt Samaria," *KS* 3, 258ff.

[120] ושמתי followed by ל cf. Gen 21:13; Exod 14:21; Jer 2:7; Isa 28:17 and BDB. For שׂום in a prophetic announcement of disaster with Yahweh as the speaker, cf. Hos 2:5; Am 8:10; Isa 42:15.

[121] Some critics have maintained that Micah did not prophesy against Samaria (cf. Wellhausen; Mays appears somewhat indecisive). Bruno, *Micha und der Herrcher aus der Vorzeit* (1923) 5ff., was the first, as far as I can tell, to vigorously argue that Micah

Sellin (KAT 12/1) has noted, Micah does not speak of a political enemy as Samaria's foe; it is Yahweh himself who executes the destruction, apparently envisioned by means of an earthquake![122]

The motivation for the threatened doom is given in v. 5a. Unlike the more extensive accusations in 2:1ff,; 2:8f.; 3:1ff.; 3:9ff.; the prophet refers only to Jacob's פשע and Israel's חטאת. Here Micah most likely does not have cultic sins in mind, for elsewhere he is concerned only with sins of society and its oppressive leaders![123] The mention of Jacob and the house of Israel in the accusation and then the specific naming of Samaria in the announcement suggests a narrowing of focus upon the capital as the locus of evil in the Northern Kingdom (cf. 3:9ff.). Here it is clear that Jacob/house of Israel means the Northern Kingdom; after 722 these terms are transferred to the Southern Kingdom, as 3:9ff. (cf. 3:8) indicates![124]

Isaiah of Jerusalem also proclaimed words of doom on Samaria and on the Northern Kingdom. He expressly names Samaria in such a context in 7:9; 8:4; 9:8; cf. 10:9, 10, 11; the city is also referred to by the words "fortress . . . of Ephraim" in 17:3; similarly, the "proud crown of the drunkards of Ephraim" in 28:1, 3 is a metaphor for the capital city. Furthermore, Isaiah uses "Israel" to denote the Northern Kingdom in 9:7 (parallel with "Jacob"), 11 (in v. 13, the phrase מישראל יהוה is probably an addition, cf. Kaiser; BHS), and 17:3. "Jacob" is used for the North in 17:4![125] "Ephraim" occurs in 7:2, 5, 9; 9:8, 20. We now turn to a brief discussion of the texts which speak of a threat to Samaria and/or the Northern Kingdom: 9:7-20 + 5:25, 26-29; 8:1-4; 17:1-6; 28:1-4; 7:7-9.

---

originally spoke of Jerusalem rather than of Samaria. Jepsen, "Kleine Beiträge," 97f., thinks that vv. 6-7 are Hosean in character and, like Bruno, understands "Jacob/house of Israel" in v. 1:5a to refer to the Southern Kingdom. With Rudolph, we take v. 6 as original to Micah in its present form. Samaria was not annihilated as described here (cf. Robinson).

[122] Differently, Rudolph.

[123] פשע "is secular and not necessarily forensic and denotes willful breach of a relationship of alliance" and means "to rebel," thus G. Quell, art. ἁμαρτία, TDNT 1, 279, 273. See also Knierim, art. חטא, THAT 1, 543, who notes that חטא is a comprehensive term for sin whose primary meaning is "to miss the goal"; the noun can be used for all kinds of sins: legal, cultic, social, etc., thus the meaning must be governed by the context. Micah's criticism of Samaria is not cultic, nor is Amos' and Isaiah's, cf. Lescow, "Micha 1–5," 83 (he excepts Am 8:14).

[124] This transfer of Jacob-Israel to the Southern Kingdom has a parallel usage in Isaiah; cf. Rost, Israel bei den Propheten, BWANT 4, 19 (1937) 46, note 2. According to Rost (pp. 45ff.) Isaiah as early as the Syro-Ephraimite crisis began to speak of the Southern Kingdom as "Israel," (8:14; cf. 1:3; 5:7; 8:18) and, like Hosea, begins to refer to the Northern Kingdom as "Ephraim" (7:2, 5, 8, 9, 17; 9:8, 20; 28:1, 3).

[125] Cf. Rost, Israel, 46, note 2. As with the word "Israel," "Jacob" is also used to denote the North (9:7; 17:4) as well as the South (2:6; 8:17). Isaiah speaks of "Judah" in 3:1, 8; 5:7; 7:6 (17); 8:8; 9:20; 22:8 (cf. Rost, 47f.). By comparison, Micah refers to Judah only once (1:9), preferring the designation "Jacob/Israel" (1:5a; 3:1, 8, 9).

1. Isa 9:7-20 + 5:25, 26-29 is probably an original poem[126] of five strophes divided by refrains (vv. 11b, 16b, 20b, 5:25b). The first four strophes (9:7-11, 12-16, 17-20, 5:25) present an "historical reminiscence" of Yahweh's past dealings with his people[127] while the final strophe (5:26-29) prophesies a coming disaster brought on by "a nation afar off," i.e., Assyria. The prophet seems to emphasize the focus of his attention by repeatedly naming the object of his dealings: Jacob/Israel; Ephraim/ inhabitants of Samaria, 9:8, 9; Israel, vv. 11, 13; Manasseh, Ephraim, v. 20. In the present literary shape of the passage, the historical reminiscence functions as the accusation, which is followed by the announcement of judgment in the last strophe (cf. Wildberger). As in Mic 1:3ff., Isaiah has prophesied disaster for the North. The motivation differs, however; Micah speaks of Israel's sins of oppression (פשׁע/חטאת), while Isaiah refers to Israel's גאוה and גדל (9:8b, 9; on the text, cf. BHS), Israel's refusal to return (v. 12), her godlessness (v. 16), and wickedness (v. 17) — a broader and more comprehensive accusation. More importantly, whereas Yahweh is presented as destroying Samaria in Mic 1:6, for Isaiah, Yahweh (referred to as "he" in 5:26) summons a foreign enemy who will "seize and carry off" (5:29), that is, take into exile![128]

2. Isa 7:7-9 are words of Yahweh which the prophet addresses to Ahaz during the time of the Syro-Ephraimite war. After an account of the political situation, vv. 1-2, and Yahweh's command to Isaiah, vv. 3-6, a kind of warning is given in vv. 7-9![129] The genre of the piece is not a prophetic account but a prophetic word combined with a description of the situation![130] The words about Syria-Damascus and Ephraim-Samaria in vv. 8a, 9a are to be taken as the subject of v. 7b ("It shall not stand, and it shall not come to pass"), which means that these powers will have no future, for they will not survive their revolt against Assyria![131] Unlike Micah's proclamation of doom against Samaria, Isaiah here connects Samaria (and Ephraim) with Syria in the doom he announces. But it is not a total destruction (cf. Mic 1:6). Nor is the reason for the impending doom in the realm of Samaria's transgressions, but rather for her political alliances, which are against Yahweh's plans. Finally, in contrast to Micah, Isaiah connects Samaria's doom with Assyria (vv. 17ff.).

3. 8:1-4 and 17:1-6 both announce judgment upon Damascus and Samaria. In 8:1f. in his first person report[132] Isaiah tells how Yahweh commanded, and he

---

[126] That these verses belong together has generally been assumed since the time of Ewald (cf. Donner, *Israel*, 70).

[127] The series of consecutive imperfect verbs refers not to future but to past events; cf. Kaiser and discussion in Vollmer, *Geschichtliche Rückblicke*, 137ff.

[128] Some date the entire passage after the Syro-Ephraimite war (e.g., Kaiser; Fohrer; Donner, *Israel*, 71). Wildberger argues persuasively for a date before this period, i.e., in the first phase of Isaiah's activity.

[129] Cf. M. Saebø , "Formgeschichtliche Erwägungen zu Jesaja 7:3-9," *Stud. Theol. Lund* 14, 1 (1960) 54ff. and see Wolff's assessment of this art. in *Frieden ohne Ende*, BibSt 35 (1960) 20f. Cf. also Kaiser.

[130] Cf. Wolff, *Frieden*, 16.

[131] Cf. Saebø , "Formgeschichtliche Erwägungen," 63f.; Wolff, *Frieden*, 21; Kaiser.

[132] Cf. Duhm.

himself executed, the inscription of a large tablet. After the report of the conception and birth of a son, and Yahweh's command to name him Maher-shalal-hashbaz (v. 3), the unit concludes with an announcement of judgment to Damascus and Samaria, which will be plundered by the king of Assyria before the child is old enough to speak (v. 4). The threat of Judah's enemies appears at the same time to be a promise of salvation to Judah, which will no longer need to fear the Syro-Ephraimite coalition![133] Similarly in 17:1ff.[134] the prophet threatens with destruction first Damascus (vv. 1f.) and then "the fortress . . . of Ephraim" (v 3aα) and the kingdom of Damascus (v 3aβ₁). Neither Yahweh nor a foreign agent is explicitly named as the agent of disaster. Vv. 4-6 announce that the Northern Kingdom ("the glory[135] of Jacob"), compared to a harvest of grain, will be cut down. Unlike Micah (1:6), these two Isaian texts link the approaching disaster upon Samaria with Damascus. Isaiah again explicitly names Assyria as the agent of doom (8:4; implicit in 17:1ff.). Unlike Micah (1:5a), Isaiah does not here give any basis for the impending disaster (unless 17:10, with its motif of "forgetting God," is to be linked to vv. 1-6, which seems to have no sound basis in the text).

4. Isa 28:1-4 proclaims "woe" against the "proud crown of the drunkards of Ephraim." V. 1 is both "an introit and a reproach"[136] against the debauchery and drunkenness (cf. 5:11f.) of her aristocracy. Divine punishment (vv. 2-4) by means of the Assyrians ("one who is mighty and strong" v. 2) must follow upon these excesses. The imagery of the passage, e.g., "overflowing waters," "being trodden under foot" (vv. 2-3) suggests violent disaster but not total destruction. Unlike the other Isaian passages we have considered here, this text is formulated in the accusation-announcement pattern, and contains elements of social critique (שׁכר, vv. 1, 3), which is combined with the hybris motif (גאוה, vv. 1, 3; cf. 9:8). Thus it is similar to Mic 1:3ff. in form and content. The judgment announced in both is destructive in nature. However, Isaiah again thinks of Assyria (28:2) as the divine agency of disaster, where Micah names only Yahweh (1:6). Like Mic 1:6ff., Isa 28:1ff. does not relate the doom to Samaria's political alliance with Syria.

Conclusion: Although they were prophets in Judah, both Micah and Isaiah had occasion to look northward and address their prophetic word to Samaria and the Northern Kingdom. A comparison and contrast of these sayings is instructive for our investigation and may be summarized as follows.

1. Both Micah and Isaiah prophesied disaster for Samaria. Whereas Micah presented this in terms of the capital's total annihilation (1:6), Isaiah speaks more generally of Samaria's fall, without specific mention of destruction (8:4; 17:3;

---

[133] Wildberger, however, cautions against seeing v. 4 as a prophecy of salvation for Judah and points to the ambivalent element in Isaiah's prophecy.

[134] Critical assessment of 17:1ff. varies widely. Gray identifies an original poem of three strophes in vv. 1-3, 4-6, 9-11; vv. 7-8 are seen as later additions (cf. Duhm). Fohrer finds in vv. 1-6 a collection of six brief sayings; vv. 7-14 are non-Isaian. Kaiser, on the other hand, thinks that none of 17:1ff. belongs to the eighth century.

[135] According to Duhm and Marti, כבוד is not original to this verse.

[136] Donner, *Israel,* 76 dates this text in the period between 733/32 and 722; Fohrer, 735-733; Kaiser argues that the text betrays Hellenistic Greek influence.

28:1ff.). On the other hand, Isaiah speaks of exile of the whole land (5:29), on which Micah is silent.

2. Micah does not view Samaria's and Israel's future in connection with Syria; for Isaiah, judgment on the Northern Kingdom is intimately linked to Damascus and Syria (7:7ff.; 8:4; 17:1ff.).

3. It is significant that for Micah, Samaria's punishment is understood solely as an act of Yahweh, acting through natural catastrophe without human agency. For Isaiah, however, doom is envisioned at the hands of a political enemy, namely Assyria, whether explicit (8:4) or implied (5:26; 7:17ff.; 17:1ff.; 28:2).

4. Both prophets find motivation for the impending doom in Israel's sins. While Micah speaks of Israel's פשע and חטאת, which we interpreted above as sins of social oppression (in parallel to Jerusalem and Judah), Isaiah's accusation is both more general and comprehensive: pride (9:8f.; 28:2, 3), lack of repentance (9:12), godlessness (9:16), drunken debauchery (28:1, 3), bring on Yahweh's wrath. Unlike Micah, the threats in 7:7ff.; 8:1ff.; 17:1ff. lack any such indictment. In these texts, Isaiah sees Damascus and Syria linked with Samaria and Israel and together both guilty of rebellion against Assyria and united against Judah, which is the reason for their coming fall.

5. Finally, one notes the difference in vocabulary which designates the Northern Kingdom. Whereas both prophets speak of Samaria (Mic 1:6; Isa 7:9; 8:4; 9:8; 28:1, 3; cf. 17:3) and use the word-pair Jacob/Israel (Mic 1:5a; Isa 9:7), only Isaiah uses the designation "Ephraim" (7:5, 9; 9:8, 20), a term Micah never uses.

2
Jerusalem and the Zion Tradition
In Micah and Isaiah

The importance the city of Jerusalem plays in the prophecy of Micah was understood and emphasized by the redactor responsible for the second אשר clause in 1:1. Micah's proclamation is presented as "the word of Yahweh . . . which he saw concerning Samaria and *Jerusalem*." Nothing in chap. 2 appears to concern Jerusalem, but in chaps. 1 and 3, two prophetic sayings are sharply focused on the capital city: Jerusalem is named in 1:9, 12b (13b, which speaks of the "daughter of Zion" is a secondary addition), and the parallel Zion-Jerusalem occurs in 3:10 and 12. Our task in this chapter is to analyze Mic 1:8ff. and 3:9ff. (Part A) and draw a comparison with Isaiah texts which also take up the theme of Jerusalem and relate to the Zion tradition (Part B).

It must be stated that some debate attends the interpretation, especially the date and origin, of the "Zion tradition" and also how or whether Isaiah's prophecy is influenced by it. A brief word about this tradition will therefore prove helpful.

The phrase "Zion tradition" has come to designate a tradition complex encompassing a group of closely related motifs which center around Zion and Yahweh's relationship to the city. The history of this tradition, especially its origin and signficance, has been dealt with in a number of scholarly monographs and articles, especially in about the past three decades.[1] In what is perhaps the basic work on the subject, E. Rohland analyzes the tradition according to four main motifs: (1) Zion is the peak of Zaphon, the highest mountain; (2) the river of paradise flows out of it; (3) God has defeated the assault of the waters and the chaos at Zion; (4) there God has defeated the kings and their peoples. To these J. J. M. Roberts adds a fifth: the defeat of the nations.[2] Many scholars trace

---

[1] To list the most significant: Edzard Rohland, *Die Bedeutung der Erwählungstraditionen Israels für die Eschatologie der Alttestamentlichen Propheten* (Diss. Heidelberg, 1956) 142; G. von Rad, *Old Testament Theology* 1, 46–47; 2 156–159; John Hayes, "The Tradition of Zion's Inviolability," *JBL* 82 (1963) 419–426; Josef Schreiner, *Sion-Jerusalem. Jahwes Königssitz* (1963); H.-M. Lutz, *Jahwe, Jerusalem und die Völker,* WMANT 27 (1968); F. Stolz, *Strukturen und Figuren im Kult von Jerusalem,* BZAW 118 (1970); J. Jeremias, "Lade und Zion," *PbTh* (1971) 183–198.

[2] J. J. M. Roberts, "Zion Tradition," *IDBSup,* 985f., following H. Wildberger, "Das

the roots of the Zion tradition back to the pre-Israelite inhabitants of Jerusalem, the Jebusites. This view has not gone uncontested, especially by G. Wanke,[3] who argues that the Zion tradition arose first in the post-exilic period. Wanke in turn has been criticized by H.-M. Lutz.[4] The discussion has been furthered by two significant articles by J. Jeremias and J. J. M. Roberts. Jeremias investigated the role of the ark in the history of the Zion tradition, concluding that the ancient Yahweh war ideology connected with the ark became combined with Canaanite traditions and led to the formation of the Zion tradition.[5] This article was unfortunately not taken into account by Roberts, whose study of the origins of this tradition led him to the view that the tradition, though not post-exilic, is not related to the ancient Jebusite ideology but derives from a combination of Baal and El mythology together with the glorification of Zion in the Davidic-Solomonic era.[6]

In the following discussion it is assumed that the Zion tradition is not a later, postexilic phenomenon; and it will be shown that Micah and Isaiah reflect evidence not only that the tradition existed before their time, but has influenced, negatively or positively, their prophetic message.

The following questions will guide our comparison:

(1) What is the form and function of the texts having to do with Zion-Jerusalem?

(2) How and in what way is the Zion tradition reflected in their respective messages?

(3) What significant themes or motifs are connected with these texts?

(4) How do Micah and Isaiah envision Zion's future?

A. MICAH

1. Disaster Comes to Zion

The first text to occupy our attention in this chapter is Mic 1:8-16. We are above all interested in what may be learned about Micah's attitude toward

---

Völkerwallfahrt zum Zion, Jes. II 1-5," *VT* 7 (1957) 62-81 . The texts which offer the most important background material are the "Zion Psalms" 46, 48, 76. These Psalms exhibit a variety of closely related similarities of content and structure (on which see esp. Jeremias, "Lade und Zion," 189ff.). The central motifs of the Zion Psalms are: Yahweh is in the midst of Zion (Ps 46:6), or her palaces (48:4); he dwells in Zion (46:5; 76:3; 87:1); Zion is the city of Yahweh, or the city of our God (46:5; 48:2, 9), the city of the great King (48:3) (cf. Jeremias, 191).

[3] *Die Zionstheologie der Korachiten in ihrem traditionsgeschichtlichen Zusammenhang,* BZAW 97 (1966) 70ff.

[4] Jahwe, 213-216; cf. also J. Jeremias, *BiOr* 24 (1967) 365f.

[5] "Lade und Zion," 183-198.

[6] "The Davidic Origins of the Zion Tradition," *JBL* 92 (1973) 329-344.

Jerusalem-Zion as reflected in these verses. Since the text is notoriously difficult to reconstruct, we omit offering a full translation of it with critical notes and refer to the recent commentaries of Rudolph and Mays (cf. also BHS) for full consideration of recent conjectural emendations.

The delimitation of the passage has been discussed above, chap. 1, pp. 13f. We take vv. 8–16 as a unit. In vv. 8–16 only v. 13b (including the following לכן in v. 14) appears to be secondary.[7] Although v. 16 is regarded as secondary by some,[8] no convincing reasons require its deletion from the unit.

What is the *form* and *function* of this passage? First, let us note the various elements. In v. 8 the prophet, not Yahweh (as in v. 6), speaks in the first person, expressing his intention to lament with four cohortative verbs.[9] The motivation for his lamentation is not found in the foregoing passage (vv. 2–7) but in v. 9, introduced by כי, which gives the reason first in a noun clause and then in two verb clauses (perfs.).[10] This "self-summons" (Selbstaufforderung) to lament, followed by a motivation introduced by כי corresponds closely to the genre "a summons to communal lament."[11] Further, the verbs ספר and ילל hiph. are typical of the vocabulary of the genre![12]

V. 16 also seems to represent an example of this form. In v. 16a two imperatives (fem. sing.) summon to mourning rites (קרחי וגזי), with the motivation

---

[7] Cf. e.g., Rudolph; Mays.

[8] Cf. e.g., Fohrer, "Micha 1," 73; Lescow, "Micha 1–5," 55, 68, sees v. 16 as a later threat to Jerusalem, from the period of her capitulation, and relates it to 4:9f., 11f., 14. With Rudolph and others, we consider v. 16 to be genuine.

[9] ספר, "to wail, lament," BDB; on ספר as a designation of lament in the context of mourning rites, see C. Hardmeier, *Texttheorie und biblische Exegese*, BEvTh 79 (1978), 207ff.; ילל hiph., "to howl" (BDB); the parallel of these two verbs also occurs in Jer 4:8; Joel 1:13. The singing of dirge could be accompanied by going bare-headed (the turban was removed) and barefoot (שולל Q) cf. Ezek 24:17, 23 and Jahnow, *Das hebräische Leichenlied im Rahmen der Völkerdichtung*, 1923, 6). With the expression . . . אעשה מספד ואבל, cf. Isa 32:12 and Am 5:16. For a recent and significant discussion of the mourning metaphor as employed in the prophetic announcements of judgment, see C. Hardmeier, (*Texttheorie*). According to Hardmeier, Mic 1:8 is not an explicit introduction to a mourning song; rather, he finds in v. 8a "die Kundgabe einer konkomitierenden, symbolischen Ausdruckshandlung," 357f.

[10] The placement in a sentence of an indicative verb first (v. 9bβ) without a ו is typical of lamentations; cf. Lam 1:2, 3, 7, etc.; Jer 47:7 and K. Schlesinger, *VT* 3 (1953) 386; also Hos 4:6; 10:7; and Wolff, BK XIV/1, 97.

[11] See Wolff, "Der Aufruf zur Volksklage," *Ges.St.*, ThB 22 (²1973) 392ff. The three elements of the genre are: 1) summons to mourn in the imperative (usually in a series); 2) the naming of the addressee by the vocative; 3) the motivation introduced by כי or על followed by the perf. In Mic 1:8, the imperatives are replaced by cohortatives; there is no vocative (the general summons to lament can also occur without the vocative; cf. Wolff, ibid., 396); and the כי clause sustains the same function as in the summons to communal lament. For a critical discussion of Wolff, see Hardmeier, *Texttheorie*, 342ff.

[12] Cf. Jer 4:8; 49:3; Joel 1:13 and Wolff, "Aufruf," 400.

introduced by עַל. A single imperative repeats the summons in v. 16b, followed
by a כִּי clause and the perfect. Though the vocative is not always present in the
form, here it may have become lost, as is suggested by the meter and by the lack
of a connection for the feminine suffixes in the verbs. Thus the passage (vv. 8-16)
is introduced and concluded by the lament motifs presented as the prophet's own
lament or a call to lament.[13]

The lament theme is also found in the body of the unit. V. 10 (בְּכוֹ אַל cf.
BHS) contains a summons to "weep" and "roll yourselves in the dust," the later
being a rite of mourning for the dead. V. 11bβ mentions the wailing (מִסְפַּד) of
Beth-ezel, which picks up v. 8. The call to sound the trumpet in v. 11a (cf. BHS)
though it usually summons to flight before the enemy (cf. Jer 4:5f.)[14] is here
connected with the theme of lamentation (cf. Joel 12:15).[15] If one emends the
beginning of v. 12 to read אִיךְ (cf. BHS), it has the character of a dirge. Finally,
the passage is replete with paranomasia, or word-play, which is frequently used
in death-laments.[16]

Certain expressions recur in vv. 10ff. which lend the passage a kind of
stereotyped character. The expression יוֹשֶׁבֶת plus the name of a town occurs in
vv. 11a, bα, 12a, 13a, 15a — always at the end of a line. Also characteristic is the
direct address to these towns and their inhabitants, both in the form of a warning
(אַל תַּגִּילוּ v. 10a conj. BHS) and in the form of exhortations (vv. 10aβ [cf. BHS],
10bβ, 11, 13, 16). The command in v. 13a, "harness the steeds," is reminiscent of
the "Aufforderung zur Flucht."[17]

To what genre of prophetic speech do vv. 8-16 belong? The passage has been
designated a "Triumphslied"[18] as well as "herald's warning of invasion,"[19] but the
dominance of the elements of lament has led scholars to call the text a lament

---

[13] Hardmeier, *Texttheorie*, 360f., though he relates Mic 1:8-16 to past events, nevertheless maintains that the text is a mourning song which is a "fiktiven Trauerausdruck mit
der Funktion der Unheilsankündigung" (v. 16). Hardmeier discerns two different perspec-
tives in the function of the mourning metaphor in Judean 8th cent. prophecy, both of
which are present in Mic 1:8-16: 1) the function of announcing by means of a fictitious
mourning, a future disaster (Mic 1:8, 16; cf. Am 5:2; Isa 3:25-4:1; 32:9-14); 2) the function
of referring to a real disaster which has already happened (Mic 1:9-15). I find this distinction in Mic 1:8-16 to be artificial and unconvincing. The difficulty of finding past *and*
future events in 1:8-16 can be avoided when the whole piece is dated before 701 and viewed
as the proclamation of a coming disaster.

[14] Cf. Bach, *Die Aufforderungen zur Flucht und zum Kampf,* WMANT 9 (1962) 19ff.

[15] Joel 2:15 is the only passage where the call to sound the trumpet is directly connected
with a summons to lament, cf. Wolff, "Aufruf," 394.

[16] Cf. W. L. Holladay, "Form and Word-play in David's Lament over Saul and
Jonathan," *VT* 20 (1970) 156ff.

[17] Cf. Bach, *Aufforderungen,* 20; Jeremias, "Deutung," 338.

[18] Bruno, *Herrsher,* 38.

[19] R. E. Wolfe, IB 6; N. Gottwald, *All the Kingdoms of the Earth* (1964) 208f.

(*Klage*),[20] lamentation (*Klagelied*),[21] or a dirge (*Toten-, Leichenklage*).[22] For the sake of precision in the use of form critical terminology, the lament as complaint should be distinguished from the lament as dirge.[23] The more appropriate term here is dirge, as the form elements (see above) and the vocabulary suggest ("mourning," "going barefoot and naked," etc.) words which belong to the mourning rites for the dead.[24] And our passage is a good example of the prophetic adaptation of the dirge to suit a specific purpose: the reason for the song is not the death of a person, but the destruction of a political entity. But what is the precise *function* of this prophetic dirge?

In his detailed and important article on this pericope, K. Elliger concluded that Micah with these words refers to a past event, namely, the assault of Sennacherib's troops upon the Judean contryside and the humiliation of Jerusalem in 701.[25] He sees here a genuine lament which reveals the prophet's sympathy and compassion for his countrymen in an hour of great distress. Though this interpretation is appealing and has found several followers (e.g., Weiser; W. Beyerlin, *Kulttraditionen,* 12), there are a number of items which speak against interpreting this lament as referring to a past event, whereby the prophet truly mourns the fate of his nation. The prophetic adaptation of the dirge, singing the calamity of a nation or political group instead of a person, in all other examples refers to a *future* event.[26] The perf. verbs are therefore to be understood as *perfectum propheticum* (vv. 9, 11bα, 12b, 16bβ). The classic example of a prophetic dirge in Am 5:1-3 speaks as though the "virgin Israel *has* fallen, no more to rise," but thereby announces *impending* doom, not a past catastrophe. As in Am 5:1ff. there is no reference to the guilt of Judah and Jerusalem here, which is typical of the prophetic dirges.[27] Moreover, the paranomasia would be meaningless if Micah were referring to a past distress.[28] Vv. 8-16, therefore, is not a genuine lament[29] over a past event, but rather the *announcement of a coming destruction* which is clothed in the form of a dirge. Indeed, the prophetic use of

---

[20] Duhm, "Anmerkungen," 83; Weiser; Jeremias, "Deutung," 337.

[21] Budde, "Rätsel," 79; Sellin; Robinson; Lindblom.

[22] Jahnow, *Leichenlied,* 6, 21, and passim; Elliger, "Heimat," 57; Smith.

[23] Cf. B. Childs, *Isaiah and the Assyrian Crisis* (1967) 22, note 6. On the distinction between a Totenklage and a Notklage (complaint), see C. Westermann, "Struktur und Geschichte der Klage im AT," *Ges. St.* 266ff.

[24] Cf. Jahnow, *Leichenlied,* 6, 21, 24, and passim; also Stählin, κοπετός ("Die Totenklage im AT") *ThW* 3, 835ff.; but see Hardmeier's comments, *Texttheorie,* 358.

[25] Elliger, "Heimat," 61.

[26] Cf. Fohrer, "Micha 1," 78; Donner, *Israel,* 103, states: "Der Text schildert den Anmarsch des Feindes nicht, sondern kündigt ihn an." Cf. also Jeremias, "Deutung," 337.

[27] Cf. Westermann, *Basic Forms,* 202f., notes in his concise discussion of the prophetic lament that the death-lament, "without the trace of a reason," can graphically depict the irrevocable judgment Yahweh brings upon Israel.

[28] Cf. Jeremias, "Deutung," 337f.

[29] Cf. Fohrer, "Micha 1," 73.

the dirge does not comfort, but disturbs; instead of calling forth sorrow and pity, it announces divine judgment upon its audience as though that judgment brings death to them.[30]

The judgment Micah announces in vv. 8-16 is to strike several towns in the Judean Shephelah — some of which are identifiable (see the commentaries) — and especially Jerusalem. It is now our task to look more carefully at the verses concerning the threat to Jerusalem.

Vv. 8-16 refers to Jerusalem at three significant points, dividing the passage into three sections, each ending with the naming of Jerusalem (v. 9b, 12b) or an address to Jerusalem (Zion) (v. 16) — presuming at this point that our interpretation of v. 16 (see below) is correct that Zion is addressed here.

> a. "For incurable is the wound from Yahweh;[31]
> indeed, it comes to Judah,
> it reaches to the gate of my people,
> to Jerusalem" (v. 9).

The motivation for Micah's mourning and wailing is given in v. 9 (the first כי introduces a noun clause; the second כי introduces two verbal clauses, the subject of which is the noun clause).

The word מכה can denote a "plague" (Num 11:33, Deut 25:59, 61), "slaughter" (Jos 10:10; 1 Sam 16:19) or, as here, "sickness, wound" (Lev 26:21; 1 Kgs 22:35, etc.). Following the events of 701, Isaiah described Judah's condition as that of an extremely ill person with "bleeding wounds" (1:6; cf. Jeremiah's laments, 14:17; 15:18; also 30:12). There is no mention of a political enemy as the source of the wound. Micah speaks of Yahweh as its author.[32] Two parallel clauses indicate the goal of the approaching doom: it "comes (באה) to Judah, reaches (בגע) to the gate of my people, to Jerusalem."[33]

Micah calls the Southern Kingdom "Judah" only in 1:9 (1:5b is secondary).[34] The sequence in Isaiah is invariably Jerusalem-Judah (3:1, 8; 5:3; 22:21); the reverse sequence is found only in secondary texts (1:1; 2:1; 36:7 = 2 Kgs 18:22; cf. Amos 2:5, secondary). The sequence in Mic 1:9 places emphasis on Jerusalem, for it is the last part of the sentence and is thus rhetorical rather than geographical (cf. Keil): *Jerusalem* is the ultimate goal of divine judgment.

---

[30] Cf. Stählin, *ThW* 3, 838f., Jahnow, *Leichenlied*, 164.

[31] Read (מכת יהוה) with Elliger, "Heimat," 14; Mays, et al.

[32] The approaching threat to Judah and Jerusalem is *divine* judgment (cf. 1:6; 2:3), as in 1:12b. Micah clearly intends to express a confrontation between Yahweh and Judah/Jerusalem.

[33] בוא frequently is used to indicate the approaching of a catastrophe (often in prophetic perfect) in prophetic judgment speeches (usually in the announcement, seldom in the accusation), cf. Preuss, art. בוא, *ThWAT* 1, 551ff., with a list of examples.

[34] Rost, *Israel bei den Propheten*, 19, unpersuasively argues that here "Judah" refers to the North Kingdom as does "Jacob/Israel" (1:5a), an expression which is transferred to Judah *after* the fall of Samaria. Rather, the use of "Judah" in 1:9 suggests that this passage *precedes* 722, thus explaining this single use of Judah in Micah.

The phrase "gate of my people" (שַׁעַר עַמִּי) stands in apposition to
Jerusalem and was probably a popular expression for the capital city (cf. Ob 13).
In Ruth 3:11 the expression presumably refers to the place where the citizens of
the town gather rather than to the "town council" (Gerlemann, BK XVIII).[35] As
a fixed expression it should *not* be interpreted as an indication of Micah's
sympathy and sorrow over the approaching distress to Judah and Jerusalem.[36]

The concluding line of the motivation (v. 9bβ) emphasizes that the capital
city is the final and most important goal of the "wound of Yahweh." The entire
verse must have troubled Micah's audience, for the words of v. 8 would seem to
announce the death of a person. Instead, the incurable blow reaches to the
capital, the heart of Judah.

b. "For calamity comes down from Yahweh to the
gates[37] of Jerusalem" (v. 12b).

Introduced by כִּי, v. 12b again names Jerusalem as the object of Yahweh's
judgment. V. 12b belongs not with the following "Aufforderung" in v. 13 (Duhm)
but is the motivation for v. 12a (Smith; Sellin; Robinson). The contrast is
between Maroth and Jerusalem; between טוֹב and רַע. The threat from Yahweh
"comes down" (יָרַד cf. 1:3, where Yahweh *himself* "comes down"; cf. 2 Kgs 1:10,
12, 14; Isa 34:5). The calamity which comes down מֵאֵת יהוה (cf. Gen 19:24) is
indicated by the word רַע, "evil, distress, calamity" (BDB) and also denotes
divine judgment in Micah 2:3. Micah's opponents in 3:11bβ seem to respond
directly to such an announcement, when they say, "No evil (רָעָה) will come upon
us."

The goal of the calamity, prefixed by the preposition לְ, is the "gates of
Jerusalem." V. 12b obviously picks up v. 9b and is similar in wording and
function. Again the prophet names Yahweh as the agent of danger which will
strike Jerusalem. It is significant that Judah is not mentioned again; the
prophet's focus is narrowing down to the capital, as the climax in v. 16 suggests.
Thus a second time divine judgment is announced upon Jerusalem; no political
foe is named.

c. "Make yourselves bald, and cut off your hair,
for the children of your pleasure.
Enlarge your baldness like the vulture's,
for they shall go forth into exile" (v. 16).

[35] Whether a more specific meaning is implied, such as market place (Marti), meeting
place (Keil; Weiser), or judicial tribunal (Smith), is difficult to say.
[36] Unlike Hosea, where "my people" always voices God's compassion for his people; (cf.
2:3, 25; 4:6, 8, etc. and Wolff, BK XIV/1 on 4:6). On עַמִּי in Micah (and Isaiah) see the
excursus below, chap. 4.
[37] *GST* read the plural; cf. BHS.

In v. 16 the dirge reaches its conclusion. Neither the deletion of the verse as secondary[38] nor the transposition of 4:14 after v. 16[39] recommends itself. The similarity of v. 16 — according to both form and content — with v. 8f. speaks strongly in favor of taking v. 16 as the original conclusion to the passage.

A vocative in v. 16 has apparently become lost, as is suggested not only by the meter but by the lack of an antecedent for the feminine suffixes. To whom are the feminine imperatives addressed? The "land of Judah,"[40] "Samaria,"[41] as well as the "house of Israel"[42] have been suggested. We assume here that the imperatives are intended to address Jerusalem,[43] whom Micah summons to "make yourself bald," a typical mourning rite for the dead (cf. Am 8:10; Isa 22:12; Jer 16:6). For whom Jerusalem is to mourn is indicated by the על clause. The בני תענוניך (cf. Songs 7:7; Eccl 2:8) are most probably the inhabitants of Jerusalem. The last clause (v. 16bβ) gives the reason for Zion's mourning: her inhabitants will go into "exile" (גלה II).[44] The threat of exile appears in prophetic speeches not infrequently (cf. Am 5:5, 27; 6:7; 7:11, 17; Jer 1:3; etc.); only once did Isaiah speak of exile (5:13), but there it is not merely Jerusalem but the entire nation (עמי), including nobility and the multitude. Yahweh is not named in v. 16, as in vv. 9b and 12b, but he is frequently the one who brings into exile (Am 5:27; Jer 29:4, 7; Ezek 39:28).

Thus the dirge concludes with a summons to Jerusalem to mourn for the coming exile of her inhabitants. As in the beginning (vv. 8f.) and middle (v. 12b), the focus is upon the capital city in v. 16. These three parts provide the structure upon which the entire passage is built, giving it a three-fold division: vv. 8–9, 10–12, 13–16. Each part ends with a כי clause formulated in the perfect which announces impending judgment upon Jerusalem, especially emphasized in vv. 9b and 12b by the final position of "Jerusalem" in the sentence.

What is the approximate date of this piece? Lindblom and Wolfe agree in favor of 711; Sellin, especially Elliger, and Weiser find the passage related to the events of 701, when Sennacherib marched into the Southern Kingdom. Though no ultimate certainty is possible, the late date of 701 is to be met with great skepticism; as Donner has forcefully argued, an earlier date of 724–22 is to be preferred.[45]

Let us now briefly summarize the main thrust of these words concerning Jerusalem in 1:8–16.

---

[38] Cf. e.g., Mays.
[39] Beyerlin, *Kulttraditionen,* 18f.
[40] Wellhausen; Nowack.
[41] Riessler, *Die kleinen Propheten* (1911).
[42] Duhm, "Anmerkungen," 84.
[43] E.g., Smith; Sellin; Weiser; see especially Rudolph.
[44] Cf. Westermann and Albertz, art. גלה *THAT* 1, 418ff.
[45] Donner, *Israel,* 102f.; cf. also Rudolph. For a review of the matter of the date, see Hardmeier, *Texttheorie,* 358f.

1) This prophetic speech is largely clothed in the form of a dirge, as the predominance of the dirge elements and the summons to lament indicate. The function of this prophetic adaptation of the dirge is not to lament a past catastrophe, but to announce an impending threat. Corresponding to other instances of a prophetic death-lament, there is no accusation of guilt to provide the motivation of the announcement.

2) Although Judah is named in v. 9b and certain towns in the Judean countryside are mentioned (vv. 10ff.), the primary goal of the threat Micah announces is the capital city, which is referred to no less than three times (vv. 9b, 12b, 16 by implication) in each case in the context of an explicit announcement of judgment in the perfect. The structure of the passage also underlines this: each of the three parts (vv. 8-9; 10-12; 13-16) culminates in an explicit threat to Jerusalem (vv. 9b; 12b; 16b).

3) The author of the approaching disaster is Yahweh himself, who is named no less than two times (vv. 9b, 12b). The "incurable wound," the calamity (רע), comes down from him. Yahweh presumably is the one who "takes into exile" (cf. Am 5:27). Thus Micah emphasizes that it is Yahweh who stands opposite Jerusalem with his judgment. There is no mention whatsoever of a hostile political force.

4) Totally absent in this passage is any allusion to the Zion tradition. Jerusalem does not stand under Yahweh's protection; rather, it is *he* who brings the calamity. Yahweh does not dwell in Zion, but instead sends down his judgment from heaven. Thus Micah in this announcement of divine judgment upon Zion appears to stand as an opponent of the Zion tradition's concept of the city's inviolability.

2. Zion is Destroyed

We turn to a second text in which the Jerusalem theme is of especial importance, Mic 3:9-12.

v. 9	Hear this, you heads of the house of Jacob
	and rulers of the house of Israel;
	who abhor justice
	and pervert everything that is right;
v. 10	who build[a] Zion with blood
	and Jerusalem with wickedness.
v. 11	Her heads render judgment for a bribe,
	her priests teach for gain,
	her prophets prophesy for money.
	And they trust in Yahweh, saying:
	"Is Yahweh not in our midst?
	Misfortune will not come upon us."
v. 12	Therefore on your account
	Zion will be plowed as a field;
	Jerusalem will become a heap of ruins,
	and the mountain of the house will belong
	to the "animals"[b] of the forest.

Textual notes:

a   Read בני cf. BHS.

b   Read לבהמות with Rudolph; Wolff, *Mit Micha reden,* 25, note 4; cf. Mic 5:7.

a. The "summons to hear" (שמעו נה) in v. 9 marks the clear beginning of a new unit which is concluded with v. 12. Arguments for a combination of several pieces which were secondarily united into the present unit have been unconvincing;[46] with recent critics, we take vv. 9–12 to be an original *rhetorical* unit.[47]

Following the opening summons (imperative plur.) in v. 9a the guilt of the ראשים/קצינים is described in v. 9b by a def. plur. participle followed by a finite verb (cf. *Ges.-K.* par. 116x) and continued in v. 10 by a second participle. The summons to hear should be form-critically distinguished from the two-part "Lehreröffnungsformel"[48] (cf. Mic 1:2; 6:2 [conj. cf. BHS]) which is never followed by an accusation in participial style. There is no need to suppose that the participles were originally preceded by "Woe" (Robinson), for the combination of summons + participle is typical of prophetic speech: cf. Am 4:1; 8:4; Isa 28:14 (the formula later functions to announce salvation in Isa 46:3, 12; 48:1; 51:1, 7). The accusation begun in v. 9b, 10 continues in v. 11a with three strictly parallel verbal clauses; the previous direct address is replaced by the third person plur. and the participles (v. 9b, 10) have become finite verbs. The actions of the rulers, priests, and prophets make them culpable, for they perform their respective functions (ישפטו; יורו; יקסמו) "for" (ב-pretii, cf. *Ges.-K.* par. 119p) monetary gain.

A new thought is added in the continuation (note the ו) of the accusation in v. 11b, having two parts: (a) v. 11bα, false trust in Yahweh (ישענו ועל יהוה) which is intended to form a contrast to the accusation voiced in v. 11a; (b) v. 11bβγ, a quotation of the prophet's opponents, introduced by לאמר,[49] and formulated in the first person plur., which consists of two elements: (1) a rhetorical question introduced by הלוא and (2) a declaration in the imperfect. Thus the accusation, commencing in v. 9b and reaching a climax in the quotation in v. 11b, is an "expanded"[50] form, which has three different parts, each with a different grammatical structure signaling a different theme: vv. 9b–10, injustice (participles); v. 11a, misuse of office (imperf. verbs); v. 11b, false trust (quotation of opponents).

---

[46] Cf. Robinson; Lescow, "Micha 1–5," 49, notes 14 and 15.

[47] Cf. Rudolph; Mays.

[48] The "summons to hear" has been given a thorough analysis by Hardmeier, *Texttheorie;* see 320ff. and esp. 307ff. This form-element can introduce a variety of genres: a motivated judgment speech (Am 4:1–3); judgment speech without motivation (Am 5:1–3), etc., cf. pp. 247f., note 28.

[49] On the prophets' citation of their opponents' words, see H. W. Wolff, "Das Zitat im Prophetenspruch," *Ges. St.,* ThB 22 (²1973) 38–129. The quotation brings the listeners to attention, dramatizes the accusation, and heightens the effect of the indictment (cf. p. 60).

[50] Cf. Westermann, *Basic Forms,* 184.

The לכן in v. 12 signals the change to an announcement of judgment. Unlike Mic 2:3, no messenger formula follows the לכן;[51] instead of a first person Yahweh speech (cf. 1:6; 2:3), the announcement is formulated in three clauses in the passive. The style returns to the direct address of vv. 9f.: it is "on account of you" (בגללכם)[52] that disaster comes to Jerusalem.

Vv. 9-12 present a typical, two-part Gerichtswort exhibiting the following structure:

v. 9a   Introduction: summons to hear; naming of the addressee
v. 9b-11   Complex accusation, climaxing in the quotation of Micah's opponents
v. 12   Announcement of judgment

b. Unlike 1:8-16, this passage focuses only on Jerusalem, leaving Judah out of the picture entirely. In vv. 9-12 the central importance of the capital city is emphasized in several ways. The parallel words Zion-Jerusalem[53] occur both in the accusation (v. 10) and also in the announcement (v. 12). Reference to Zion is underscored by the thrice repeated fem. suffs. in v. 11a: "*her* rulers, *her* priests, *her* prophets." It is noteworthy that Micah, having established the guilt of these leading circles, announces judgment not only upon them, but upon the city itself (v. 12). Just as the rulers, priests and prophets are connected with Zion (v. 11a), so the city's future is related to their guilt (בגללכם v. 12).

The prophet underscores the wickedness of Zion by means of four different motifs: (1) The city's system of justice has been perverted and twisted by its leaders. The ruling classes "abhor " and "twist all that is הישרה" (v. 9b). (2) The city itself has been built on corruption and oppression. It is a city built with דמים, with bloodguilt,[54] probably meaning that the constructing of elegant (private rather than public) buildings has been done at the expense of the goods and the lives of the poor. Although others spoke of Jerusalem as a bloody city (Jer 22:17; cf. עיר דמים in Ezek 22:2ff.; Nah 3:1; cf. Hab 2:12), Micah was apparently the first prophet to describe the city of David in such an antagonistic manner. (3) V. 11a continues to underline Zion's corruption. Zion's rulers, priests, and prophets perform their official duties for bribes (שחד) and money; these acts of favor to the rich ultimately result in oppression and injustice to the

---

[51] In Jer 26:18 the same announcement is introduced by the messenger formula, but without a לכן. Budde, "Micha 2 und 3," *ZAW* 38 (1919/20) 22, thinks the messenger formula originally belonged after לכן בגללכם in 3:12; also Sellin.

[52] בגלל seldom occurs in prophetic speech; cf. Jer 11:17 and 15:4 where the word also connects a threat with its reason. Further, cf. Gen 12:13; 30:27; Deut 1:37; 18:12; 1 Kgs 14:16.

[53] According to Fohrer (art. Σιών, *TDNT* 7, 296) all other parallels of Zion-Jerusalem are late.

[54] On דמים as bloodguilt, cf. Num 35:33, Deut 17:18; etc., and Gerlemann, art. דם in *THAT* 1, 448-451. The social critique of this passage is considered in detail below, chap. 4.

poor. (4) V. 11b contrasts the guilt of Zion's leaders with their confession of faith in Yahweh. Here, a more detailed exposition will take us a step further in understanding the Zion theme in Micah.

(a) Micah accused his opponents of "trusting in Yahweh" וְעַל־יהוה יִשָּׁעֵנוּ v. 11bα).[55] שָׁעַן (niph.) followed by עַל means "to lean, support oneself upon" (2 Sam 1:6; 2 Kgs 5:18; Jgs 16:26). Here it is used in the figurative sense of "to rely on, trust in" and is synonymous in meaning with the word בטח (they stand parallel in Isa 31:1; 50:10; Prov 3:5). For Micah this is *false* trust, which provides a false sense of security, as the quotation of his opponents in v. 11bβγ illustrates.

(b) The quotation in v. 11bβγ is a response to Micah's preaching, disputing his claims that divine judgment is imminent. The two-part structure consists, first, of a rhetorical question, הֲלוֹא יהוה בְּקִרְבֵּנוּ, formulated in the first pers. plur. A negative assertion follows: לֹא־תָבוֹא עָלֵינוּ רָעָה. These words express a belief in Yahweh's divine presence in Jerusalem which guarantees the city's safety. But does v. 11bβγ merely reflect the popular piety of Zion's inviolability? Or does it directly pick up ancient Jerusalemite tradition?

W. Beyerlin has argued that the words in v. 11bβ reflect the language of theophany, rooted in the Sinai tradition, which became incorporated in the Jerusalem cultic tradition.[56] That the words stemming from Micah's opponents are rooted in Jerusalem cultic tradition may be accepted as correct. But a brief examination of v. 11bβ and γ will show that these words reflect a different history of tradition than the Sinai complex.

(1) יהוה בקרבנו is a noun clause[57] with Yahweh as subject, with a suffixed adverb as predicate. This expression, or formula, occurs in the Old Testament in a wide variety of contexts,[58] but its primary significance is in connection with

[55] Isaiah also uses the word in a negative sense: reliance on "oppression and perverseness" (30:12), or on "horses and chariots" (31:1).

[56] *Kulttraditionen*, 39. Beyerlin connects the words יהוה בקרבנו with 1 Sam 4:3, where the phrase יהוה יבא בקרבנו is related to the ark. He postulates that Mic 3:11bβ points to the ark in the Jerusalem sanctuary, i.e., not the ark as cultic object, but rather to the concept of epiphany that is supposedly connected with the ark. We may note here, without extensive critique, that (1) The assumed connection between ark and theophany is problematic (for details, see Jeremias, *Theophanie*, 121ff.; R. Schmitt, *Zelt und Lade als Thema alttestamentlischer Wissenschaft* [1972] 270ff.). (2) According to the oldest information about the ark in Numbers, Joshua, and 1/2 Samuel, the ark is understood as a manifestation of Yahweh's lasting *presence*, and has nothing to do with a sudden theophanic appearance (cf. Schmitt, *Zelt und Lade*, 131ff.). 1 Sam 4:3 is not about a theophanic appearance. (3) Beyerlin also appeals to Exod 34:9 for support. Nor is this theophany language. Moses merely requests that Yahweh *accompany* Israel as she enters the promised land.

[57] The noun clause expresses a condition or state; cf. Grether, *Hebräische Grammatik für den akademischen Unterricht* (²1955) par. 94c.

[58] With man as speaker it can express an assertion of (Num 11:20; Deut 6:15), a question about (Exod 17:7), or a wish for (Exod 34:9), Yahweh's presence.

the Yahweh war tradition (Num 14:42f.; Deut 1:42, 7:21; Jos 3:5; 1 Sam 4:3). It is thus a variation of the formula יהוה עם (or יהוה בקרב) (את) and יהוה עם are used interchangeably in Num 14:42f.), the ancient assurance of divine presence in Yahweh war.[59] When the ark was brought to Jerusalem and installed in the sanctuary, the tradition of Yahweh war apparently became incorporated into the Jerusalem cultic tradition, where it found expression in the Zion tradition.[60] Whereas Yahweh was formerly "in the midst of Israel" in her "holy wars," he then became thought of as he who dwells in Zion, where he protects his people from the onslaught of the enemy. It is in the so-called Zion Psalms 46, 48, and 76 where these motifs are most vividly expressed.[61] The motif of Yahweh's presence in his city is especially emphasized in Ps 46,[62] where the refrain יהוה צבאות עמנו is sung at the end of strophe II (vv. 5–8) and strophe III (vv. 9–12) and perhaps originally after strophe I (vv. 2–4). The refrains appear to summarize the essence of the preceding strophes. This is not the language of theophany; rather, these words express praise of the *present* dwelling of Yahweh in Zion. As in Mic 3:11bβ, this is a noun clause, formulated in the first pers. plur., and it corresponds fully with the words of Micah's opponents. In the second, main strophe in Ps 46 (vv. 5–8), a statement is made which sums up the reason why the inhabitants of the city of God need have no fear: אלהים בקרבנו. Here we find precisely the same word (בקרבנו) that is used in v. 11bβ to express Yahweh's presence. There can be little doubt that it is *this* motif in the Zion tradition to which Micah's opponents appeal and upon which they base their false security. They take their stand upon the Jerusalem cult tradition which holds that Zion is the "city of God" (Ps 48:2), his holy habitation (46:5), the "dwelling place" (76:3) which he has established (48:4; cf. 87:1).

(2) The structure of the entire statement (v. 11bβγ) lends confirmation to this interpretation. The quotation in v. 11bβγ has a statement about Yahweh's presence followed by a negatively formulated assertion which gives the consequences of the divine presence. The same structure can be observed in Ps 46: "God is our refuge" (v. 2); consequence: "we will not fear" (v. 3); "God is in her midst" (v. 5); consequence: "she shall not be moved" (v. 5). This correspondence between the divine presence and divine protection can be seen further in Ps 46:7 and 8, 10 and 12; 48:4 and 5–8; 76:2f. and 4, 6f.

It thus becomes clear that Micah, in dispute with his opponents, is engaged in a *sharp polemic against the Zion tradition* and those who hold to a false security in the city's divine protection and inviolability. For he placed in the

---

[59] Cf. Wolff, *Frieden ohne Ende*, 42; further see H. D. Preuss, ". . . ich will mit dir sein," *ZAW* 80 (1968) 139–173.

[60] Cf. J. Jeremias, "Lade und Zion," *PbTh* 183–198, esp. 195.

[61] Only Pss 46, 48 and 76 should be designated as "Zion Psalms"; for the reasons, see O.II. Steck, *Friedensvorstellungen*, 9, note 5.

[62] On Ps 46, see the detailed analysis in Rohland, *Erwählungstraditionen*, 123ff.; also Jeremias, "Lade und Zion," 190ff.

strongest possible contrast to the false security (v. 11b) an announcement of judgment in v. 12. Here, picking up the "Zion-Jerusalem" terminology from v. 10, the prophet adds a third term: the mountain of the house (הר הבית). The entire city, including the temple, is subject to total annihilation, as the imagery of the verse makes clear ("plowed field," etc.).[63]

For our central concern, we may summarize as follows.

1. In this prophetic saying Micah focuses his attention on Jerusalem and her responsible circles: rulers, heads, priests, prophets. They are inextricably linked to Zion.

2. The city has been corrupted by these leaders, who pervert justice and misuse their offices for gain.

3. Micah's opponents are also guilty of false trust in Yahweh, basing this trust in slogans ultimately rooted in the Zion tradition. The prophet's accusation against them is a strong polemic and rejection of the concept of Zion's protected status.

4. The announcement of doom is not simply punishment of those groups accused, but total annihilation of the city, palace, temple and all.

5. Whereas 1:8ff. speaks of "Yahweh's blow" or "disaster" or "exile" (1:9b, 12b, 16b) coming to Jerusalem, with no accusation for a motivation, 3:9ff. brings an indictment against the responsible circles which results in the announcement of the city's complete destruction.

B. ISAIAH

1. Yahweh and Zion

Where Micah's use of the Zion tradition is both clear and consistent, Isaiah's understanding of the relation between Yahweh and Zion is more complex. To begin this analysis of pertinent Isaian texts, we group three texts together which make an explicit statement about Yahweh's relationship to Zion: Isa. 8:18; 14:32; 28:16-17a.

a. Isa 8:18.

In the unit 8:16-18 (cf. Wildberger) Isaiah, after commanding that his teaching be sealed among his disciples (v. 16), utters a first pers., confession-like[64] statement of trust in vv. 17-18a, concluding with the statement about "Yahweh Sabaoth, who dwells on Mount Zion" (השכן בהר ציון).

Yahweh is linked to Zion by the participle השכן, which grammatically may be understood to signify his continual, uninterrupted dwelling there (cf. Ges.-K.

---

[63] The date of Mic 3:9-12 is often assigned to the events of 701 (cf. Marti; Nowack; Wolfe); Sellin suggests 711, when Sargon made his expedition to punish Ashdod.

[64] The genre of vv. 16-18 is that of prophetic confession or memoir (cf. Gray; Kaiser; Wildberger), with a tone of lament (Wildberger). On 8:11-16, see Th. Lescow, "Jesajas Denkschrift aus der Zeit des syrisch-ephraimitischen Krieges," ZAW 85 (1973) 324ff.

par. 116a). Isaiah here picks up a motif that belongs to the Jerusalem cultic theology, particularly as it is expressed in the Zion Psalms (cf. השׁכן in Ps 46:5).[65]

b. Isa 14:32.[66]

In the unit 14:28-32, vv. 29-31 are addressed to Philistia, who is first warned against premature rejoicing (v. 29a) and then summoned to wail (v. 31a), with the reasons given in two כי clauses (vv. 29b, 31b). V. 32 stands in abrupt contrast to the preceding verses, for it juxtaposes the danger of Philistia with the security of Zion, and it replaces the direct address of vv. 29, 31 with a question and answer. Our interest is in the answer to the question, "What should one answer the messengers of the nations?"[67] which the prophet gives: "Yahweh has founded (יסד) Zion, and in her the poor of his people find refuge" (v. 32). The noun clause (inversion of predicate and subject; cf. Ges.-K. par. 140f., 142a) places emphasis on the subject, Yahweh. Whereas 8:18 expressed the idea that Yahweh dwells in Zion, here the imagery is that of the masterbuilder who makes secure the building by laying its foundation. Though this imagery is reminiscent of creation language (Yahweh as the one who lays the foundation of the earth)[68] Isaiah is again appropriating a motif taken from the Zion tradition.[69] The root יסד (pi. "to found, establish" BDB) and its synonym כון occur in the Zion Psalms and undoubtedly reflect ancient, pre-Israelite tradition.[70]

Zion is a place of refuge (יחסו) for the poor (concerning the "poor" in this verse, see below, chap. 4); the image is familiar from the Zion Psalms, which speak of the city as a bulwark: the habitation (משׁכן 46:5) of God is a place of refuge (מחסה, 46:2) against the waters of chaos; cf. 48:4ff., 76:3ff.

Thus, within the context of a saying addressed to Philistia, the prophet in v. 32 proclaims that Zion is a place of security for the poor (*not* the entire nation). The security is not, however, unconditional; nor is hostile attack

[65] Cf. further Pss 48:2, 4; 76:3, and literature cited in Wildberger. On the word משׁכן, cf. W. H. Schmidt, "משׁכן als Ausdruck Jerusalemer Kultsprache," *ZAW* 75 (1963) 91f.

[66] Begrich, "Jesaja 14:28-32," *ThB* 21 (1964) 124f., recognizes a three-part structure: vv. 29-30, 31, 32, but places 30a before v. 32; Gray and Fohrer delete the verse as secondary. For a thorough form critical analysis see Childs, *Isaiah*, 59ff. J. Vollmer, *Geschichtliche Rückblicke*, 193 is unconvincing in his arguments against the authenticity of v. 32.

[67] This question is not addressed to Philistia but to Judah or perhaps King Hezekiah; cf. Fohrer.

[68] Cf. H.-M. Lutz, *Jahwe*, 152.

[69] Cf. Childs, *Isaiah*, 61; cf. Rohland, *Erwählungstraditionen*, 140f.

[70] Cf. Ps 48:9, "the city . . . which God established (יכוננה); also 87:1, 5; cf. 76:3. Cf. Jeremias, "Lade und Zion," 192 and the lit. cited in note 40.

precluded.[71] It is important to note that v. 32b is "not a word of promise to Israel, but a confession of faith proclaimed by Israel to the nations."[72]

c. Isa 28:16-17a.

This text is closely related to Isa 14:32, but offers a variation on the motif of Zion's "foundation."

It is a matter of dispute whether vv. 16-17a present an originally independent saying, later placed into its present context, or whether these verses are an organic part of vv. 14-18 (vv. 14-22).[73] Vv. 16-17a are introduced by the messenger formula; Yahweh speaks in the first pers. Preceded by an accusation (vv. 14f.) and followed by an announcement (vv. 17bff.), vv. 16-17a offer a promise of salvation; no addressee is indicated.[74] Our interest is in v. 16, where Zion is the central focus; Yahweh says:

Behold, I am laying in Zion (יסד בציון)[75]
for a foundation stone, a tested stone,
a precious corner stone of a sure foundation;
whoever believes will not be in haste.

As in 8:18b and 14:32b, Yahweh is here linked to Zion; whereas Yahweh founds (יסד) Zion in v. 14:32b, here Yahweh lays a foundation stone *in* Zion. This foundation (מוסד) guarantees security for those who trust (המאמין). It is apparent that the Zion tradition is expressed here, but altered somewhat lest there be a misunderstanding, for security in Zion is to be understood only in connection with Yahweh's purpose and the demand for faith.[76] Similar to 14:32, where Zion is a refuge for the "poor," here, Zion is a place of security only for the faithful.

Here we may draw a preliminary contrast between Micah and Isaiah in relation to the Zion tradition.

(1) When Micah speaks of "Yahweh" and "Jerusalem" together (1:9, 12b), it is in an adversary relationship; Yahweh brings a "blow" or "evil" on the city.

---

[71] Cf. among others, Th. Vriezen, "Essentials of the Theology of Isaiah," in *Israel's Prophetic Heritage* (1962) 140f.

[72] Cf. Childs, *Isaiah*, 61.

[73] Cf. Procksch; Childs, *Isaiah*, 30f., for the former view; Marti; Schreiner, *Sion-Jerusalem*, 168ff., for the latter. The date of the text is disputed; Duhm thinks the text belongs to the time of Sargon's hostilities against Philistia; Donner, *Israel*, 153, ca. 705-701.

[74] For a thorough analysis of 28:14-22, see Childs, *Isaiah*, 29ff., and especially 65ff.

[75] Read יוסד instead of יסד pi., Marti; BHS; otherwise, Rohland, *Erwählungstraditionen*, 150.

[76] Rohland, *Erwählungstraditionen*, 148ff.; Childs, *Isaiah*, 67. Zimmerli, "Prophetic Proclamation and Reinterpretation," in *Tradition and Theology in the OT*, ed. D. Knight (1971) 85f.

By contrast, "Yahweh and Zion" in Isaiah belong together positively in 8:18; 14:32; 28:16. Whereas in Micah the city will lose its inhabitants in exile (1:16) or be totally destroyed (3:12), in Isaiah, Zion is where Yahweh dwells; it is founded by him and therefore is a place of safety, at least for the poor and the faithful (14:32b; 28:16).

(2) Significantly, the motif of "trust, belief" is connected with Zion in *both* Micah and Isaiah, but in remarkably antithetical ways. Micah accuses his opponents (Zion's heads, priests and prophets) of trusting (ישענו) in Yahweh's presence and fearing no evil (3:11b). Isaiah's view is in sharp contrast to Micah's: Yahweh dwells in Zion, a place of security for the poor and especially those who trust in him. The context and structure of the words of Micah's opponents is remarkably similar to Isaiah's words: cf. ישענו ... לא-תבוא עלינו רעה (Mic 3:11) with המאמין לא יחיש (Isa 28:16). In both statements, a word for trust is followed by a verbal clause introduced by לא which denies the possibility of danger. In each case, the declaration is a confession-like statement which is predicated on Yahweh's protective presence in Zion. However, it is significant that neither Micah 3:11 nor Isa 28:16 is connected with all of Jerusalem (or Judah) but with *groups* in Jerusalem: for Micah, the circles of leadership whom he accuses; for Isaiah, the faithful who are perhaps the remnant, or his disciples.

2. Yahweh Protects Zion

Here we investigate texts which give us further insight into the function of the Zion tradition in Isaiah, continuing the comparison with Micah's prophetic sayings about Zion. The texts pertinent to this theme are Isa 8:9f.; 17:12ff.; 29:1ff.; 31:4f.

a. Isa 8:9f. and 17:12-14

The basic similarity of these two texts allows us to take them together.[77] Three elements link them closely together: (1) Zion, or the nation (neither is specifically named), is under attack from an unnamed enemy (עמים 8:9; 17:12). (2) Yahweh is understood as the protector, who wards off the enemy (8:10b; 17:13). (3) The structure and motifs of each text exhibit characteristics which are dependent upon the Zion tradition.[78]

If these sayings stem from Isaiah, and we believe adequate and persuasive evidence has not yet proven their non-genuineness,[79] they contrast most distinctively with Micah's expectations about Zion's future (1:9b, 12b, 16; 3:12), a point

[77] For a thorough form and tradition historical analysis of 8:9f., see M. Saebø, "Zur Traditionsgeschichte von Jesaja 8:9-10," *ZAW* 76 (1964) 132ff.; also Lutz, *Jahwe,* 40ff.; on 17:12ff., see Childs, *Isaiah,* 50ff., 129.

[78] Cf. von Rad *OTT* 2, 156ff., who speaks of the schema evidenced here and its reflection of the Zion tradition. Further, Saebø , *ZAW* 76 (1964) 132ff., who identifies also other elements of tradition; also Kaiser; Wildberger.

[79] On the authenticity of 8:9f., see Wildberger's discussion; on 17:12ff., Childs, *Isaiah;* Lutz, *Jahwe,* 40ff.; 215.

which is evident. What is of interest for our investigation is the signficant contrast in the way the Zion tradition is used. Micah quotes (or puts in the mouth of) his opponents words (3:11bβγ) which precisely echo the Zion traditon, as we have seen above. In 8:10 Isaiah promises protection (the saying is addressed not to Judah/Zion but to the nations) with the words: "It shall not stand; for God is with us." The correspondence is thought and structure between these words and the words attributed to Micah's opponents could hardly be closer: cf. לא תבוא (Mic 3:11bγ) with לא יקום (Isa 8:10bα) and יהוה בקרבנו (Mic 3:11bβ) with כי עמנו אל (Isa 8:10bβ). The style of both formulations is the first per. plur. What for Micah is "false" trust is proclaimed as a statement of faith by Isaiah. Aside from the fact that Micah addressed the wicked leading circles and Isaiah's saying has the "nations" as its addressee (perhaps he actually addressed these words to his disciples, cf. Eichrodt), the two passages are substantively revealing with respect to the distinction between Micah and Isaiah regarding Yahweh's protective presence in Zion.

b. Isa 29:1ff.

We have already discussed this passage in relation to the elements of theophany it contains (chap. 1). The literary and form critical problems the text presents are enormous, and here we cannot call on any broad consensus among critics. Central to understanding the text is whether only vv. 1-4 are the original unit[80] or whether vv. 5-7 (or parts of them) also belong to it.[81] Vv. 1-4 present an announcement of judgment on Ariel, i.e., Jerusalem, introduced by a cry of הוי. Yahweh speaks in the first per. directly addressing the city (vv. 2-4). Divine judgment is emphasized in v. 2f. (cf. the three-fold "I": "I will distress . . . /encamp against . . . /raise siege words. . . ."). That Ariel is the goal of Yahweh's judgment is underlined by the initial "Woe, Ariel" (v. 1) and the mention of the city in vv. 2 (and 7). If we take vv. 5ff. as belonging originally with vv. 1-4, then Yahweh Sabaoth is pictured as suddenly intervening (תפקד v. 6)[82] in a theophany to thwart the "multitude of all the nations." The Zion tradition's pattern of attack-salvation is apparent. The saying presents Yahweh as the one who comes against Jerusalem, and is in this broad respect not unlike Micah 1:9, 12b. If Isa 29:1b is understood as an element of accusation against the city's cultic security,[83] we have a point of similarity with the false security of Micah's opponents

---

[80] Cf. e.g., Duhm, who sees vv. 1-4a as the original unit and vv. 5ff. as later material of varied origins. For a recent, similar view see Lutz, *Jahwe*, 100ff.

[81] Cf. Fohrer; von Rad, *OTT* 2, 155ff.; Steck, *Friedensvorstellungen*, 55, note 149; H. J. Hermisson, "Zukunftserwartung und Gegenwartskritik in der Verkündigung Jesajas," *EvTh* 33 (1973) 56, note 8: who emphasizes that v. 4a could not have originally ended the unit and that the change from Yahweh to the nations as the attacker of Zion corresponds to Isaiah's proclamation; 29:1ff. should be viewed in the light of 1:21ff., where punishment changes to salvation (through purification).

[82] The verb "to visit" (pi.) read in the positive sense, with Duhm; Procksch; Fohrer.

[83] Cf. Fohrer; Lutz, *Jahwe*, 107.

in 3:11b. It is therefore all the more significant that for Micah, the results must be total destruction; for Isaiah, the city will be punished but not annihilated, as 29:3b, 4a indicate. Here it is evident that Micah's relation to the Zion tradition is wholly negative, whereas Isaiah's relation is positive, despite a critical modification: though Zion may be punished, she will not be destroyed.

c. Isa 31:4-5.

After an introductory audition formula ("thus says Yahweh to me"), vv. 4-5 offer a series of similes (כ . . . כאשר, v. 4; כ . . . כ, v. 5) in which Yahweh's actions are compared with a lion and with hovering birds. Although in its present literary context, vv. 4-5 might be taken with vv. 1-3 and perhaps with vv. 8-9 (vv. 6-7 are commonly seen as secondary), it seems best to regard these (vv. 4-5) as originally unrelated to the surrounding verses.[84] Our interest focuses on the parallel Mount Zion-Jerusalem, which in vv. 4 and 5 are the objects of Yahweh Sabaoth's actions. V. 5 clearly presents the theme of divine protection, emphasized by the heaping up of verbs of deliverance and rescue (נגן; נצל hiph. [cf. Isa 5:19]; פסח; מלט hiph). There are, in our judgment, no compelling grounds for deleting this verse as secondary. V. 4 would then present a parallel idea: Yahweh "comes down to fight (ירד . . . לצבא) in behalf of הר ציון. In this case Mount Zion-Jerusalem is the goal of Yahweh's protective presence,[85] a motif associated with the Zion tradition. By comparison, the different perspective of Micah is visible in two particular ways: (1) The verb ירד in Mic 1:12b unambiguously brings רע מאת יהוה to Jerusalem; (2) When Micah mentions Zion-Jerusalem, it is in connection with guilt and destruction (3:9ff.); in Isa 31:4f. there is no assessment of transgression, and Yahweh's work on Zion brings rescue and salvation (cf. 14:32; 28:16; 29:5ff.).

3. Yahweh Purifies Zion

Isa 1:21-26 provides a significant basis for comparing and contrasting the Zion theme in Micah and Isaiah. The importance of this text—also for chap. 4 (below)—warrants its presentation in full.

v. 21   How the faithful city[a]
          has become a whore.

---

[84] 31:1-9 present a host of difficulties for a literary analysis, and little agreement is to be found among critics. V. 4 does not seem to continue vv. 1-3 (cf. Donner, *Israel,* 138). If v. 8a continues v. 5 (cf. Duhm), then an original unit can be found in vv. 4, 5, 8a. G. von Rad, *Der Heilige Krieg im alten Israel* (⁴1965), 60, note 100, considers vv. 1-5 a unit (vv. 1-3, accusation; vv. 4-5 divine oracle).

[85] As in 8:18; 14:32; 28:16, Yahweh does not fight *against* Zion (thus e.g., Donner, *Israel,* 138, who connects the passage with 701), but protects it. The twice occurring על in v. 4 means not "against" but "upon" (von Rad, *Krieg,* 60, note 100); otherwise, Childs, *Isaiah,* 57ff.

> She was full of righteousness,
> justice lodged in her [but now murderers].[b]

v. 22   Your silver has become dross,
        your liquor adulterated [with water].[c]

v. 23   Your rulers are rebels
        and partners of thieves.
        Everyone loves a bribe
        and chases gifts.
        They do not defend the fatherless,
        nor does the widow's case come to them.

v. 24   Therefore says the Lord, Yahweh Sabaoth, the Mighty One
        of Israel:
        "Woe! I will take out my wrath on my foes and will
        avenge my enemies.

v. 25   [I will turn my hand against you][d]
        I will smelt away your dross with lye,[e]
        and remove all your alloy.

v. 26   I will restore your judges as at the first,
        and your counsellors as at the beginning.
        Afterward you will be called the city of righteousness, the
        faithful city.

Textual notes:

a   G adds Σιών (Procksch; Gray; Kaiser follow G).
b   Delete (with Wildberger, et al.).
c   An explanatory gloss (cf. Duhm; Gray; Wildberger).
d   Delete (With Fohrer; Wildberger).
e   Instead of כבר, many critics read בכר ("in the furnace"), e.g., Gray;
    Procksch; Kaiser. The text need not be changed, however, for lye is used
    for the purpose of producing silver; cf. L. Koehler, *ThZ* 3 (1947) 232f.

Isa 1:21–26 is a unit (vv. 27f. is a later interpretation, cf. Duhm; Wildberger)
which clearly divides into three parts: vv. 21–23, the accusation, introduced by
איכה, which functions as the motivation; vv. 24f., the announcement of
judgment, introduced by לכן and an expanded "formula of divine utterance";
v. 26, a promise of restoration. The prophet in his accusation describes the fallen
character of the "faithful city," which is at first spoken about in the third pers.
(v. 21) and then addressed directly (vv. 22f.). The passage exhibits a remarkable
symmetry קריה נאמנה in v. 21 and 26 and well-balanced chiasm (cf. v. 26b with
v. 21a; v. 26a with v. 21b; v. 25 with v. 22; v. 24b with v. 23).[86]
    Elements of the dirge permeate the text: איכה (cf. Lam 1:1; 2:1); the "once

---

[86] Cf. R. Fey, *Amos und Jesaja*, WMANT 12 (1963) 64.

... now" motif[87] (vv. 21, 22, 23aα); qinah meter (vv. 21, 22, 23aα; cf. Wild-berger); and the הוי in v. 24b). Thus the passage appears to be a two-part judgment speech, concluded by a promise, which is put in the framework of a lament for the dead, or dirge. According to Hardmeier's thorough analysis, the text is, form critically speaking, a parody of an "Untergangslied" whose function is not to announce doom (like Am 5:2) but to proclaim the removal of that which has corrupted the city.[88] The importance of this insight will become clear below.

The object of the lament in v. 21 is the קריה נאמנה, which can no longer be so described, for, as the accusing words of v. 21b make clear, the city's former משפט and צדק have disappeared. The city's corruption from its former purity is pictured by three different images: the city has become a whore (v. 21); its silver has become dross; and its wine watered down (v. 22). The function of these images is to picture what has really happened to the city's leadership:[89] the שרים are rebels (סוררים) and take bribes (שחד); they do not uphold justice for the orphan and the widow (v. 23). The essence of the accusation, therefore, is social critique (on this aspect of the text see below, chap. 4). The divine wrath (v. 24b) evoked by the lack of justice and righteousness comes forth as a punishment which *purifies* (צרף, v. 25) so that the city can be restored (שוב hiph., v. 26). What is important to note for our purposes is that, although the city has become corrupt, the *city* is not to be punished or destroyed; rather, the city's *leaders* (שריך v. 23; שפטיך, יעציך, v. 26) must be removed so that new, pure leaders can come forth. The consequence of this is that Jerusalem will return to its former state (עיר הצדק קריה נאמנה v. 26).

Isaiah does not name Jerusalem or Zion directly (cf. 29:1ff.). Instead the capital is called קריה נאמנה (vv. 21a, 26b) and עיר הצדק. Moreover, the "faithful city," described as once having been filled with משפט/צדק (parallel elsewhere in Isa [1:27] 5:7, 16; [9:6] 28:17a; [32:1, 16f.], but משפט/צדקה), will again become an עיר הצדק (v. 26b). This language is most probably not Isaiah's creation but rather the appropriation of ancient tradition. The word צדק is connected with pre-Israelite Jerusalem, as can be seen in the name Melkizedek (Gen 14:18–20) and Adonizedek (Jos 10:1ff.).[90] H. H. Schmid finds in Isa 1:21ff.; Jer 31:23; Isa 60:17; Ps 17:1 the reminiscence of the God Zedek who presumably had been worshipped in Jerusalem.[91] Wildberger suggests that קריה נאמנה reflects a dependence on the Zion tradition, noting that the word קריה also occurs in Ps 48:3 to denote Zion. One might note here further that, although the word

---

[87] "In der Totenklage wird die strahlende Vergangenheit dem düsteren Jetzt entgegen-gesetzt," H.-J. Kraus, *Klagelieder*, BK XX (³1968) 26.

[88] Hardmeier, *Texttheorie*, 353f.

[89] Somewhat similarly, Hardmeier, 350.

[90] Cf. A. R. Johnson, *Sacral Kingship* (1967) 31ff.; also see N. Porteous, "Jerusalem-Zion: The Growth of a Symbol," *Fest. Rudolph*, 253ff. who sees a connection between "righteousness" and "peace" in ancient Jerusalem tradition which reflects mythological ideas attached to the city before David's time.

[91] H. H. Schmid, *Gerechtigkeit als Weltordnung*, BHTh 40 (1968) 76f.

נאמנה is not found in any of the Zion songs, its synonym כון and its derivatives
are used in connection with Jerusalem in Ps 48:9 and 87:5. Moreover, the pattern
of punishment-salvation may reflect the schema so familiar within the Zion
tradition; in line with this, Hermisson suggests that the "ideal time"
(כבראשנה/כבתחלה) could refer to the time of Zion's founding and Yahweh's
taking up residence there.[92] The point to be stressed here is that, as we have seen
in the previous Isaiah texts discussed above, Isaiah, even when he points to the
guilt connected with the city, is unable to speak in terms of its ultimate destruction. And in this regard, Isaiah's view of Zion remains rooted firmly in the
Jerusalem cultic theology.

This Isaian prophecy about Zion is analogous in several significant ways to
Mic 3:9ff., yet the differences are further evidence of the disparity between Micah
and Isaiah concerning Jerusalem. Striking similarities lie in the following:
(1) The word משפט occurs in both texts in connection with Jerusalem: "justice"
has been corrupted and destroyed (cf. Mic 3:9b משפט הישרה with משפט צדק
Isa 1:21b). (2) Jerusalem is a city in which violence and corruption rule (cf. Mic
3:10 with Isa 1:23). (3) Both texts accuse the city's officials; the close relationship
between the capital and her leaders is stressed in Micah and Isaiah by referring
to them as "her rulers" (Mic 3:11) and "your princes" (Isa 1:23, 26). (4) Both
prophets accuse the officials of שחד, the result of which is that "justice" is not
practiced: cf. Mic 3:9b המתעבים משפט and 3:11a ראשיה בשחר ישפטו with Isa
1:23b יתום לא ישפטו. Thus we see that the criticism leveled at the officials and
leaders in Jerusalem by Micah and Isaiah extends even to the vocabulary that
was used. It is, therefore, all the more remarkable that the social critique
connected with Jerusalem in both texts leads to such opposite results. For Micah,
the sins of the leaders are the reason (בגלל 3:12) for Zion's annihilation. For
Isaiah, the corruption of the officials means death *only* for the officials
themselves; the city will remain after its judgment of purification, having been
returned to its former glorious state. Finally, a point of comparison may be seen
between Mic 1:8ff. and Isa 1:21ff. Isaiah's lament over the "faithful city" expects
a time of renewal for Jerusalem, when her former status as a city of צדק will
be restored. By contrast, Micah's lament over Jerusalem expects a disaster
(vv. 9b, 12b) which does not "purge" (cf. Isa 1:25) simply the officials but which
ultimately results in the loss of *all* the city's inhabitants.

4. Yahweh Punishes Zion

In parts 1, 2, and 3, we have examined the Isaian texts which present Yahweh
as founder, protector, and purifier of Zion-Jerusalem. Yahweh might purify her,
or permit her to be punished, but in a positive relation to the Zion tradition:
these Isaian texts see Yahweh as ultimately preserving Jerusalem. Here we come
to a fourth group of texts in which Isaiah speaks of Zion as the object of political

---

[92] Hermisson, "Zukunftserwartung und Gegenwartskritik in der Verkündigung Jesajas," *EvTh* 33 (1973) 68f.

threat and/or divine punishment, *without* Yahweh's defense or last minute intervention.

The older critical notion of Zion's absolute inviolability in the theology of Isaiah has now been largely given up.[93] Yet it remains to be asked whether Isaiah *expressis verbis* proclaimed the destruction of the city, with its temple and palace. The texts which appear to speak directly of Jerusalem's collapse are astonishingly meager. In this category we place the fragment 5:14 + 17 and 32:9-14.[94]

a. Isa 5:14 + 17

This text is usually understood as a fragment; perhaps originally a verse crying "woe" preceded what is in v. 14, which is an announcement of disaster introduced by לכן.[95] Vv. 15-16, a later addition, separate vv. 14 and 17, which belong together. Probably belonging to Isaiah's early period,[96] the text proclaims doom on "her nobility" and "her multitude," "her throng," and those who "exult in her." The four occurrences of the fem. sing. suff. most likely referred originally to Jerusalem.[97] If this is correct, the picture here is of the death of the capital's inhabitants, who must go down into Sheol. V. 17 continues the threat, but with a different picture: lambs, etc. shall feed among the "ruins."[98] Vv. 14 and 17 are apparently a threat of doom to the city's nobility (v. 14) and the city itself (v. 17). Remarkably, however, the text is only a fragment. Jerusalem is not named; its

---

[93] J. Pedersen, *Israel* III-IV, 552ff. and O. Procksch, *Theologie des Alten Testaments* (1950) 189, understood Isaiah to maintain that Jerusalem would not be overcome because it was the dwelling place of Yahweh. Th. Vriezen properly cautions against this view: "Essentials in the Theology of Isaiah," *Fest. Muilenburg*, 138ff. Huber, in line with this (correctly, in our opinion), concludes that Isaiah proclaimed not an unconditional inviolability of Zion but a condition—the condition being that of trust in Yahweh (*Jahwe, Juda und die anderen Völker beim Propheten Jesaja*, BZAW 137 (1976) 239.

[94] Thus also Hermisson, "Zukunftserwartung," 70, note 40. W. H. Schmidt, *EvTh* 37 (1977) 271, includes also such texts as 29:4; 22:14; 3:8. We have understood 29:4 differently (see above, pp. 56f.) as a text illustrative of Yahweh's punishment followed by a turning point of grace. 3:8 is not an announcement of doom on Jerusalem-Judah but rather the *motivation* for the announcement in 3:1-7 (cf. Wildberger). 22:14 is not a direct announcement of destruction for Zion; rather its inhabitants, who have reacted to the withdrawal of Assyrian troops in 701 with rejoicing, will be punished: "till you die." Cf. Huber, *Jahwe*, 38, who thinks that there is no explicit threat of conquest and destruction of Jerusalem in Isaiah, as in Mic 3:12. He notes texts which seem to include the taking of Jerusalem *without* naming the city directly (3:8; 3:25f.; 6:11; 8:14; 32:13f.). Of these we are chiefly interested in 32:13f., which is more specifically focused on Jerusalem than the other texts.

[95] Cf. Duhm; Gray; Wildberger; somewhat differently Fohrer.

[96] Cf. Wildberger; Duhm suggests 711.

[97] Cf. Duhm; Gray; also Hermisson, "Zukunftserwartung," 70, note 40, thinks עלז בה supports the connection with Jerusalem and the cities mentioned in Isa 22:2 and 32:13.

[98] Read נדים instead of גרים, cf. BHS; Wildberger. The text is somewhat uncertain.

destruction is suggested but not specifically portrayed. The picture of a "ruins" replacing the city is comparable to Mic 3:12: Jerusalem becomes a heap of ruins (נרים) where "animals" will be found. And, as in Mic 3:9ff., Isaiah here connects Jerusalem's destruction with the sins of the nobility, though here it is their pride and self-security (עלז, cf. Wildberger), not their works of oppression, which bring their fall.

b. Isa 32:9-14

Thought by some critics to be the last word Isaiah had to proclaim,[99] this text combines the form elements of a "didactic opening formula" (v. 9) with a "summons to lament" (vv. 11f.) addressed to the complacent women, who are to mourn for a coming destruction of fields and houses of the קריה עליזה (v. 13). The accusation, clear though made indirectly, is expressed in the words descriptive of the women (שאננות, בטחות vv. 9, 11) and the reference to "joyous city," probably an allusion to 22:22,[100] where Isaiah reprimands Jerusalem for its (inappropriate) joy over the withdrawal of the Assyrian troops. The motivation for the mourning (ספד) is given in a series of על clauses (vv. 12b-13a) and כי clauses (vv. 13b-14) which function as the announcement. The climax of the announcement is in v. 14; clearly, the prophet has Jerusalem in mind, for he prophesies that "the palace will be forsaken, the populous city deserted; the hill and watchtower will become dens forever, a joy of wild asses, a pasture of flocks."[101] The structure of the saying indicates that its focus is on Jerusalem, not on the land or the nation.[102] Here, there is no longer any future expectation of a new beginning[103] for Zion (1:21ff.), nor is there a word about Yahweh's protective presence (14:32; 28:16; 31:4f.). The imagery of v. 14 indicates that the destruction of the capital city will be total.

In this text we have several interesting parallels to Mic 1:8ff. and 3:9ff. The elements of the dirge in Mic 1:8, 16 and 32:11f. function to announce and anticipate, by means of lamentation, a future disaster.[104] The two passages share the same form (summons to lament, i.e., sing a dirge) in Mic 1:16 and Isa 32:11f., and the vocabulary is that which is typical of the form (cf. ספד in Mic 1:8 and Isa 22:12). The accusation of complacency (Isa 32:9-11) corresponds to the false trust motif in Mic 3:11b. Parallel to Micah's announcement of exile (גלה 1:16) is

---

[99] Thus Fohrer; Duhm, on the other hand, dates the passage in the earliest time of Isaiah. The great difference between 1:21ff. and 32:9ff. speaks against Duhm's supposition. Kaiser regards the passage as late; the arguments are not persuasive.

[100] Cf. Fohrer.

[101] On the textual problems of v. 14, cf. BHS. Debated is whether to eliminate עד-עולם (thus Duhm) or not (thus Hermisson, "Zukunftserwartung," 70, note 40).

[102] Contra Kissane; Kaiser.

[103] Cf. Hermisson, 70.

[104] Hardmeier, Texttheorie, 361f., 373.

Isaiah's proclamation that the "palace will be forsaken, the populous city deserted" (32:14). Further, according to both Micah (3:12) and Isaiah (32:14) the ultimate end of Jerusalem comes in total destruction: the city will no longer exist. It should be noted that here Isaiah appears to avoid specifically calling the city "Zion" or "Jerusalem," as also in 1:21ff. and 29:1ff., unlike Mic 3:10, 12, which emphasize that the goal of disaster is the capital by naming Zion-Jerusalem *twice*. In Isa 32:9ff. we have, then, a significant analogue to Mic 3:9ff. It should not, finally, escape notice that elements or motifs of the Zion tradition are totally absent from Isaiah's word of destruction on Jerusalem, indicative of a change in his perspective.

An Isaian text (10:27bff.) which belongs under the theme of "Yahweh's Punishment of Zion" is compared with Mic 1:10ff. in the following Excursus.

EXCURSUS II

A COMPARISON OF MIC 1:(8f.)10ff. AND ISA 10:27bff.

Isa 10:27b, with the words עַל מִפְּנֵי־שָׁמֶן, commences a new unit which Wildberger, for example, sees concluded in v. 33 (and possibly v. 34). But the arguments for understanding v. 32 as the end of the passage are weighty and persuasive.[105] The saying *reports*, with verbs in the perfect, the advance of an unnamed enemy which, apparently departing from Samaria,[106] passes through several towns on its way to Jerusalem.[107] The report of the march is interrupted in v. 30, where the prophet momentarily addresses the towns of Gallim, Laishah, and Anathoth, summoning them (imperative verbs) to respond to the danger which passes in their midst. After the resumption of the report in v. 31, the climax of the text comes in v. 32, with an announcement in the imperfect: "On this very day, halting at Nob, he will shake his fist (יְנֹפֵף) at the mountain of the daughter[108] of Zion, at the hill of Jerusalem." Critics are in disagreement as to whether this refers to the events of 701,[109] the period of the Syro-Ephraimite crisis,[110] or 715, the time of Ashdod's rebellion.[111]

The realism of the text suggests that the saying is not a vision of the future but a report or description of an enemy's attack or approach to Jerusalem. Although there is no accusation to motivate the threat, under the assumption that v. 33 does not belong to the unit, v. 32 may be understood to be a prophetic announcement

---

[105] Cf. especially Gray; also Kaiser, who is followed by Childs, *Isaiah*, 62.

[106] Read שֹׁמְרוֹן instead of שָׁמֶן; cf. BHS; Wildberger.

[107] D. L. Christensen, "The March of Conquest in Isaiah 10:27c–34," *VT* 26 (1976) 389f., argues that the enemy ("he" in the text) is Yahweh the Divine Warrior and that the text reflects ancient war motifs. See this art. for further bibliography.

[108] Read (Qere) בַּת instead of בֵּית.

[109] Fohrer; Kaiser.

[110] Donner, *Israel*, 35ff.

[111] Cf. Wildberger's weighty arguments opposing Donner's interpretation.

of disaster upon the capital. Whether Isaiah here is calling for repentance or for faith[112] is certainly not indicated in the text.

The passage bears apparent similarity to Mic 1:(8f.)10ff. Duhm remarked about the similarity, though he judged Isa 10:27bff. to be "Leer vom Inhalt," less impressive than the Micah text, and non-genuine. According to Marti, Isa 10:27bff. is an "imitation" of Mic 1:10ff. Are the texts in fact so closely related?[113]

Certainly similarities are immediately apparent: (1) Both passages seem to indicate a route taken by an approaching enemy, though the routes are different. (2) In both the towns named are directly addressed in the imperative (cf. Isa 10:30 with Mic 1:10ff.). (3) A reaction to political danger is voiced in both (cf. Isa 10:29b with Mic 1:12a). (4) The description of events is in the perfect. (5)Paronomasia is evidenced in Mic 1:10ff. and Isa 10:30. (6) Neither text contains an accusation of guilt. (7) Finally, both texts portray Jerusalem as the goal of the threat.

There are significant differences, however. (1) The form of the texts is basically dissimilar, for the framework of the Micah text is a dirge; elements of such a death lament are missing in Isa 10:27bff. (2) According to our interpretation of Mic 1:8ff. above (pp. 43f.), the perfect verbs are to be understood as referring to a future event, not to a past march of an enemy. Isaiah reports the real approach of a political foe. (3) Significantly, the impending disaster Micah announces stresses that Yahweh is the agent (vv. 9b, 12b). The threat bearing down on Jerusalem in Isaiah, though left unnamed, should be understood as a political foe. (4) Whereas Mic 1:16 speaks of an exile, Isa 10:32 indicates only that an attack is imminent, not whether it will be successful. Despite the interesting and remarkable similarities in the two texts, there is no evidence to suggest that one prophet was influenced by or borrowed from the other; nor can it be established that they are both dependent upon some form or pattern of prophetic speech.

In this section (Part B) we have attempted a brief analysis of the most pertinent texts relating to the Zion tradition in Isaiah. For convenience sake and to avoid too long a discussion, we grouped the texts into four categories in order to highlight the essential motifs and contours of these texts. It is evident, as previous scholarship has abundantly shown, that the Zion theme in Isaiah is complex, certainly not uniform, and exhibits a kind of dialectic and ambivalence. Nevertheless, it should be clear that Isaiah is without doubt dependent upon the Zion tradition, but also that he alters and adapts it to suit a particular situation and time. Thus he can speak of Zion's security—but for the poor or faithful. He speaks of its strength against foreign powers, yet he knows Yahweh can both punish the city but not ultimately destroy it—though even this view appears to have finally changed after 701. Micah's relationship to the Zion tradition, by contrast, is unambiguous. The city will be totally destroyed; all those who hold to Zion's inviolability have a false security rooted in an equally false trust. It might appear that the prophecy of Micah and Isaiah stand totally

---

[112] Thus Kaiser, who relates the passage to 30:15; 28:16.

[113] This is assumed by others, e.g., Robinson; cf. Allen, *The Books of Joel, Obadiah, Jonah and Micah,* NICOT (1976).

in antithesis to each other. It is true that Micah sees no hope for the future of Zion, but at the end of his career Isaiah apparently expressed this same view (32:9ff.). As far as Isaiah's view of Zion's security is concerned, it is clear that this view is related to trust in Yahweh; Zion as a place of refuge is for those who believe. Micah directed his words to a different audience. He spoke to those who had a false faith, based on the dogma of Zion's insecurity, whereas Isaiah addressed those who refused to believe at all. This difference in their circle of addresses accounts for some of the contrasts in their message. Yet the fact remains that Micah and Isaiah have essentially a different stance toward the Zion tradition. Even when Isaiah can speak about its demise in chap. 32, we note that he cannot call the capital by its name, Zion or Jerusalem, but can only say allusively (and ironically): the "joyful city" (v. 13), the "populous city" (v. 14).

Summary Conclusion

1. Micah's words relating to the Zion tradition are couched unambiguously in sayings which announce Jerusalem's destruction (3:12) or the exile of its inhabitants (1:16). A prophetic mourning song (dirge), without accusation, prophesies doom for Zion, whereas a prophetic judgment speech condemns and then dooms to annihilation the capital city. Isaiah, too, makes use of the mourning song form in 1:21ff. and 32:9ff., the latter in many respects comparable to Mic 1:8ff. In addition, Isaiah's words about Zion occur in a wide variety of forms: confession-like statements, 8:18; 14:32; words expressing security in the face of attack, 8:9f.; 17:12ff.; promises of security for the faithful, 28:16; sayings which announce danger to Jerusalem but protection by Yahweh (29:1ff.; 31:4f.); but significantly, there is *no* passage comparable to Mic 3:9ff. in which the city is accused and condemned to destruction.

2. The Zion tradition is taken up in the sayings of both Micah and Isaiah. Micah's relation to this circle of theological ideas is overwhelmingly negative: Zion and its leaders will be totally destroyed (3:9ff.). Isaiah would appear to stand in the strongest contrast to this, for he proclaims a security in Zion from the assault of the nations (8:9f.; 17:12ff.; cf. 31:4f.), and even when Yahweh punishes the city, he ultimately saves it from destruction (29:1ff.); his punishment is really only "purification" (1:21ff.). Yet for Isaiah this is not an absolute: ultimately, only those who believe will find rest and refuge there (14:32; 28:16). Thus, whereas Micah has a *polemic* against the Zion tradition's concepts of Yahweh's presence and protection, Isaiah modifies the tradition to correspond with his call for faith.

3. Micah connects with his judgment on Zion a critique of the officials and their oppression of the people; indeed, the injustice and avarice of the rulers, including priest and prophet, corrupt Jerusalem and require its absolute devastation (3:9ff.). Isaiah, too, portrays Jerusalem in terms of the oppression and wickedness of its leaders. It is therefore all the more remarkable that for Isaiah, this requires purification of the city and the destruction of the wicked, but *not* the destruction of the city itself, which will be restored to its former perfection

(1:21ff.). In addition to the social critique theme, Micah strikes out at the "false trust" of the city's leading circles: they believe Zion will endure and offer security. They "believe," but it is a false faith because their lives are enmeshed in the evils of a wicked society. Isaiah, on the other hand, knows nothing of this kind of false trust; rather, he *calls* for trust in Yahweh, not political alliances, and *for* those who trust, he presents Zion as a refuge.

4. Finally, regarding Zion's future, it need only be said that Micah expects the exile of Jerusalem's inhabitants and the disappearance of the city from history. Isaiah, having held to a hope for Zion's continued, even renewed existence, finally sees a future as dim as Micah's (Isa 32:9ff.).

3
Prophetic Conflict and Opposition
in Micah and Isaiah

It was inevitable that the word of Yahweh as proclaimed by his prophets would meet opposition. Indeed, the prophetic literature attests to a lively and continuing conflict both of *prophet against prophet(s) and people against prophet.* In addition to the texts in Micah and Isaiah to be discussed below, passages in Jeremiah, Ezekiel, Zephaniah, and Zechariah[1] give evidence of intense disputes between the prophet and groups of prophets and other opponents. Not infrequently the opponents are simply called "the *nebiim,*" and the context is a polemical one.[2] Remarkably, Hosea and Amos contain no record of disputation with prophetic groups; according to H. W. Wolff, Hosea can speak positively of "the prophets" with whom he is thought to form an "Oppositionsgemeinschaft."[3] On the other hand, the classical prophets could be opposed by non-prophetic individuals or groups; cf. the attempts to silence them (Am. 7:12f. [2:12]; Mic 2:6; Isa 30:9ff.) and to thwart their work (Hos 9:7b; Isa 28:9f.; Jer 2:30; 5:12f.; 7:25; 17:15; 25:4; 26:5; 29:19; 35:15; 44:4f., 16; Zech 1:4ff.; 7:7–12).

> Here we may briefly note some of the antecedents in the Old Testament of such prophetic conflict. Perhaps one such example is to be found in the narrative about Miriam and Aaron's dispute with Moses (Num 12:1ff.).[4] In this text we have a kind of inner-prophetic dispute about whether Yahweh speaks *only* through Moses (v. 2) and thus has to do with prophetic authority. Further, in addition to the

[1] Cf. Jer 2:8; 5:31; 6:10ff.; 8:10ff.; 14:13ff.; 23:9ff.; 26:7ff.; 28–29; for Jeremiah, see Thomas Overholt, *The Threat of Falsehood,* StBTh 2nd series 16 (1970); Ezek 13:2ff.; 14:9; 22:25 (Eng 28), and see especially K. Carley, *Ezekiel Among the Prophets,* StBTh 2nd series 31 (1975), 26ff., 76ff., and passim; Zeph 3:3f. and Zech 13:2ff.

[2] Cf. R. Rendtorff, art. προφήτης, *TDNT* 6, 805.

[3] Cf. Hos 6:5; 9:7f.; 12:11, 14 and H. W. Wolff, "Hoseas geistige Heimat," *Ges. St.,* 232ff. Hos 4:5b is thereby understood as secondary (Wolff, BK XIV/1). The *nebiim* are mentioned in Am 2:11f.; 3:7, passages generally thought of as stemming from Deuteronomistic redaction. If Am 7:14 is understood as a rejection of the title *nabi* (see Wolff's discussion, BK XIV/2), could this imply a polemic against an official circle of prophets?

[4] The date and unity of Numbers 12 is problematic. Driver, *Introduction to the Literature of the Old Testament* (⁷1963) 62, assigns the passage to E; Noth, *Überlieferungsgeschichte des Pentateuchs* (1948) 139f. sees here a complex growth of tradition.

conflict between Elijah and the Baal prophets (1 Kings 18), 1 Kings 13 tells of the prophet from Bethel who claims to be on a par with the man of God from Judah: "I also am a prophet as you are" (v. 18). According to Crenshaw, the story illustrates the great difficulty presented when two prophets equally claim divine inspiration for their message.[5] The passage most instructive in this context is the narrative about Micaiah ben Imlah in 1 Kings 22.[6] Here we find the following important elements: 1) *nabi* stands against *nebiim;* 2) Micaiah prophesies doom (v. 8, 17, 18), while the 400 prophets expect salvation (vv. 6, 11f.); 3) the question of prophetic authority is raised (who possesses רוח־יהוה, v. 24? who has stood in the council of Yahweh, vv. 19ff.?); 4) whose word proves true (vv. 28, 37f.; cf. Deut 18:22; Jer 28:9)? 5) the term שקר is used (for the first time?) in connection with a group of salvation prophets (v. 22f.); 6) the term שלום, though not directly spoken by the salvation prophets, is surely the implied message they proclaim (cf. vv. 6 and 11f. with v. 26b); 7) the *nebiim* and their representative Zedekiah are enticed and led by Yahweh's direction (vv. 20–23). One or more of these elements play an important role in the prophetic texts having to do with prophetic conflict in the 8th century and later, and therefore can be important in clarifying and understanding them.

Scholarly discussions of prophetic conflict are often placed under the heading "true and false prophecy" (the expression "false prophet" does not occur in *M*).[7] Much of this discussion has focused on what distinguishes a "true" from a "false" prophet. G. Quell clearly stated the importance of the problem in the opening words of his book, *Wahre und falsche Propheten:*

Das Kernproblem der Prophetie, nicht allein ihrer weit verzweigten Geschichte, sondern ihrer aktuellen Autorität ist erfasst, wenn die Frage gestellt wird: Was ist ein wahrer, was ist ein falscher Prophet?[8]

The question, not insignificant for the theology of the Old Testament,[9] has been treated especially in terms of elucidating the *criteria* for judging what is true and

---

[5] On the importance of this text for the question of true-false prophecy, cf. J. Crenshaw, *Prophetic Conflict,* pp. 39ff. and the bibliography cited there; but see A. Jepsen, "Gottesmann und Prophet: Anmerkungen zum Kapitel 1. Könige 13," in *PbTH,* 171ff.

[6] The significance of 1 Kings 22 for the true-false prophecy theme is well known and frequently discussed in the literature. On the text and its interpretation, see among others, J. Gray, *I and II Kings* (1967); G. Quell, *Wahre und falsche Propheten,* 71ff.; E. Würthwein, "Zur Komposition von I Reg 22:1–38," in *Das ferne und nahe Wort,* BZAW 105 (1967) 245ff., who presents a persuasive analysis of the narrative: vv. 5–9, 13–17 (18), 22–28 are the oldest layer; vv. 10–12, 24–25, a second layer; vv. 19–21, a third layer (251f.). Würthwein considers the general background, not the details, to be historical. The Gattung is a saga, with a Märchen-like framework. See H. Seebass, "Micha ben Jimla," *KuD* 19 (1973) 109ff., for a different interpretation.

[7] The word πσευδοπροφήται sometimes translates what *M* has only as נביאים: for example, *G,* Jer 6:13; 33:7f., 11, 16; 34:9; 35:1; 36:1; the corresponding passages in *M,* Jer 6:3; 26:7f, 11, 16; 27:9; 28:1; 29:1.

[8] G. Quell, *Wahre und falsche Propheten: Versuch einer Interpretation* (1952) 9.

[9] G. von Rad, "Die falsche Propheten," *Ges. St.* 2, 220.

what is false. Here we may note in passing the recent work of E. Osswald, J. Crenshaw, and an article by J. Sanders. Osswald critically examines the following criteria: 1) manner of revelation; 2) prophet's awareness of his commission; 3) ethical actions; 4) content of the message; 5) fulfillment; 6) time when prophecy comes to an end.[10] But the difficulties in applying these criteria to the message of the prophets are well-known. As a result of these difficulties, at least in part, Crenshaw has perceived two basic tendencies emerging from the pertinent literature: 1) "the trend toward denial of valid criteria for distinguishing the false from the true prophet"; 2) "the attempt to understand the reasons for the phenomenon of false prophecy, particularly the human ingredient of all prophecy."[11] Sanders attempts to take the discussion a step further by devoting attention especially to what he calls "hermeneutics," namely, "the ancient theological mode, as well as literary technique, by which that application was made by the prophet, true or false, that is, how he reads his 'texts' and 'contexts' and how he related them."[12] But a thorough review of these issues and of the now lengthy literature on true-false prophecy is *not* our purpose here; both Crenshaw and Sanders offer extensive summary of the scholarly discussion.[13]

In the following pages, the focus is upon two parts: texts in Micah and Isaiah which show them in conflict and dispute with other prophetic opponents (Part A); texts which give evidence of opposition to the work of Micah and Isaiah (Part B). We shall therefore examine texts which are the earliest examples of Israelite classical prophetic disputation. The intention here is to compare and contrast Micah and Isaiah on this theme. The results should not only help us further to discern the relationship of the words of one prophet with the other, but should also provide a partial background to prophetic conflict in later prophetic material. The ensuing discussion will be guided by the following questions:

1. What kind of *forms* of prophetic speech do Micah and Isaiah utilize in the passages pertinent to this theme?

2. Who are the prophetic opponents which Micah and Isaiah speak of? How are they characterized?

3. What has provoked the opposition of Micah and Isaiah to other prophets?

---

[10] E. Osswald, *Falsche Prophetie im AT* (1962) 12ff. See also G. Münderlein, *Kriterien wahrer und falscher Prophetie: Entstehung und Bedeutung im AT,* Europäische Hochschulschriften XXIII, Bd. 33 (1974). Münderlein's study does not develop or test distinguishing criteria. Given the fact that there are no general, unambiguous criteria, his goal is to examine the function of the arguments used by the prophets, and the context and redaction of the arguments (p. 22).

[11] J. Crenshaw, *Prophetic Conflict: Its Effect Upon Israelite Religion,* BZAW 124 (1971) 49ff.

[12] J. Sanders, "Hermeneutics in True and False Prophecy," in *Canon and Authority* (eds.) G. Coats and B. Long (1977) 22.

[13] J. Crenshaw, 13–22; Sanders, 22–31.

4. What is the theological context out of which their opponents speak? Can one discern how the נביאים relate to ancient Israelite tradition?

A. CONFLICT WITH THE נביאים

1. Micah

That Micah carried on passionate and aggressive disputes with prophetic opponents is abundantly clear from two passages: 3:5-8; 3:9-12 (cf. also 2:11)[14] The נביאים are named twice, in 3:5aβ and 6bα; in v. 7 the prophets are called "seers" (חזים) and "diviners" (קסמים). In 3:9-12, which is addressed to an audience wider than only the "prophets," the נביאים are expressly named in the accusation along with "rulers" (ראשים) and "priests" (כהנים). Mic 2:11 also reflects Micah's opposition to the popular prophets, where he sarcastically refers to them as a מטיף, a "preacher" whom "this people" find acceptable. The root נטף hiph. ("to drop, drip" BDB), can be used of prophetic discourse (cf. Am 7:16; Ezek 21:2 נבא/נטף) and occurs also in 2:6. With these three texts (Mic 3:5ff.; 3:11; 2:11) we are on solid footing for the beginning of our investigation.

We begin our study with Micah's unequivocal attack on the נביאים in 3:5ff., a text which Quell appropriately labeled a "Kampfdokument."[15]

a. Mic 3:5ff.

v. 5   Thus Yahweh has said against the prophets[a]
        who cause my people[b] to go astray,
    who, when they have something to eat,
        cry out: "Peace."
    But he who does not put (anything) into their mouth,
        against him they sanctify war.

v. 6   Therefore it shall be night to you without vision
        and darkness[c] to you without divination.
    The sun shall go down upon the prophets,
        and the day darken for them.

v. 7   The seers[d] shall be ashamed
        and the diviners confounded.
    All of them shall cover their moustache,
        for there is no answer from God.

[14] According to A. S. van der Woude, "Micah in Dispute with the Pseudo-Prophets," *VT* 19 (1960) 256f., Mic 2:12f. contains a "prophecy of weal" which, though not a part of a disputation, may derive from a discussion between the pseudo-prophets and Micah. Van der Woude offers, however, no good grounds against the quite evident fact that vv. 12f. presuppose the exile (cf. esp. Smith; also Robinson; Mays, who shows that vv 12f. are not even a rhetorical unit).

[15] G. Quell, *Wahre und falsche Propheten,* 116.

Textual notes:

a   The expression עַל־הַנְּבִיאִים following the messenger formula poses
     certain problems. On the possible original wording of the beginning of
     v. 5, see below, p. 72. The עַל can be translated "concerning" (thus the
     RSV; Robinson and Weiser: über) or "against" (Nowack, Sellin:
     "wider"); G = ἐπὶ τοὺς προφήτας. ἐπί + acc. can have a hostile intent; cf.
     Bauer-Arnt-Gingrich, *A Greek-English Lexicon of the NT* (Chicago: The
     Univ. of Chicago Press [1952] 288); cf. Hos 12:11 (context indicates that
     here it means "to"; G = πρός) and Jer 14:15; 23:15 for similar expressions.

b   The word עַמִּי does not seem to fit with the introductory "Thus has
     Yahweh said," for one would expect עַמּוֹ (or אֶת עַם יְהוֹה] cf. Sellin;
     BHS). On the other hand, if the divine speech is understood to begin
     with the part. הַמַּתְעִים there is no problem, and one could translate:
     "Thus has Yahweh said against the prophets: 'Those who lead my people
     astray . . .' " (cf. Robinson's translation). The apparent grammatical
     infelicity relates, however, to the question of the original wording of v 5.

c   Read וַחָשְׁכָה with BHS; Rudolph.

d   G = οἱ ὁρῶντες τὰ ἐνύπνια, which limits the seers to those who have dreams;
     cf. Rudolph.

(1) This passage is a severe indictment against opponents who are *prophets,*
as the repeated naming of the addressee makes clear (v. 5a, 6b, 7a). When or
where Micah spoke these words is not indicated, though one would guess that,
in the light of 3:9–12 where the *nebiim* are mentioned in connection with Zion-
Jerusalem, the scene is the capital city.

Although v. 5 clearly is the beginning of a new rhetorical unit,[16] as the new
theme and addressee show, the ending is less clear. V. 8 is often taken as the
original ending,[17] but v. 7 is rather to be understood as the conclusion.[18]

---

[16] Smith thinks of chapter 3 as one symmetrical poem of seven strophes. While most
scholars reject this and see in chapter 3 three different units (3:1–4, 5–8, 9–12), it is less clear
whether the present shape of chapter 3 stems from their belonging to the same legal procedure (Sellin) or from the redactor (Lindblom). Rudolph suggests that they were not
spoken on the same occasion, since they partly overlap; rather, chapter 3 is a kerygmatic
unit that refers to the lack of responsibility of the leaders in Jerusalem.

[17] E.g., Nowack; Sellin; Robinson; Weiser; most recently Rudolph and Mays.

[18] It is true that v. 8 provides a logical conclusion to vv. 5–7 in that Micah's vocation
as Yahweh's prophet stands in strongest contrast to the *nebiim.* But one must ask
a) whether it is a part of the original rhetorical unit or b) whether Micah (thus Lindblom)
or a redactor later placed v. 8 in its present position. In favor of b) speak the following:
1) the strong adversative וְאוּלָם (cf. Gen 28:19; Exod 9:16; Num 14:21; 1 Kgs 20:23; Job 1:11;
etc.), which does not occur elsewhere in the prophetic corpus, appears to have a redactional
function of tying v. 8 with the foregoing verses; 2) the sudden change to the first person
style in v. 8 suggests that it did not originally continue v. 7, which speaks of Micah's

V. 5 is an accusation against the prophets, introduced by the messenger formula (m — f) כה אמר יהוה. But in all likelihood this is a secondary formulation.[19] It seems highly probable that the original beginning of the passage was the "woe cry."[20] Perhaps the m — f originally introduced the announcement of judgment in vv. 6–7 (as in 2:3). In this case the form of the text, together with Mic 1:3ff.; 2:1ff.; 3:1ff.; and 3:9ff., strongly suggests that the accusation in v. 5 is

---

opponents in the third person; 3) the announcement of judgment in v. 7 appears to be the climax of the saying; v. 8 is unexpected.

V. 8 has the nature of a personal *reflection* by the prophet on the nature of his prophetic office and calling (delete the phrase את־רם יהוה with most commentators and BHS); its particular form is "without parallel in the Old Testament" (thus Mays; this raises the question of its being an original word from Micah; cf. F. Stolz, "Der Streit um die Wirklichkeit in der Südreichsprophetie des 8. Jahrhunderts," *WuD* 12 [1973] 17, note 35). It seems to me that there are two possibilities for the origin of v. 8: 1) it could represent part of a debate Micah had with his prophetic opponents; in this case, it would be his response to their words which went unrecorded; 2) v. 8 could be words Micah spoke only to his disciples, for the verse does not have a direct address to his opponents, which one might expect if he were speaking in the heat of disputation with them (note that 3:5ff. addresses the prophets, while v. 8 speaks about Jacob and Israel [i.e., the Southern Kingdom] — a broader scope is thus explicit). An additional possibility is that v. 8 originally belonged *after* 2:11. Here the juxtaposition of the "preacher for this people" and Micah is even more powerful; moreover, the phrase רוח ושקר כזב in v. 11 could well have prompted a later hand to add את־רוח יהוה in v. 8; also, cf. 1) the parallel that would result between העם הזה (v. 11) and ישראל־יעקב (v. 8); 2) the contrast between "I will preach to you of wine. . . ." (v. 11) and "I am filled with power, — justice and might to declare to Jacob his transgression. . . ." (v. 8).

[19] It is not typical of 8th century prophecy for the m-f to introduce a two-part judgment speech (*Gerichtswort*) (Westermann, *Basic Forms*, 180), although it is possible (e.g., Am 1:3, 6, 13; 2:1, 6; 3:12; cf. Wolff, BK XIV/2, 165); nor does Yahweh speak in the 1st person in the saying. In addition, the m-f does not appear to fit with the עמי (one would expect עמו ; see above textual note b on 3:5). Critics offer several reconstructions of the text: 1) delete the m-f (a) and replace it with הוי (Robinson), or (b) have the passage begin with על הנביאים (Smith), or (c) repeat the ואמר from 3:1 (Lescow, "Redaktionsegeschichtliche Analyse von Micha 1–5," *ZAW* 84 [1972] 48, "And I said to the prophets"). 2) Retain the m-f but change על to הוי (Budde, "Micha 2 und 3," *ZAW* 38 [1919/20] 20; Quell, *Wahre und falsche Propheten*, 116). 3) Have v. 5 begin with the definite plural participle (Mays).

[20] "Woe to those who lead my people astray." Several form critical factors support this reconstruction: 1) In the prophetic literature, the (mostly plural) participle, descriptive of the evil deeds of the addressee, is frequently preceded by הוי (examples cited by Wolff, BK XIV/2, 285, note 1; see also E. Gerstenberger "The Woe-Oracles of the Prophets," *JBL* 81 [1962] 251). 2) Micah used the woe-cry in 2:1ff., a passage similar in form to 3:5–7. 3) The impersonal formulation of v. 5 is typical of the woe-cry, unlike the personal formulation of the "Hear this" formula in 3:1 and 9. This would presuppose that על־הנביאים in 3:5 does not originally belong here; it may have been inserted because of its occurrence in v. 6, or perhaps the redactor had in mind the similar introductory phrase in Jer 14:15 and 23:15.

the *prophet's word* and the announcement in vv. 6–7 is the *divine word* (as in 1:6; 2:3).[21]

The *accusation* in v. 5 begins with a general statement ("who lead my people astray") in participial style which Micah seems to prefer (cf. 2:1; 3:2, 9b, 10). Continuing the participial style (def. plur.), v. 5bα provides an explication of *how* the prophets "lead astray" (the part. followed by *waw apodosis* + perf. verb expresses a condition, "when" cf. Ges.-K. 116w and 159i). V. 5bβ, also a conditional construction (אשר) clause in the imperf. followed by perf. clause, cf. Ges.-K. 159f.) concludes the accusation. Thus in v. 5b two conditional clauses which are antithetically parallel (peace-war) elucidate and interpret the initial charge in v. 5a, to which they are grammatically and substantively subordinate.

The *announcement* in v. 6a, introduced by לכן (cf. 2:3, 5; 3:12), shifts from the third person to the personal style of address (לכם 2x) and is formulated as two synonymously parallel noun clauses. V. 6b, two verbal clauses in the perf., has the function of further explaining v. 6a; the synonymous parallelism in v. 6 is expressed in almost chiastic fashion (v 6a: night-darkness; v. 6b: sun-day). The *result* of the "divine intervention" of v. 6 is expressed in v. 7a, where the subject of the three verbal clauses (perf.) is not the הנביאים named in v. 6b but החזים/הקסמים, nouns which pick up the language of v. 6a (חזון/קסם). The abrupt changes from the third person in v. 5 to second person in v. 6a and then back to the third person in vv. 6b–7 is perhaps due to the liveliness of the prophet's public delivery (Nowack), or reflects the legal procedure in which the prophet can speak about the accused party to the assembled court and then *to* the accused party.[22] The speech reaches its climax in a final note of judgment in the כי clause in v. 7b, which is a terse restatement and interpretation of v. 6ab: the absence of visions/divination (v. 6a) and the darkness which is to descend upon the *nebiim* (v. 6b) is given further elucidation by way of the reason expressed in v. 7b: "because there is no answer from Elohim."

The *form* of Mic 3:5–7 shows that it conforms to the basic, two-part prophetic judgment speech, but with a certain amount of development in both the accusation and the announcement of judgment. The structure of the saying may be presented as follows:

v. 5α   Introduction (original formulation uncertain)
v. 5αβ   Accusation
v. 5b   Development of accusation
         (Transition = לכן)
v. 6   Announcement of judgment: divine intervention

---

[21] Recently, Hoffman, *Die Intention der Verkündigung Jesajas,* BZAW 136 (1974), 3ff., calls into question this distinction, only in Isaiah, between *Jahwewort* and *Prophetenwort* as formulated by H. W. Wolff in his "Die Begründungen der prophetischen Heils- und Unheilssprüche," and "Das Zitat im Prophetenspruch," in *Ges. St.* 9–35 and 36–129, respectively.

[22] Cf. Boecker, *Redeformen,* 71ff., 143ff.; cf. 3:9ff.

v. 7a   Results of the intervention
v. 7b   Climax (כי clause) of announcement

Thus Micah makes use of a typical prophetic form of speech to announce
Yahweh's impending judgment on the prophets. Now we proceed to a close
examination of the content of the saying.

(2) Who are Micah's opponents? Why does he stand in conflict with them?
We may conveniently deal with these questions by examining (a) the terms Micah
uses to designate the opposition, (b) their actions, and (c) their words cited by
Micah.

(a) If we exclude the phrase על־הנביאים in v. 5a as part of the redactional
introduction, then Micah names his opponent once as הנביאים (v. 6b) and then
as החוים ("seers") and הקסמים ("diviners") (v. 7aα). The root חזה has the
primary meaning of "to see visions,"[23] whereas קסם denotes the practice of
divination; deriving from the Arabic *qasma* (to cut, divide), it expresses the idea
of "to distribute by casting lots."[24] It is remarkable that the words חוים and
קסמים stand together with נביאים as designations for Micah's opponents. One
could assume that the prophet intends to distinguish between three classes or
groups of prophets, but no clear evidence supports such a supposition. The
terms are to be seen as more or less synonymous,[25] as is suggested by (1) the
parallelism of the terms, (2) the fact that it is the *nebiim* who will be deprived
of "vision" and "divination" (v. 6) and (3) the language of 3:11, where the *nebiim*
are said to practice divination (יקסמו). Thus we find no necessary polemic in
Micah's *use* of either חוים or קסים to designate his opponents.[26]

---

[23] Cf. Num 24:4, 16, etc., and D. Vetter, art. חזה, *THAT* 1, 535. Occasionally a *nabi* is
identified as a seer: 2 Sam 24:11; 2 Kgs 17:13; Ezek 7:26; Lam 2:9, cf. J. Jeremias, art. נביא,
THAT 2, 9f. The redactors responsible for the superscriptions to some of the prophetic
books thought of these men as seers (e.g., Isa 1:1[2:1]; Am 1:1; Mic 1:1).

[24] Cf. I. Mendelsohn, "Divination," *IDB* 1, 857. The term can designate various forms
of inquiry into the future: 1) the use of headless arrows in a quiver, each representing
several possibilities; 2) consulting the teraphim; 3) examination of the livers of sacrificial
victims; cf. Ezek 21:26f. and A. R. Johnson, *Cultic Prophet*, 32ff.

[25] Cf. Weiser; Mays; also Jepsen, *Nabi*, 43, who emphasizes that the use of seer and
diviner alongside nabi does not mean other classes of prophets but rather characterizes
their particular function; cf. Ezek 13:9.

[26] Later the Deuteronomist regarded divination, like all magical activity, as forbidden,
and placed the diviner in sharp contrast to the *nabi* (Deut 18:10ff.; cf. Lev 19:26). Critics
are not in agreement as to whether divination was always a pejorative term in Israel (thus
Mays), or was at one time a valid method of inquiry into the divine will (e.g., Sellin;
Johnson, *Cultic Prophet*, 34f., esp. note 1 on p. 35). In any case, Micah does not condemn
divination per se, but the abuse of the prophetic office (cf. Ezek 13:6, 9; 22:28), as 3:5b,
11aβ make clear. Stolz, "Der Streit," 24f. gives consideration to whether קסם has some
connection here with necromancy. He is unable to offer convincing data which would show
that Micah (and Isaiah) intend to accuse their prophetic opponents of participating in
necromancy. See also A. Guillaume, *Prophecy and Divination among Hebrews and Other*

(b) Micah's accusation against his prophetic opponents begins with the participial phrase הַמַּתְעִים אֶת־עַמִּי. In the Old Testament Yahweh is said to "lead astray" (תעה hiph.) as a form of divine punishment;[27] the Wisdom tradition refers to "going astray" (by rejecting reproof, Pr 10:17; or by being led astray by the wicked, Pr 2:26; cf. Pr 28:10, where the synonym שעה occurs). Particularly do the prophetic indictments speak of "misleading," where the subject can be the leaders (Isa 3:12; 9:15; Jer 50:6; cf. 2 Kgs 21:9), a spirit of harlotry (Hos 4:12), or lies (Am 2:4). But it is above all the *nebiim* who are accused of "leading my people astray," a phrase that occurs, in addition to Mic 3:5, in Jer 23:13, 32; Ezek 13:10. The verb תעה is an "important term for sin and for its consequences";[28] in Mic 3:5 it is a general accusation which becomes specifically defined in v. 5b, especially in the words attributed to the opponents in v. 5b, the meaning and background of which we must now consider.

(c) According to v. 5b הנביאים "lead my people astray" in that they

Proclaim שלום when they are given something to eat,
but they sanctify war against him who puts nothing
in their mouth.

In what does this "leading astray" consist? Some scholars find nothing more than an ethical problem here: the greedy prophets practice their profession for monetary gain; their oracles are conditioned by what they receive; thus what they preach is geared to their self-interest instead of to their duties and obligations.[29] Or, one finds in the passage a critique of social ills. Münderlein's recent study argues that the prophets are like the other leaders of society who do harm to the poor (cf. 2:1ff.; 3:1ff.; 3:9ff.) because they are unable to pay for their oracles.[30]

Although each of these interpretations helps explain Micah's opposition as voiced here, the central issue has not yet been seen. The most significant part of the accusation is to be found in the quotations of the prophets' words,[31] though

---

Semites (1938) and B. Long, "The Effect of Divination upon Israelite Literature," *JBL* 92 (1973) 489–497, who discusses how divination practices influenced the shaping of specific genres of Old Testament literature.

[27] Isa 30:28, object: "the people"; Isa 63:17, object: "chiefs"; Ps 107:40, Job 12:24, object: "princes."

[28] J. Sawyer, art. תעה *THAT* 2, 1056; see also H. Braun, art. πλανάω *TDNT* 6, 233ff. According to John 7:12, Jesus' opponents thought of him as "leading the people astray."

[29] Wellhausen; Marti; Sellin; Lindblom; Bruno, *Herrscher,* 67f.; Quell, *Wahre und falsche Propheten,* 117ff.; Rudolph; Hossfeld-Meyer, *Prophet gegen Prophet,* 46ff.

[30] Münderlein, *Kriterien wahrer und falscher Prophetie,* 24f.

[31] Cf. H. W. Wolff, "Das Zitat," 94, emphasizes that the quotation is "das wichtigste Stück in der Begründung, weil es die deutlichste Form der Begründung ist." This is certainly true of Mic 3:5. Westermann, *Basic Forms,* 61, clarifies how the quotation in prophetic speech forms is a development of the accusation, which applies especially to Mic

in effect it is only one word: "they preach 'shalom'." This is characteristic of
Micah, as he quotes his opponents with relative frequency (2:4, 6f. [11]; 3:11),
which indicates that he engaged in heated and lively debates with those whom
he opposed.[32] Moreover, as Lindblom has emphasized, it was the *content* of the
preaching of these *nebiim* that was their principal characteristic.[33] We may
therefore understand this passage as reflecting what must have been an intense
disputation between Micah and the *nebiim:* they preach שלום when according
to Micah it is a time of Yahweh's judgment. As recent studies have noted,
especially those by van der Woude and Crenshaw, the prophets' quotation of
their opponents can be an important source for discerning their theological
stance.[34] This leads us to a necessarily brief look at the word שלום in this
context.

That the word is of considerable import is indicated by the fact that in later
classical prophecy שלום was a characteristic motif of the "salvation prophets," as
its frequency on their lips attests (Jer 6:14; 8:11; 14:13; 23:17; 28:9; Ezek 13:10, 16).
Micah was the first to oppose the *nebiim* for the preaching of שלום.

α. What is the meaning of the term shalom in this context? According to von
Rad, the root meaning is "well-being, with a strong emphasis on the material
side."[35] Mitton states: "the root meaning . . . seems to be completeness, wholeness
(cf. Akkadian *salamu,* to be faultless, healthy, complete)."[36] When the word is on
the lips of the prophets, its sense may be ambiguous, expressing a variety of
concepts, in Eisenbeis' view, such as Wohlergehen, Wohlfahrt, Wohlbestellsein,
Glücklichsein, politischer (?) Friedenzustand, etc.[37] Westermann's suggestive
study concludes that what shalom means when uttered by the prophets is Heil

---

3:11, where the quotation brings to a climax a complex accusation; in 3:5, however, the
quotation is the central point of the accusation rather than a development of a preceding
thought. The conditional clauses in v. 5b ought to be seen as subordinate to the quotation.

[32] Here קרא introduces the quotation, a typical introductory term (see H. W. Wolff,
"Das Zitat," 43, note 32) which can have the technical meaning of "to proclaim" in the
prophetic literature (e.g., 1 Kgs 13:32; 2 Kgs 23:16f.; Isa 40:2, 6 and further references in
C. Lambuschagne, art. קרא, *THAT* 2, 668f.). 2:4 and 3:11 introduce the quotation with
a form of the verb אמר, while in 2:6 the opponents' words are indicated by יטיפון (see
below, pp. 92ff.) "thus they preach"; 2:11 contains no such introductory verb, which must
be supplied. Quotation of opponents' words in each of these cases should be seen as
deriving from a "lebhafte Auseinandersetzung" (Wolff, 46 and passim.).

[33] J. Lindblom, *Prophecy in Ancient Israel,* 213.

[34] A. S. van der Woude, "Micah in Dispute with the Pseudo-Prophets," *VT* 19 (1969)
244–260. Though van der Woude is above all interested in Micah's disputations with the
false prophets, he completely passes over Mic 3:5–7 in his discussion of the prophets' words
as cited by Micah. Crenshaw, *Prophetic Conflict,* passim.

[35] G. von Rad, art. εἰρήνη, *TDNT* 2, 402.

[36] C. L. Mitton, art. "Peace," *IDB* 3, 705.

[37] W. Eisenbeis, *Die Wurzel šlm im AT,* BZAW 113 (1969) 166f.

(not as in Heilstaten or Heilsgeschen) in the sense of Wohlergehen. Hence, what they proclaim is not an act of divine intervention, but a condition.[38]

β. Can we discern the tradition historical roots of the shalom motif as found in the mouth of the *nebiim?* There appears to be a scholarly consensus that what we have here is cultic prophecy in which the prophets in Jerusalem were consulted for the sake of securing personal as well as corporate welfare.[39] But what about the theological tradition behind this? As far as I am able to determine, it was von Rad who first posed this question of the shalom preaching of the "false prophets."[40] Von Rad himself answered as follows: the pseudo-prophets, who had a connection with the official cultus, exhibit in their preaching a "national-religiöse Heilserwartung" which received its legitimation from the covenant theology of the Bundeskult. Thus, when the prophets announced salvation, their message was a representation of the covenant promises. But it is not covenant theology which stands behind the proclamation of shalom, as Kraus' critique of von Rad has shown; rather, it is the traditions associated with David and Jerusalem.[41] Against Von Rad, Kraus argued that shalom prophecy stems from the state cult, which has its legitimation and support in the institution of the monarchy. The Royal Psalms and the ideology of the Nathan Oracle (2 Samuel 7) provide the appropriate context for understanding the roots of shalom prophecy: "Shalom ist der *eine* Hauptgedanke im Königsritual."[42] From this it follows that the David tradition is *one* aspect of the roots in tradition of shalom prophecy.

The other aspect is to be traced to the tradition associated with the city of Jerusalem and Yahweh's divine residence there. The "Jerusalem cult tradition," which Steck has attempted to delineate and which he calls a "reflektiert-geschlossene, theologische Konzeption," has as its central idea the relationship of Yahweh to Mt. Zion and the city of Jerusalem.[43] The key to this tradition, Steck contends, lies in the fundamental assertion that Zion is the divine mountain, where Yahweh dwells and reigns.[44] The shalom *motif* is one element of this larger "theological conception," for shalom was (1) connected with pre-Israelite, Jebusite

---

[38] C. Westermann, "Der Friede im AT," *Ges. St.* 2, ThB 55 (1974) 220. In addition, see H. H. Schmid, *šalôm "Frieden" im Alten Orient und im AT* (1971) 112ff., for a complete bibliography of studies on *shalom.*

[39] See for example A. Johnson, *Cultic Prophecy,* 49, and also note 2; J. Jeremias, *Kultprophetie,* 7: ". . . dass es den Kultpropheten primär oblag, Heil (שׁלום) für Israel herbeizuführen, ist gesichertes Ergebnis der Forschung," who cites Ps 74:9; Ezek 7:26; Lam 2:9. J. Lindblom, *Prophecy in Ancient Israel,* 215: ". . . one of the major tasks of these cultic prophets was to announce shalom in the interest of the royal house and official policy, to encourage the people, and by the power of their prophetic words, influence the course of events in a favorable direction."

[40] G. von Rad, "Die falschen Propheten," 215ff.

[41] H.-J. Kraus, *Prophetie und Politik,* Theol. Ex. Heute NF 36 (1952) 43ff. Kraus disputes von Rad's use of Exod 20:18ff. and Deuteronomy 18 in this connection.

[42] Kraus, ibid.

[43] O. H. Steck, *Friedensvorstellungen,* 1f., note 9.

[44] Steck, 14.

Jerusalem, where the God *Salem* was apparently worshipped;[45] (2) shalom is often closely connected with Jerusalem in the Psalms;[46] (3) Yahweh, who according to the Zion Psalms dwells in and protects his city, is the author of shalom for his cultic community.[47]

The Jerusalem salvation prophets of Micah's time, whose theme is shalom, hold fast to the *Jerusalem cult tradition,* which continually reinforced the idea that Yahweh guarantees the safety of the city, its king and people. It seems exceedingly probable that behind the passage Mic 3:5-7 lies an intense scene of disputation, in which Micah announces doom for the city, its leaders, and the *nebiim* (cf. 3:9-12). The *nebiim* can announce shalom, a false security which can only result in the removal of their prophetic gifts (vv. 6-7). Micah's accusation is to be understood as a strong *polemic* not only against the false security promoted by the shalom proclamation but also *against the traditions* which stand behind and inform such preaching.[48]

γ. The accusation is completed in v. 5bγ, where the *nebiim* are said to proclaim the opposite of shalom. When they are given nothing to eat, i.e., when they are not paid by someone,

They sanctify war against him (וקדשו עליו מלחמה).

The phrase קדש מלחמה occurs infrequently (Jer 6:4 [without מלחמה in 22:7; 51:27; cf. Isa 13:3] and Joel 4:9). The background of such language would seem to be the "holy war" tradition,[49] although this exact wording does not occur in

---

[45] Cf. esp. F. Stolz, *Strukturen und Figuren im Kult von Jerusalem,* BZAW 118 (1970) 215ff.; for extensive bibliographical information on this point, Schmid, *šalôm,* 86, note 135 and Steck, *Friedensvorstellungen,* 12 (note 13), 25f.

[46] Ps 122:7ff., "Pray for the *shalom* of Jerusalem. . . . *Shalom* be within your walls and security within your towers. . . . *Shalom* be within you." The connection of peace with security in Jerusalem is made explicit.

[47] The cultic community could pray for and expect the blessing of *shalom* from Yahweh: cf. Ps 29:11 "May Yahweh give strength to his people; May Yahweh bless his people with *shalom*"; Ps 85:9, "Let me hear what God will speak, for he will speak *shalom* to his people"; cf. v. 11 and see esp. Schmid, *šalôm,* 70, who sees an original Canaanite song which has been transferred to Yahweh. F. Stolz, "Streit um die Wirklichkeit," 13ff., thinks he finds grounds for asserting that the prophetic announcement of *shalom* has its place in the oracle of salvation (*Erhörungsorakel*) given in response to the lament of the individual, community or king.

[48] Münderlein, *Kriterien,* 23ff., is correct in emphasizing that the concern for the morality of the *nebiim* plays a subordinate role in the accusation. But his conclusion that there is no explicit dispute over the content of the *nebiim's* preaching is incorrect and does not at all reckon with the fact that Micah's central concern is with their message, cf. 3:5b ("they proclaim" קרא); 3:11b ("they say" לאמר); in an ironic context, words are put into the mouth of the מטיף (2:11aβ).

[49] Bach, *Die Aufforderungen zur Flucht und zum Kampf im alttestamentlichen Prophetenspruch,* WMANT 9 (1962) 88.

any of the narrative reports of holy war. Soggin's[50] contention that these prophets preached a kind of holy war in which Yahweh would bring nations *against* Israel is not founded on compelling evidence and has found little acceptance (cf. e.g., the commentaries). In terms of the question of the relationship of the *nebiim* to ancient tradition, there are no grounds for concluding that ancient holy war tradition influenced these prophets whom Micah opposed. The language is rather to be taken in a metaphorical sense with strong sarcastic overtones,[51] meaning the prophets can also threaten doom of every sort (Sellin). The point here in Micah's accusation is that his prophetic opponents are arbitrary and act from self-interest.

(3) The *nebiim* who thus mislead the people can expect nothing other than Yahweh's punishment. What kind of judgment is to come upon them?

The announcement of judgment, signaled by the לכן in v. 6, now directly addresses Micah's opponents. Two main thoughts are expressed here. (a) These prophets will no longer prophesy. This is made clear by the synonymously parallel phrases "night without vision/darkness without divination" (v. 6a)[52] and "the sun shall go down/day shall be dark" (v. 6b). Since Yahweh can reveal his will to a prophet through visions and dreams (Num 12:6ff.; Hos 12:11; Jer 23:28), he can also withdraw these means of revelation (Lam 2:9). This withdrawal is underscored by the twice repeated מ of separation (cf. *Ges.-K.* 119w) in v. 6a. The expression "sun goes down" is used elsewhere figuratively for calamity, ignorance and confusion.[53] Thus these prophets are not condemned to death, as in Jeremiah (6:15; 8:12; 14:15; 23:15, 40; 27:15; cf. Ezek 14:9), or as Deuteronomic law required (13:5; 18:20); rather, their revelations are to come to an end. (b) This means that Micah does not dispute their authority as legitimate prophets (unlike Jeremiah, cf. 14:14; 23:2; 27:15; 28:15; 29:9); he claims that by the misuse of their prophetic functions, they have become disqualified as prophets and their authority is to be taken away.[54] The prophets will become "ashamed and confused"[55] as a *result* of this divine judgment. To symbolize this shame they "will

---

[50] J. A. Soggin, "Der prophetische Gedanke über den Heiligen Krieg, als Gericht gegen Israel," *VT* 10 (1960) 82f.

[51] Cf. QUELL, *Wahre und falsche Propheten,* 117, 118, note 1; Mays; Hossfeld-Meyer, *Prophet gegen Prophet,* 48. Wellhausen, followed by Marti, speaks of "Privatrache" on the part of the prophets. Bruno, *Der Herrscher,* 64, rejects this interpretation; he stresses that those who do not pay *cannot* pay and therefore it cannot be "revenge."

[52] Regarding the word "darkness," Marti says, "Es ist kein Gedanke an Nachtgeschichte in diesem Ausdruck; sondern Nacht und Finsternis sind Bilder für das Unglück, das herein bricht. . . .["]; cf. Am 5:8. On the expressions "night" and "darkness" in this context, see Hossfeld-Meyer, *Prophet gegen Prophet,* 170, note 22.

[53] Cf. Jer 15:9, Ketib; Ezek 32:7; Isa 60:20; Joel 2:10; 3:4; 4:15; cf. Am 8:9.

[54] See esp. J. Jeremias, "Die Vollmacht des Propheten im AT," *EvTh* 31 (1971) 316.

[55] The word-pair also occurs in Jer 15:9; Pss 35:26; 40:15; 70:3; 71:24; Job 6:20; cf. Zech 13:4, where "every prophet will be ashamed," not because of a lack of revelation, but rather "of his vision."

cover their moustache," a common sign of mourning (cf. Ezek 24:17, 22; Lev 13:45). This part of the verse serves to emphasize that Micah's opponents are to be thoroughly discredited in that they will be deprived of their authority and prophetic function.

The passage is brought to its conclusion by the כִּי clause (v. 7b), which seems to function as the reason for the mourning spoken of in v. 7a. The expression מַעֲנֵה אֱלֹהִים occurs only here in the OT and apparently has no particular roots in Israelite tradition (Wellhausen). In addition to v. 7b, the word מַעֲנֶה occurs only in Wisdom texts (Pr 15:1, 23; 29:19; 16:1; Job 32:3, 5; cf. also Sir 4:24; 20:6).[56] The announcement of judgment on the "heads and rulers" in the previous saying (3:4) also culminates in the same idea, though the wording is different: "but he [Yahweh] will not answer them" (וְלֹא יַעֲנֶה אוֹתָם). The word אֱלֹהִים in v. 7b is remarkable. It does not mean to include "other gods," i.e., the spirits consulted by the medium;[57] rather, it refers to the divine revelations from Yahweh, which will now cease.[58] Thus v. 7b reiterates the thought of v. 6 and confirms the interpretation that these prophets had once been, in Micah's view, legitimate speakers for Yahweh.

b. Mic 3:11

Micah speaks of the נְבִיאִים also in 3:11, where they are linked with the רָאשִׁים and the כֹּהֲנִים. The *nebiim,* like the rulers and priests, are expressly connected with Zion; they are "her prophets" (fem. suff.). It is not unusual for prophets and priests to be mentioned together.[59] It may be assumed that here we have to do with temple prophets.[60] The *nebiim* are accused of two things:

---

[56] On the theological context and importance of the concept of Israel's answer, see C. Barth, "Die Antwort Israels," *PbTh* 47 and passim.

[57] As suggested by Ehrlich, *Randglossen* 5, 279; Duhm, "Anmerkungen," 86; Sellin; Robinson; Lindblom.

[58] Thus Rudolph, who thinks the phrase makes an ironic allusion to the prophetic title "Gottesmann." It is instructive to compare 3:5–7 with 1 Samuel 28, where Saul inquires of Yahweh, but receives no answer either by dreams, Urim, or the prophets (v. 6). In the light of 1 Sam 16:14; 18:12; 17:11, this means that the Spirit of Yahweh was no longer with Saul (cf. R. Knierim, *EvTh* 30 [1970] 129). Like Saul, the *nebiim* have their charisma taken away (Mic 3:6–7). The glossator who added אֶת־רוּחַ יְהוָה in 3:8 probably also understood the passage in this way: the *nebiim* no longer have the spirit of Yahweh, but *Micah* does.

[59] See O. Plöger, "Priester und Prophet," *ZAW* 63 (1951) 157ff. (now in *Aus der Spätzeit des AT* [1971] 7ff.) for a thorough consideration of texts where priest and prophet occur together.

[60] The naming of priest and prophet together does not *necessarily* imply that the reference is to cultic prophecy; see the appropriate caution in R. Rendtorff, art. προφήτης *TDNT* 6, 806, who stresses that the simple equation that a nabi equals a cultic prophet (and thus an official profession) is not supported by the passages where priest and prophet are linked. On the other hand, the shalom prophets are surely to be connected with the temple (3:5), and it is these whom Micah has in mind also in 3:11.

(1) They perform their duties for money (בכסף), which does not mean that they are paid for their oracles, but that they have subordinated their office to avarice (Mays) (cf. 3:5b). (2) With the rulers and priests, they are guilty of false trust in Yahweh and take their stand on the Zion theology's dogma of Yahweh's presence and the city's inviolability (v. 11b). Behind the quotation (לאמר) attributed to the *nebiim* and the others, we may discern what must have been a disputation between these groups and Micah.[61] The placement of the word *nebiim* last in the series (rulers, priests, prophets) may emphasize that it is especially the prophets who are spokesmen of the dogma of Zion's security. The shalom preaching of the prophets in 3:5b and the words quoted in v. 11b are in essence an expression of the same false security: peace rather than disaster. Unlike 3:5ff., where divine judgment is directed only to the prophets, there the prophets will perish together with rulers and priests in the destruction of Zion, a destruction that they themselves bring on (v. 12).

c. Mic 2:11

V. 11 is a part of the larger context of 2:6-11, which is analyzed below, pp. 91ff. Here our interest centers on the use of the word מטיף and its verbal root נטף. The verse begins with לו, which expresses a condition (*Ges.-K.* par. 151c) which may be understood impersonally: "if a person . . ." The prophet states:

If one would go about in the spirit and deceive with lies[62]
    (saying) "I will preach (אטף) to you of wine and strong drink"--
He would be a preacher (מטיף) for this people.

The statement is generally recognized as ironic and sarcastic. Micah speaks not of נביאים but of מטיף, a term underscored here by its verbal form (אטף), which has been used to characterize Micah's own preaching in v. 6 (אל-תטפו).[63] Although v. 11 is formulated as a condition, it may be understood as a kind of accusation against his opponents, for it no doubt shows how Micah perceived them. Having characterized them as preachers of shalom, yet whose oracles are governed by the pay they receive (3:5b) and who perform the duties of their office for financial gain and who trust (falsely) in Zion's security (3:11), here Micah indirectly accuses them of "going about in the spirit" (הלך רוח), which perhaps means ecstatic spirit-possession of the old *nebiim*,[64] and also of speaking lies

---

[61] See below, p. 93, and footnote 105.

[62] Some critics see a grammatical difficulty in the phrase הלך רוח ושקר כזב. Smith takes שקר as modifying רוח ("spirit of falsehood"). Ehrlich, followed by Sellin and others, reads כָּזָב instead of כְּזָב and construes it as the object of the verb אטף, and also makes the text read in the first person ("If I would go about . . ."). Rudolph understands רוח and כזב as hendiadys ("windy lies").

[63] On the verb נטף, see below, pp. 93f.

[64] Thus Mays, with passages.

and deceit. The word שקר, perhaps first connected with the *nebiim* in 2 Kings 22 (רוח שקר) and later to become a chief attribute of the *nebiim* in Jeremiah, means "aggressive deception aimed at harming the neighbor"; the word כזב, "to lie," emphasizes that their preaching does not correspond to the truth.[65] The quotation put into the mouth of the מטיף (v. 11b), "I will preach to you of שכר and יין" (note the word-play שקר/שכר) suggests that Micah's opponents are both frivolous and given to strong drink, which is not befitting to their office. Such "preachers" speak to their audience about "subjects that please" (Mays). The implication is clear: the *nebiim* are false prophets because they do not speak of Yahweh's demands and his righteous judgment.

To summarize: It is evident from Mic 3:5-7, 11; and 2:11 that Micah opposed prophetic groups which he referred to as נביאים, חזים, and קסמים; or, in sarcastic tones, he could speak of them as a מטיף. His attack upon them took the form of accusations against their theology: they preach shalom and falsely trust that disaster cannot come upon Jerusalem and are thus rooted in the Jerusalem cultic traditions; against their avarice and greed (3:5b, 11aβ); against their lives of deceit and general debauchery (2:11). The punishment for the *nebiim* will be executed along two lines: on the one hand, they will be silenced, with their authority withdrawn (3:6f.); on the other, they will ultimately perish in Zion's destruction, which they together with the priests and rulers have caused (3:12). In the judgment speeches in 3:5ff. and 3:9ff., Micah illustrates the guilt of the *nebiim* by quoting their words; behind this style of the accusation stands genuine and heated debate between two prophetic positions: judgment vs. salvation.

2. Isaiah

Like Micah, Isaiah found himself in conflict with prophetic opponents. Yet only a few passages attest to such a conflict. Nevertheless, these texts are important ones, and an analysis of them will enable us to draw certain comparisons with the pertinent Micah texts. The word נביא occurs only four times in Isaiah: in 3:2, with קסם; in 9:14; in 28:7, parallel with כהן; in 29:10 (plur.) parallel with החזים. In addition, the words ראים and חזים stand parallel in 30:10. With the exception of 30:10, the נביא, חזים, קסם, are found in a context of critique or judgment. Therefore they are the object of our investigation here. 30:10 is treated below in Part B. We begin with the fullest and most important of these passages, 28:7-13.

a. Isa 28:7-13

This prophetic saying will provide us with an introduction to Isaiah's unequivocal attack on his prophetic (and priestly) opponents. Here we shall give

---

[65] Cf. Klopfenstein, art. כזב *THAT* 1, 819. שקר and כזב also occur together in Isa 28:15, where the context is the false trust in political treaties with Egypt.

particular attention to the *form* of this text, the reasons for the disputation in evidence here, and to Isaiah's message as it relates to our theme of prophetic conflict.

Vv. 7–13 constitute one part of a larger literary complex in chap. 28 which may be divided into several originally separate units: 28:1-4, 5-6, 7-13, 14-22, 23-29 (cf. Kaiser), material which reveals an involved process of transmission and redaction. Our unit begins in v. 7 with these words:

> And also these reel with wine
> > and stagger with strong drink;
> priest and prophet reel with strong drink,
> > they are confused with wine,
> they stagger with strong drink,
> > they err in vision,
> > > they stumble in giving judgment.

V. 7 commences with the connective phrase וְגַם־אֵלֶּה which links it with 28:1-4. If the phrase, together with the rest of v. 7a, is a redactional addition, then the original unit probably began with v. 7b.[66] V. 7b brings Isaiah's *accusation* against priest and prophet (not directly addressed but spoken of in the third person) for drunkenness and the resultant inability to attend to "visions" and "giving judgment." Introduced by כִּי, v. 8 continues the accusation with a descriptive statement in the perfect tense which underscores the extent of the religious leaders' debauchery. The drunkenness theme breaks off sharply with vv. 9-10, a quotation in which priest and prophet now address Isaiah. Vv. 9-10 are formulated first as a rhetorical question (twofold מִי)[67] and then as a mocking, nonsense statement.[68] These verses appear to be a disputational statement, as the

---

[66] The new rhetorical unit which begins here continues neither vv. 5-6 (non-Isaian material) nor vv. 1-4, a saying against Samaria. Vv. 7ff. exhibit signs of redactional activity, although no consensus among critics has emerged. Duhm considers vv. 7-8 to be a later, though Isaian, addition to vv. 9ff. According to Kissane, v. 7a is the original part of the verse, v. 7b being a later addition. Kaiser sees secondary material in v. 7a but also in v. 7bα₂β. We take only v. 7a as secondary (cf. Childs, *Isaiah,* 28); the literary connective וְגַם־אֵלֶּה and the taking up of the language of v. 7b indicate this clearly enough.

[67] A. van Selms, "Isaiah 28:9-13: An Attempt to give a New Interpretation," *ZAW* 85 (1973) 32, terms vv. 9-10 a "motivated interrogative sentence" whereby a question is introduced by an interrogative particle or pronoun followed by a sentence begun with כִּי, which motivated the question. He sees this as the Hebrew version of *reductio ad absurdum;* cf. 1 Sam 17:43.

[68] The precise meaning of v. 10 is probably not to be ascertained, in spite of continuing attempts to understand it. For summaries of critical opinions see Fohrer; Kaiser. Special studies of the verse are found in the following: W. W. Hallo, "Isaiah 28:9-13 and the Ugaritic Abecedaries," *JBL* 77 (1958), 324 ff., and more recently, A. van Selms, *ZAW* 85 (1973) 332ff. Van Selms attempts to understand the unintelligible words as Assyrian phrases which Isaiah could have learned from fugitives in exile. But it seems best, in the light of v. 9, to understand v. 10 as words of derision and scorn against Isaiah's prophecy;

rhetorical question and derisive tone suggest. Form critically, the quotation, though an integral part of the accusation, does not function to elucidate or further substantiate the accusation (as e.g., in Isa 5:9; 5:19; 29:15; Am 6:13; 8:5f.; Mic 3:5, 11); rather, it reflects an argumentative discussion between Isaiah and his opponents (see below),[69] although the encounter now seems to be viewed from a certain distance.[70]

The prophet's announcement of judgment is introduced by a deictic כִּי in v. 11 and continues until v. 13a; v. 13b is most probably a later addition.[71] V. 11 threatens coming disaster in a somewhat indirect manner: he (Yahweh is not named but implied) will speak to this people in a foreign tongue, i.e., the Assyrian army will attack.[72] V. 12 places in starkest contrast to v. 11 a quotation (אֲשֶׁר אָמַר אֲלֵיהֶם) from Yahweh illustrating or rather summarizing his previous offer of "rest" and "quiet"[73] (cf. 7:4; also 30:15), which then concludes on an

---

cf. G. Pfeiffer, "Entwöhnung und Entwöhnungsfest im AT: der Schlüssel zu Jesaja 28:7–13," *ZAW* 84 (1972) 341ff.

[69] Vv. 9–10 clearly exhibit marks of a disputation speech. Note especially the double question introduced by מִי (on such questions in the disputation, cf. esp. R. Melugin, "Deutero-Isaiah and Form Criticism," *VT* 21 (1971) 332f., who cites Exod 4:11; 2 Kgs 18:35 = Isa 36:20; Job 38. Isaiah's opponents mean to rebuff him with the rhetorical question, which implies that the answer is: "Certainly not us, who need no instructing word from you." The text indicates that, as in other examples of disputations, Isaiah's words to which they respond are not placed immediately before their disputing questions (v. 9).

[70] Thus B. Childs, *Isaiah*, 28.

[71] Cf. Duhm (who sees an addition only in the last three words of v. 13b); also Eichrodt; Hossfeld-Meyer, *Prophet gegen Prophet*, 55. Not only do the words of v. 13b seem to be taken from 8:15, but, form critically, with v. 13b, the saying contains a second announcement of judgment. Stolz, "Der Streit um die Wirklichkeit," 22, note 53, takes v. 11 as still a part of the accusation. But v. 11 is clearly an announcement of impending doom. Kaiser thinks both v. 12 and v. 13 are secondary expansions, but he advances no convincing arguments for this radical a deletion. It seems best to take only v. 13b as secondary, for with the quotation, the saying is rounded off and reaches a climax; nothing more need be said.

[72] There is no agreement on the date of our passage: Scott suggests a time prior to the revolt of Ashdod (711) or after Sargon's death in 705. Fohrer locates it during the third period of Isaiah's activity (716–711). Kaiser dates it during the period of Judah's revolt against Assyria, 703–701. The place of the disputation is often assumed to be in the temple during sacrificial activities (cf. e.g., Fohrer). W. Dietrich, *Jesaja und die Politik*, 155, suggests rather (following Procksch) that the situation was a meal during which there was a discussion between *a* priest and *a* prophet and Isaiah concerning foreign policy.

[73] The exhortation (*Mahnwort*) in v. 12aα₃, הַנִּיחוּ לֶעָיֵף, is interpreted by Stolz, "Der Streit," 21, to mean that priest and prophet have failed in their responsibility to "make rest for the weary," which he connects with their work in the temple (sacrificial offerings and answering petitions with oracles [Klageerhörung]); this he places in the context of prophetic social criticism (similarly Hossfeld-Meyer, *Prophet gegen Prophet*, 54). On the exhortation in v. 12aα₃, see G. Warmuth, *Das Mahnwort*, BET 1, 68: the exhortation here

accusatory note: "but they would not listen" (v. 12b). The result of rejecting Yahweh's words brings the announcement to a close in v. 13a, which repeats the words spoken by the priest and prophet in v. 10, turning them into a word of doom.[74] Those who refuse (vv. 9-10) to accept Isaiah's message and to obey Yahweh's call to "rest" (v. 12a) will experience divine wrath from a conquering power whose language is unintelligible to them (v. 11, 13a).

The form of vv. 7b-13a is thus a two-part judgment speech. Its particular Isaiah structuring, however, is to be seen especially in the inclusion of two quotations (vv. 9-10, 12-13a) which, though they contrast with each other, lend the saying a certain symmetry. The saying is somewhat intricately constructed, as the relationship between individual verses shows.[75]

Isaiah names as his opponents כֹהֵן and נָבִיא (v. 7b), a phrase which does not occur elsewhere in Isaiah, nor in Hosea (4:5aβ is a gloss) and Amos, but once in Micah (3:11) and frequently in Jeremiah (2:26; 26:7, 11, 16; 32:32; in reverse order in 6:13; 8:10; 14:18; 23:11). The priest and prophet are connected with the temple cultus, and thus one may speak of "cultic prophet" as Isaiah's opponents.[76] The accusation of "drunkenness"—also found in Isa 5:11f., 22; 28:1, 3; 29:9—is common property of OT prophecy (cf. Hos 7:5; Am 4:1; 6:6) and is not infrequently mentioned in the Wisdom tradition (e.g., Pr 20:1; 21:17; 23:20-21, 29-35; 31:4-7); but only Isaiah and Micah (2:11) include this motif with their

---

has the function of calling attention to past failures, establishing guilt, and provides a motivation for the announcement in v. 13 and v. 11.

[74] The structure of the announcement (vv. 11-13a) is unusual: the announcement of disaster in v. 11 is followed by a quotation formulated as a Yahweh-speech introduced by a variation of the messenger formula (v. 12). V. 13aα₂, picking up the exact words from v. 10, illustrates what was already said in v. 11 by putting the words of priest and prophet into Yahweh's mouth. Westermann (*Basic Forms,* 171) understands this structure in terms of a developed announcement of two parts: intervention of God (v. 11) and the results (presumably v. 13). Fey, *Amos und Jesaja,* 132, identifies in vv. 11-13 a tripartite structure (also in 30:15-17; in the early and middle period: 5:1-7; 8:5-8a; 17:10-11): Yahweh's offer— Israel's rejection—Yahweh's withdrawal. He notes that in Amos only the last two parts of this structure are present.

[75] The phrase יוֹרֶה דֵעָה in v. 9 picks up פְּלִילִיָּה in v. 7 just as שְׁמוּעָה picks up בְּרָאָה. Note the chiasmus that results:

vision (prophet)	give judgment (priest)
teach knowledge (priest)	audition (prophet)

The phrase וְהָיָה לָהֶם דְּבַר־יְהוָה in v. 13 corresponds to יְדַבֵּר אֶל־הָעָם הַזֶּה in v. 11. And v. 13aα₂.₃ precisely repeats v. 10 (minus the introductory כִּי).

[76] Cf. O. Plöger, "Priester und Prophet," *ZAW* 63 (1951) 185 and passim; A. Johnson, *Cultic Prophet,* 61; J. Lindblom, *Prophecy in Ancient Israel,* 207f.; Fohrer; F. Stolz, "Der Streit," *WuD* 12 (1973) 20f., speaks of these prophetic opponents as "Kultpropheten, Kultfunktionäre, or Kultbeamten." Here, however, we may leave aside the much disputed issue of whether a prophet connected with the temple cult is a "cultic official."

opposition to the prophets. Here the result of such debauchery is the inability to perform priestly and prophetic duties.[77] They are unfit for their religious tasks.

Priest and prophet are pictured as strongly opposed to Isaiah's preaching (vv. 9–10). Here we must inquire into the precise function and meaning of vv. 9–10. In spite of the obscurity of v. 10, it is clear that the quotation presented here is a scornful rejection[78] of Isaiah and his prophetic activity which stems from confrontation and disputation: these opponents refuse to be "instructed in knowledge" (יורה דעה) and to have the "message explained" (יבין שמועה) to them.[79] Since vv. 9–10 do not pick up the accusing words in vv. 7b–8, to what to they respond? According to Lindblom, these derisive words refer to "the message of disaster" which the opponents regard as "pure nonsense."[80] This would then mean that here, as elsewhere in OT prophecy, the issue is that of the salvation prophets (with the priests) opposing Isaiah's prophecy of doom. This is not, however, the sense of vv. 9–10, which in no way refers to the prophet's proclamation of disaster. The refusal to "be instructed" and its scornful tone do *not* suggest opposition to approaching judgment. To what then do they refer? The words of Yahweh in v. 12 can help clarify the matter. Here a message of "rest and quiet," and by implication "salvation," summarizes an important motif in Isaiah's message.[81] This is refused, however, by "this people" (העם הזה), which

---

[77] The prophet errs in his "visions" (בראה BHS). פלִילִיה means the priest's "giving of a decision" (BDB, 813) and is used only here in connection with priests. Note the chiasmus in v. 7b: priest-prophet; vision-decision.

[78] This rejection can be understood in terms of doubt cast on Isaiah's "Vollmacht" as, e.g., in Isa 5:19; 30:10; Jer 5:13, etc.; Ezek 12:27; Mic 2:6f., etc., as suggested by J. Jeremias, art. נביא *THAT* 2, 23; see also idem, "Die Vollmacht des Propheten im AT," *EvTh* 31 (1971) 305ff., which, however, does not discuss Isa 28:7ff. Isa 5:19 is said to be an example of an indirect questioning of the prophet's authority, 306, note 1.

[79] On the words יורה דעת as the work of the priest, see J. Begrich, "Die priesterliche Tora," *Ges. St.*, ThB 21, (1964) 232ff.; H. W. Wolff, " 'Wissen um Gott' als Urform der Theologie," *Ges. St.*, 183ff., esp. 187: "דעת in Hosea's view is the particular and decisive function of the priest . . . the essential content of the priestly office." This may be applied to Isa 28:9 as well. שמועה can mean "report," e.g., 1 Sam 2:24; Isa 28:19; Jer 51:46; Ezek 21:12 (eng. 7), cf. BDB, 1035; in Isa 28:9 it means the prophet's oracle or "audition" (cf. Duhm) and thus, by extension, "vision." Kissane understands it to mean "warning"; Kaiser translates "revelation." Isaiah's priestly and prophetic opponents ascribe priestly and prophetic functions to him.

[80] Lindblom, *Prophecy,* 201.

[81] Here Isaiah uses three words for the concept of "rest" or "quietness": המרגעה from רגע II "be at rest, repose," BDB, 921, occurs only here in the OT. The root נוח occurs in the hiph. form הניחו and in the noun המנוחה. In 30:15, the substantive נחת is parallel with שקט (cf. 7:4 for שקט) and בטח, and is connected with the word ישע. On the vocabulary in 28:12 and 30:15, see Fey, *Amos and Jesaja*, 129ff., who emphasizes the dialectic between Isaiah's proclamation of doom in his early period (2:11, 17, chap. 6; 8:13–15; 10:5f.) and his offer of salvation in his late period. For a study of "rest" in Isaiah,

probably includes other leaders with the priests and prophets:[82] they "will not listen" (ולא אבוא שמוע). The phrase ולא in v. 12b underscores the rejection voiced by Isaiah's opponents in vv. 9–10. The mocking question "Whom will he teach?" etc. is in fact a refusal to listen. Also 30:15ff., which undoubtedly belongs to the same period of Isaiah's work, is remarkably similar in form and content: "in returning and rest you shall be saved . . . but you would not" (ולא אביתם; cf. 28:12b). The priests and prophets, allied with the other leaders (cf. 3:2f.), reject Yahweh's means of salvation and instead support a policy of security based on military devices (30:16; 31:1) and help from Egypt (31:1).

The disputation which stands behind our passage therefore shows Isaiah in strong conflict with priest and prophet *not* over his preaching of disaster but over his proclamation of "rest and quiet."

Is it possible to place v. 12 into a broader tradition historical context? The "rest" motif in Isaiah has been shown to belong to the Holy War tradition (cf. 7:4; 30:15 and especially G. von Rad, *Der Heilige Krieg*, 57). The connection between 28:12 and 30:15 and between 30:15 and 7:4 suggests that one root of 28:12 is to be found in the tradition of *Holy War*. That Yahweh "gives rest to his people" is often said in connection with the *Conquest tradition* (e.g., Deut 3:20; 12:9f.; 25:19; Jos 1:13, etc.; Ps 95:11) but there we have above all to do with Deuteronomistic theology (cf. von Rad, "There Remains Still a Rest for the People of God," in *The Problem of the Hexateuch and other Essays* [1966] 94ff. Von Rad does not discuss Isa 28:12 in this context.). But our verse is *not* related to this circle of concepts at all (cf. F. Stolz, art. נוח *THAT* 2, 46; R. Fey, *Amos und Jesaja*, p. 131, note 5, leaves the question open). It might be supposed that the word מנוחה refers to Zion theology, especially since Psalm 132 can speak of Yahweh's "resting place" (למנוחתך, v. 8; זאת מנוחתי, v. 14), meaning Zion. However, this is slim evidence for such a connection; moreover, Psalm 132 is probably later than our passage and many critics do not reckon it among the Zion Psalms (46, 48, 76, cf. Gunkel-Begrich, *Einleitung*, 42; E. Gerstenberger, "Psalms," in *OT Form Criticism*, 216). Nor is the "rest" motif directly attested in the complex of motifs which belong to the Zion tradition (for a summary of such, see Steck, *Friedensvorstellungen*, 13ff.). On the other hand, it would appear that in Isaiah a connection is made between the idea of "rest" and Zion as the *place* where this rest is to be found. This has been argued especially by Keller and Hossfeld-Meyer,[83] who call attention particularly to Isa 14:32 and 28:16, texts which speak of a "refuge for the afflicted" and "a foundation for those who believe" in Zion. If this

---

see C. Keller, "Das quietistische Element in der Botschaft des Jesaja," *ThZ* 11 (1955) 81ff. On the "rest" motif in Isaiah, G. von Rad (*OTT* 2, p. 160) says: "When Isaiah speaks in this way (Isa 30:15) he is thinking not only of an inward condition of the soul but also of an attitude which must be expressed in a perfectly definite mode of political conduct."

[82] The phrase העם הזה refers neither to all of Judah (as in 6:9f.; 8:6, 11f., thus Kissane) nor to the people of Jerusalem (thus Hossfeld-Meyer, *Prophet gegen Prophet*, 55) but most probably denotes all the leaders (cf. Duhm; Eichrodt) of Jerusalem, with the priest and prophet (cf. 30:15f., where the message of rest and quiet is connected with the leaders).

[83] C. Keller, *ThZ* 11 (1955) 93ff.; Hossfeld-Meyer, *Prophet gegen Prophet*, 54.

understanding is correct, then we have the very remarkable and interesting possibility that Isaiah's prophetic and priestly opponents, insofar as they embrace and promote the political maneuvers and policy of the rulers, refuse to embrace the concept of Zion as a place of rest and therefore security.

This text exhibits several parallels with Micah's attack upon the *nebiim*. As in Mic 3:11, Isaiah names the נביא together with the כהן (sing. instead of Micah's plur.) in context of accusation. Their guilt lies not in their avarice and greed (Mic 3:5b, 11a) but in their drunkenness (Isa 28:7b). Micah, too, associates the "preachers" with יין/שכר (Isaiah uses the same word-pair), but only Isaiah speaks of the consequences of their debauchery: they are unable to fulfill their official duties. Whereas only Micah expressly links the prophets (and priests) to Jerusalem, both Micah and Isaiah connect the *nebiim* with a larger circle of rulers (Mic 3:11; cf. "this people" in Isa 28.10). In both Micah and Isaiah, the *nebiim* are threatened with punishment. Whereas only Micah speaks of a judgment which deprives the *nebiim* of their revelations (3:6f.), both prophets announce an explicit punishment which embraces more than the *nebiim:* Micah speaks of Jerusalem's destruction only (Mic 3:12); Isaiah expects the invasion of a foreign power (28:11), which by implication strikes Jerusalem and Judah.

The prophetic judgment speech form is evident in Mic 3:5ff.; 3:9ff.; and Isa 28:7ff. And common to all three texts is the quotation of the opponents' words as a part of the accusation. This shows that both our prophets engaged in genuine disputation with their opponents. What is significant here, however, is the difference in the substance of the debates. Micah's prophetic opponents are shalom prophets (3:5b) who hold to the Zion dogma of the city's invulnerability and reject his prophecies of doom (3:11b). Isaiah's opponents, on the other hand, reject his proclamation of "rest" and salvation, apparently refusing to find their security and that of the nation in their trust in Yahweh, preferring the false security of political alliances (cf. 30:15; also 30:1ff., 12ff.). Thus we see that the lines of battle with the *nebiim* are drawn on two different fronts in Micah and Isaiah.

b. Isa 3:1ff.

We must look briefly at 3:1ff., a text which speaks of נביא and קסם who, along with other leading circles in Jerusalem, face prophetic indictment and Yahweh's wrath. The new unit, which begins in v. 1 and concludes with v. 9a,[84] is a two-part judgment speech marked by the absence of direct address and, except, for v. 4, is not formulated as a Yahweh speech.[85]

---

[84] With Fohrer; Kaiser; Wildberger; Duhm takes vv. 1–9 + 12 as the unit; vv. 10–11 are secondary. Scott, on the other hand, divides 3:1–15 into three original units: vv. 1–7; 8–12; 13–15.

[85] The announcement, introduced by הנה followed by a present participle, with יהוה צבאות האדון as subject (cf. 8:7; 10:33; also 28:2), is given in vv. 1–5; vv. 6–7, continuing the announcement, provide a vivid example of conditions resulting from the judgment (cf.

The announcement of judgment (vv. 1–5, less the gloss in v. 1b, cf. Duhm, et al.) speaks of a reversal of Jerusalem and Judah's orderly way of life, for Yahweh is "removing" (מסיר cf. 1:25; 3:18; 18:5) "stay and staff," i.e., authorities and other influential and leading circles,[86] which will result in civil and political chaos. Whether Isaiah is thinking of anarchy,[87] or an internal military collapse,[88] or outside attack from the enemy,[89] is not clear. What is important for our purposes is that (1) Isaiah includes the נביא in his list of leaders and that (2) the קסם is mentioned together with the "prophet." It must now be asked whether there is an implicit polemic here against these leaders and in particular against the prophet and diviner. On the one hand, this list of leading circles (noticeably absent are king and priest) seems to be merely a neutral naming of those who constitute the "staff and stay" of the people.[90] On the other hand, there are several indications which suggest a different interpretation. (1) Isaiah apparently reserves the word נביא for his prophetic opponents. It is not a neutral term.[91] (2) The קסם receive no sympathetic word from Isaiah, for he places divination under his critical eye in 2:6 (emended text),[92] where diviners and "soothsayers" (ועננים) are lamented as the reason Yahweh has rejected his people. (3) In 3:2f. the prophet and diviner are loosely grouped together with the "magician" (חרשים) and the "charmer" (לחש), who are representatives of popular superstition and magic.[93] (4) Finally, the זקן (//קסם 3:2) is elsewhere indicted by Isaiah

---

Wildberger); the motivation, introduced by כי and formulated in the perfect, is given in vv. 8–9a.

[86] Cf. Duhm; Gray; on the phrase משען ומשענה see Wildberger, who calls attention to Isaiah's use of שען for "false trust" (שען [10:20] 30:12; 31:1) and the false reliance upon the authorities implied by the word שען in 3:1a.

[87] Duhm.

[88] Wildberger.

[89] Fohrer.

[90] This is the conclusion reached by Hossfeld-Meyer (*Prophet gegen Prophet*, 51), who find no negative evaluation of prophet and diviner in this text.

[91] Cf. 28:7 and the discussion above, p. 85.

[92] Many critics read some form of קסם in v. 6a (instead of מקדם) which then provides a parallelism with עננים (e.g., Duhm; Fischer; Eichrodt; Wildberger; differently, Fohrer. Note the possible emendations in BHS).

[93] It is clear from Isa 2:6 (emend.) and 3:2f. that Isaiah takes a negative view of divination (despite Johnson, *Cultic Prophet*, 33ff., who argues that divination was a legitimate prophetic activity) and associates it with the realm of magic, a forbidden activity in Israel (cf. only Lev 19:26; 1 Sam 28:8f.; Deut 18:10f.). What must be exphasized here is that Isaiah connects the נביא with the קסם, which in turn is associated with the magical arts (parallel to עננים in 2:6, a term which belongs in the sphere of magical practices; see Wildberger). He could therefore easily say what Jeremiah proclaimed a hundred years later: "Do not listen to your prophets, diviners, your dreamers (cf. *G, S, V*), your soothsayers, or your sorcerers, . . ." (Jer 27:9).

as an oppressor of the poor (3:14, along with the שרים who themselves are
"rebels," 1:23). And the שפטים in Isaiah are by implication "wicked" judges who
must be restored to Jerusalem after she is purified (1:26). These considerations
make it quite likely that here Isaiah knows himself to stand in opposition to
prophets *and* diviners; they are not only linked with other leaders whom he
elsewhere criticizes (cf. 1:10; 3:14; 9:15) but especially with magicians, charmers
and soothsayers, all illegitimate links to the divine realm. Perhaps one can, with
Scott, speak of "false prophets" here in 3:2.[94] Admittedly the polemic against
prophet and diviner is an indirect one. Nevertheless, 3:2, together with 2:6,
indicates that Isaiah's opposition to the prophets and diviners is real.

As in Mic 3:6f., "prophet" and "diviner" stand under Isaiah's prophetic
indictment (3:2; cf. 2:6 emended text). The implications of the words משען
ומשענה are that the prophet, diviner, and the other leading circles, are *not* to
be relied on for security and guidance. This is not unlike Micah's contention that
the *nebiim* are arbitrary and therefore unreliable spokesmen for the divine word,
for they can be "bought" (3:5b). However, we can detect a distinction in the way
Micah and Isaiah use the word קסם. For Micah, as we have seen, קסם is nothing
more than a synonym for נביא (cf. 3:6f.; cf. 3:11a נביאיה . . . יקסמו). For Isaiah,
the קסמים are viewed negatively; they belong in the same class as the magicians,
charmers, etc. (cf. 3:2f. and 2:6 emend. text). Finally, the inner structure of Isa
3:1ff. presents us with an interesting reversal in comparison with Mic 3:9ff. In the
latter text, the leading circles have incurred Yahweh's wrath and therefore the city
will be destroyed. In the former, Jerusalem (and Judah) "have stumbled" (כשלה
v. 8) and therefore the leading circles will be destroyed, i.e., "removed" (מסיר,
3:1).

c. Isa 9:14 and 29:10

In a prophetic saying concerning the Northern Kingdom (9:7-20) at the time
of a threat to her from Assyria (cf. 5:26 and Wildberger), we find another
reference to the *nebiim:* "The elder and the honored man is the head, and the
prophet who teaches lies (נביא מורה-שקר) is the tail" (v. 14). As in 3:2, the נביא
is mentioned together with the זקן; here the context is one of announcement
(v. 13) and accusation (v. 15). Of interest for our question is the phrase "prophet
who teaches lies," which connects the נביא with the שקר motif, as we found in
Mic 2:11. The formulation here is that the prophet "teaches" (מורה) lies,
probably meaning that the *nebiim* give deceitful oracles,[95] which are destructive
of the people and lead them astray (v. 15). But the verse looks like an addition
to v. 13 which attempts to explicate what is meant by "head and tail" (cf. Marti;
Duhm; Gray; Wildberger), though some regard the verse as genuine (e.g.,
Procksch; Fohrer). If the verse is taken as genuine, it would indicate that both

---

[94] Scott, *IB*, 5.

[95] Fohrer translates "Propheten und Lügenlehrer," and sees here a reference to prophets,
on the one hand, and priests who give oracles, on the other.

Micah and Isaiah viewed the *nebiim* as liars who deceive the public and lead them astray. But the contribution of 9:14 to our question remains somewhat inconclusive. In 29:10, the word הנביאים and החזים can be unquestionably regarded as glosses, for they have been added to a saying which has nothing to do with prophets.[96]

B. OPPOSITION TO THE PROPHETIC MESSAGE

Not only did Micah and Isaiah stand in vocal opposition to the נביאים, as we have seen; they themselves experienced direct opposition as well. Here we turn our attention to a brief discussion of the opposition Micah and Isaiah faced. The aim of the following paragraphs is to assess this topic in the broader context of prophetic conflict and especially to compare two texts, Mic 2:6f. and Isa 30:8ff., in the light of the following questions: (1) Who opposed these two eighth century prophets? (2) On what basis? What is the nature of this opposition?

Antagonistic and hateful opposition to Yahweh's prophets is of course not new with Micah and Isaiah. In the 9th century, for example, Jezebel went so far as to "cut off the prophets of Yahweh" (1 Kgs 18:4).[97] Elisha was mocked (2 Kgs 2:23), and one of his disciples could be characterized as a "mad fellow" (2 Kgs 9:11). Micaiah ben Imlah was insulted by the prophet Zedekiah and imprisoned by the king of Israel (1 Kgs 22:24ff.). The book of Amos records how Amaziah, priest of Bethel, attempted to silence Amos and drive him from the king's sanctuary — to no avail (Am 7:12ff.; cf. the redactional piece in Am 2:12). Hosea quotes his opponents, who state: "The prophet is a fool! The man of the spirit is mad" (Hos 9:7b), which were "insulting words born out of an intensely hostile situation"[98] (cf. also Hos 12:1).

1. Micah 2:6f.

That Micah's preaching provoked his audience to oppose his message is clear from 2:6f. Before we look carefully at these verses, first a brief discussion of the larger unit is necessary.

a. The text of 2:6-11 is notoriously corrupt and can be reconstructed only with some difficulty. V. 6 begins a new rhetorical unit,[99] although the abrupt

---

96   Cf. Duhm; Kissane, et al.

97   On the "violent fate of the prophets," see O. H. Steck, *Israel und das gewaltsame Geschick der Propheten,* WMANT 23 (1967).

98   II. W. Wolff, *Hosea,* Hermeneia.

99   Some critics connect vv. 6-11 more or less closely with 2:1-5 (Smith; Sellin; Rudolph). Although vv. 6-11 presuppose Micah's preaching of doom, that need not be understood as a continuation of 2:1-5. The present arrangement of the chap. is due to the redactor; cf. Mays. The following considerations support this: (1) The abrupt beginning of v. 6 in the jussive does not link with vv. 1-5. (2) The subject matter of vv. 6-7 does not pick up anything specific in vv. 1-5; vv. 6-7 merely presuppose Micah's doom preaching. (3) There are obvious form critical differences between the two texts. (4) The word לאלה (v. 6) need

beginning suggests that something may have been lost in the text's transmission
(Wellhausen). The unit ends in v. 11, where the words אַסֹף and מַטִּיף pick up the
multiple usage of the root נטף in v. 6.

Characteristic of this text is the obvious *alternation* in voices. Micah's
opponents speak first in vv. 6f. A word of accusation, spoken now by the prophet
and directly addressed to his opponents, follows in vv. 8f![100] Micah is no longer
the speaker in v. 10a;[101] rather, he quotes his opponents, who issue a threatening
command (plur. imperatives) to the "women" of v. 9. V. 10b presents difficulties.
Jeremias thinks the words were originally Micah's accusation (which probably
read: "For the gain of the slightest thing, you pledge with a ruinous pledge"),
now re-formulated so as to apply to Judah at the beginning of the exilic period![102]
Micah speaks in v. 11;[103] the statement is not a direct accusation. It has a sarcastic
tone and what seems to be a note of detached reflection ("if a man . . ."), which
in effect is an accusing word about his prophetic opponents (מַטִּיף). The
dialogical pattern of the passage may be expressed as follows:

v. 6bα	Opponents speak: Command to silence
vv. 6bβ-7	Opponents speak: Defense of secure position
vv. 8-9	Micah speaks: Accusation
v. 10a	Opponents speak: Threat (as command)
v. 10b	Micah speaks: Accusation
v. 11	Micah speaks: Indirect accusation

We may now summarize the form critical characteristics of this passage as
follows. These verses, which group themselves into four smaller units (vv. 6-7,
8-9, 10, 11), do not give the impression of an original rhetorical unit, but rather
of a *sketch* of a longer, heated exchange or debate between two parties. Not
everything said in the debate is repeated here, as the lack of connection between
the smaller units would indicate (e.g., vv. 8-9 do not seem to be a direct response
to vv. 6-7)![104] The prophet quotes the words of his opponents (vv. 6-7, 10a; cf.

---

not point to the previous verses; אלה can point to what follows (cf. Nowack); alternatively,
it could point to words which are not recorded here (cf. Budde, "Micha 2 and 3," *ZAW*
38 (1919/20) 8.

[100] Wolff, *Mit Micha reden* (1978) 59, 62, finds Micah's voice already in v. 7b.

[101] Wellhausen, followed by Marti, sees in v. 10a a continuation of Micah's words which
now announce impending judgment as exile from the land.

[102] Jeremias, "Die Deutung," 339f.; followed by Rudolph; Mays.

[103] Rudolph suggests that v. 11 originally did not belong to the previous verses. The
verse, though connected with v. 6 by the root נטף, gives the appearance of being a
fragment.

[104] Robinson; Quell, *Propheten,* 135, have also pointed to the fragmentary character of
the passage.

11aβ, a simulated, ironic quotation), as also in 2:4, 3:5b, 11bβ, alternating his own words with theirs. The counter-argument of the opponents in v. 7, obviously in response to Micah's (here unrecorded) previous words of doom, are formulated in a series of rhetorical questions. Characteristic of this passage is that neither the messenger formula nor an announcement of judgment is found. Instead the text embraces a variety of form-elements: prohibition and command (vv. 6a, 10a), accusation (vv. 8f., 10b) and a conditionally formulated sentence, ironic in tone, which may be understood as a kind of accusation (v. 11). These various elements indicate that the passage belongs to the form critical category of the *disputation*.[105]

b. The command to silence: Mic 2:6abα. V. 6 contains a quotation of the prophet's opponents. This is indicated by the word יטיפון ("thus they preach"), which is functionally equivalent to קראו in 3:5 and לאמר in 3:11 (cf. also 2:4). The opponent's words then read: אל-תטפו ... לא-יטפו לאלה (v. 6abα). This is a warning not to preach, given a particular intensity by two different syntactic formulations—first אל with the jussive (vetitive), then לא with the imperfect (prohibition)—a grammatical change which heightens the force of the warning.[106] V. 6abα may be translated

"Do not preach," thus they preach,
　"one should not preach of such things."

It is noteworthy that the root נטף (hiph.) occurs here no less than three times. נטף is used in a figurative sense for prophetic discourse (cf. Am 7:16; Ezek 21:2, 7, where it stands parallel with נבא). The term is not used here neutrally, but bears a sarcastic, biting and passionate tone (cf. 2:11), suggesting the picture of a mad prophet "foaming at the mouth."[107] The use of נטף in the plural suggests two things: (1) Micah's use of the word יטיפון may indicate that his

---

[105] Thus also Westermann, *Basic Forms,* 201, and van der Woude, "Micah in Dispute with the Pseudo-Prophets," *VT* 19 (1969) 247. On the disputation form, see J. Begrich, *Studien zur Deuterojesaja,* ThB 20 (²1969) 48ff., who lists the following texts as examples of the "Gattung": Am 3:3-6, 7-8; 9:7; Isa 10:8-11; 28:23-29; Jer 8:8; and Malachi passim. For Deutero-Isaiah: 40:12-17, 18-20, 25-26; 44:24-28, etc. On the disputation, Begrich observes: (1) it is to be distinguished from the prophetic judgment speech, although their intention is related; (2) the aim is to convince the opponent with reasons to change their opinion and weaken their objections; (3) it derives from the secular sphere; (4) it contains question and counter-assertion. For an analysis of Begrich's study, see Westermann, "Sprache und Struktur der Prophetie Deuterojesajas," *ThB* 24 (1964) 124ff., who thinks that the disputation is not a Gattung, but a Redeform, since Begrich's texts exhibit such varied characteristics.

[106] The imperfect with לא is a stronger and more emphatic prohibition than the jussive with אל; cf. *Ges.-K.* par. 107o. A parallel construction is found in Am 5:5 (see Wolff, BK XIV/2). On אל with the jussive as a vetitive, see W. von Soden, *Grundriss der Akkadischen Grammatik,* AnOr 33 (1952) par. 81h, i.

[107] Contra Wellhausen; Marti; Nowack; with Jepsen, *Nabi,* 11; Robinson; Quell, *Wahre*

opponents in this disputation are a group of *nebiim*[108] (though not exclusively, since the accusation in vv. 8-9 picks up the motif of social and economic oppression, which must apply to the oppression by the rich and the ruling classes). (2) The words תטפו and יטפו, since they are plurals, indicate that Micah stands together with other prophets, of whom he is no doubt the leader![109] Thus we have a "Redeverbot" directed to Micah, which indicates that his proclamation drew intense opposition and hostility by opponents who attempted to silence him.

    c. The opponents' words: vv. 6bβ, 7. After the "command to be silent" (v. 6abα), the quotation of the opponents' words continues in vv. 6bβ, 7. Formulated as an indicative statement (imperfect) followed by a series of four rhetorical questions, the passage may be translated:

v. 6bβ	Insult will not overtake us[a]!
v. 7	Should this be said,[b] O House of Jacob?
	Is the spirit of Yahweh shortened?
	Are these his doings?
	Do not his acts[c] benefit
	those who walk uprightly?[d]

Textual Notes:

a   Cf. BHS, ישגנו=יַסִּגֵנוּ; otherwise, Rudolph; Mays.

b   Some read הארור instead of האמור (e.g., Sellin; Robinson; BHS; Mays; rejected by A. Ehrman, "A Note on Mic 2:7," *VT* 20 [1970] 86f.). Van der Woude, "Micha II 7a und der Bund Jahwes mit Israel," *VT* 18 (1968) 390 suggests האמיר, which he thinks is a term. tech. for covenant-making. But the text is understandable as it stands (thus also Rudolph).

c   Cf. BHS and most commentators.

d   Following Mays' translation.

    In the declarative statement לא ישגנו כלמות, the opponents express confidence in their *security;* the following rhetorical questions (introduced by ה; הלוא ... ה; אם) have the function of providing the *reason* for their confidence:

---

und falsche Propheten, 135; Jepsen compares נטף with the word משגע in Hos 9:7: "The prophet is a fool, the man of the spirit is mad (משנע)." On the interpretation of this verse, see Wolff, BK XIV/1.

[108] In every other case where the word נטף hiph. is used in its figurative sense, its subject is always a prophet(s); cf. the interpretations of Jepsen, *Nabi,* 11; Quell, *Propheten,* 135 (who thinks Micah battles with two different parties of prophets); van der Woude, "Micah in Dispute," 247; Crenshaw, *Prophetic Conflict,* 37; Stolz, "Der Streit," 18.

[109] Cf. Lindblom, *Prophecy,* 204; otherwise Quell, *Propheten,* 135f., who thinks two opposing groups of prophets are represented here, exclusive of Micah. Evidence for this, however, is lacking.

doom does not come, because Yahweh is patient and does good to the upright. Is it possible to discern the tradition historical background of these words? Some see a general reflection of the election traditions of ancient Israel (e.g., Sellin). Beyerlin thinks Micah's opponents take their stand on Yahweh's deed of salvation at the Exodus, guidance in the wilderness, and gift of the land.[110] Van der Woude finds reference to the Sinai covenant,[111] while Lescow suggests that this is ancient confessional language as well as allusion to the Landnahme tradition.[112] While some of the terminology of the opponents' words may vaguely be found to allude to elements of ancient salvation history or confessional statements, the fact that such different interpretations emerge indicates that a different answer is needed.

The essence of the opponents' counterargument is a rejection of any prophecies of doom and the affirmation that they are *secure.* This is expressed by the words לא ישגנו כלמות (v. 6bβ). The rhetorical questions are subordinate to this primary statement, functioning as its motivation. The sentence is strikingly similar to 3:11b in form and substance:

(3:11bγ) לא תבוא עלינו רעה

We note that both statements (1) are quotations, which are expressed by opponents, among whom the *nebiim* no doubt stand out; (2) are formulated in the first person plural (v. 6bβ, emend. text); (3) are introduced by לא, followed by the imperfect, and negate or contradict a statement by Micah; (4) express confidence in their present security before Yahweh, who protects from all disaster (רעה; כלמוה). Cf. 2:7 with 3:11bβ!

---

[110] Beyerlin, *Die Kulttraditionen,* 71ff., focuses on the word מעלליו and cites Pss 77:12 and 78:7 as evidence that the word refers to the salvation-history traditions. One crucial point stands in the way of this interpretation. The context in Mic 2:7 indicates that here the מעלל refers *not* to Yahweh's deeds of salvation, but deeds of judgment, which Micah has proclaimed.

[111] Van der Woude, "Micah in Dispute," 247, reads האמיר instead of האמר and translates: "Yahweh affirmed . . . ," which he sees in the light of Deut 26:17f. as referring to covenant making. Also בית יעקב is understood as reflecting the Sinai covenant. The unnecessary change in the text (cf. Willis' critique, "Mic 2:6–8 and the 'People of God'," *BS* NF 14 [1970] 79, note 26) and the questionable early date of such covenant theology in the Deuteronomic text (cf. L. Perlitt, *Bundestheologie im AT,* WMANT 36 [1969] ad loc.) do not recommend this interpretation.

[112] Th. Lescow, "Micah 1–5," 52, sees in the phrase הקצר רוח (v. 7a) an allusion to the ancient confession that Yahweh is "slow to anger" (ארך אפים Num 14:18, Nah 1:3, etc.) and, with the word ייטיבו, recalls a motif belonging to the conquest tradition (Num 10:29, 32; Jos 24:20; 1 Sam 2:32, etc.). The latter interpretation is dependent on an unnecessary change in Micah, which as it stands is perhaps reflective of Wisdom concepts (הישר and cf. Prov 2:7, 21, and further texts in Mays). Moreover, if one understands v. 7b as words Micah speaks (cf. Wolff, *Mit Micha reden,* 62), Lescow's interpretation meets even further difficulty.

The close correspondence in form and substance between 3:11bβγ and 2:6bβ, 7 suggests that the false security identified in 2:6bβ, 7 is rooted in the same Zion theology. Thus it is neither salvation-history tradition nor Sinai covenant which informs the views of Micah's opponents, but rather the Zion tradition.

2. *Isaiah 30:9ff.*

The reception of Isaiah's preaching was not any less negative than Micah's. The rulers of Jerusalem "scoffed" at his prophetic activity (28:14), and we have already seen in 28:9f. how prophet and priest directly contested his word of salvation. But the most explicit rejection of Isaiah's work is to be found in 30:9ff., a text upon which we now focus our attention.

Following Yahweh's command to Isaiah that he make a written record of his message (v. 8, cf. 8:16), which is the beginning of a new unit, the passage continues by giving the reason for such a writing:

v. 9 For they are a rebellious people,
        lying sons;
    sons who will not hear
        the instruction of Yahweh,
v. 10 Who say to the seers:
        "See not,"
    and to the prophets:
        "Prophesy not to us what is right.
    Speak to us of pleasant things,
        prophesy illusions.
v. 11 Leave the way,
        turn aside from the path;
    let us hear no more
        of the Holy One of Israel."

The new unit which begins in v. 8 with Yahweh's command to Isaiah ends not with v. 14 or v. 17, but with v. 11.[113] In the light of our theme, our discussion is limited to vv. 9-11. Introduced by כִּי, which ties it as a motivation to v. 8, v. 9 is an accusation against "rebellious people" (עַם מְרִי) who are unwilling to hear the תּוֹרַת יהוה. It is formulated as a noun clause (v. 9a) which is followed by an asyndetic relative clause (v. 9b). Vv. 10f. is a quotation, prefaced by the words אֲשֶׁר אָמְרוּ, consisting of two parts: two negative commands or warnings (לֹא followed by imperatives v. 10a) which are balanced by a series of exhortations (v. 10b-11).

---

[113] Cf. Childs, *Isaiah,* 36. Vv. 12-14 represent a prophetic judgment speech (accusation; announcement) which has a different style (direct address) and a different, though not unrelated, accusation (v. 12). Kaiser contests the genuineness of vv. 12-14 (and vv. 9-11), but not convincingly.

The speakers of the quotation are characterized as עם מרי and נבים
כחשים. The situation is clearly that of a disputation between two groups. Those
addressed by the quotation are prophets, who are not called נביאים but ראים
and חזים![114] It may be assumed that here Isaiah is to be included among these
"seers," for Isaiah himself is pictured as a visionary in Isa 6:1ff. (אראה; cf. the
superscriptions in 1:1 and 2:1), and he reserves the word נביא for his prophetic
opponents (28:7, cf. 3:2)![115] Those who speak to the seers attempt to command
them to silence with the words לא תראו/לא תחזו (v. 10a). This "Redeverbot" is
qualified by the word נכחות: do not prophesy to us what is "right."[116]

Who are, precisely, the speakers who are quoted here? To what are they
objecting in the preaching of Isaiah the seer and those associated with him?
To take the second question first, we might assume that Isaiah's opponents
desire that he cease his pronouncements of judgment; that instead he preach
shalom to them![117] At first glance this could be indicated by the word חלקות
("smooth things"). But the clue to the question is to be found rather in the phrase
תורת יהוה, which the opponents refuse to hear (לא אבו שמוע, v. 9b). The word
תורה is here best understood against the background of Isaiah's "preaching
against foreign policies of alliances and revolt, advocating instead quiet reliance
on Yahweh's might and governance,"[118] as is suggested by 28:9, where Isaiah's
preaching is rejected (מי יורה דעה), teaching which has to do with "rest"
(מנוחה), a motif found also in 30:15 ("rest and quietness"). The close link
between 30:9 and these texts is further indicated by the phrase לא אבו שמע
which occurs in each text (28:12; abbreviated in 30:15 לא אביתם). This interpretation is strengthened when we note who the speakers of 30:10f. are. They are called
עם מרי and בנים כחשים. Although עם might mean the entire nation (1:4;
6:5, 9, 10; 7:17) the context does not suggest this understanding. The "sons" who
are rebellious are rather the rulers, who are also called בנים in 30:1, described
as those who make their own political plans without seeking Yahweh's
counsel (v. 2). Further, the rejection of Isaiah's preaching in 28:9f., where we also

---

[114] חזים can stand parallel to נביאים as well (Am 7:12, 14; Mic 3:7; also 2 Kgs 17:13
[probably secondary, as in Isa 29:10]). חזים and ראים are thought to be synonymous (thus
Lindblom, *Prophecy*, 90). Johnson, *Cultic Prophet*, 12, however, argues that the root חזה
is used more for visions accompanied by an audition than is ראה. For a general discussion,
see Vetter, art. חזה, *THAT* 1, 533ff.

[115] Cf. Wildberger, 5. Isaiah probably expresses solidarity with other seers and vision-
aries here (cf. Donner, *Israel*, 161; Fohrer; Fey, *Amos und Jesaja*, 118).

[116] The word נכחות is at home in the wisdom tradition (Pr 8:9; 24:26; Sir 11:21) as Wolff
(*Amos' geistige Heimat* [1964] 30) and others have shown. Jensen, *The Use of tôrâ by
Isaiah*, CBQ, Mon. Series 3 (1973) 115ff., argues that Isaiah deliberately uses Wisdom
terminology in vv. 9ff. (pointing especially to the terms תורה, דרך and אחר) in order to
dispute with the royal advisers.

[117] Cf. Duhm; Crenshaw, *Prophetic Conflict*, 35.

[118] J. Jensen, *The Use of tôrâ by Isaiah*, 116.

identified political leaders as part of the opponents, suggests that in 30:9ff., it is the rulers who stood opposed to the seers![19]

If we compare Mic 2:6f. and Isa 30:9ff., it is immediately clear that the texts and the situations behind them are analogous. Both prophets met a vigorous antagonism against their preaching. The words of Mic 2:6 אל־תטפו correspond to Isa 30:10 לא תראו . . . לא תחזו, absolute commands to stop prophesying, but which are not unique to Micah and Isaiah, as the language of Am 2:12; 7:13; Jer 11:21 shows. Further, in both texts a situation of genuine dispute is reflected, as the quotations of the opponents' words indicate. Those who oppose Micah and Isaiah see both prophets as members of a larger group, as is indicated by the plurals in Mic 2:6 (תטפו) and Isa 30:10 (תראו/תחזו). Further comparison shows, however, two differences that are evident. (1) For Micah, the חזים and the נביאים are viewed together and the words are used synonymously. For Isaiah, a distinction is made between the two terms: the נביאים are his opponents; the חזים (and ראים) are those legitimate prophets to whom Isaiah sees himself linked and against whom the rulers stand opposed (30:10). (2) Whereas Micah (and those allied with him) is opposed because of his announcements of judgment (2:6f.; 3:11bγ), Isaiah's message is rejected because it offers תורה of Yahweh (30:9), which is a word of dependence and trust on Yahweh for the nation's security (30:15; 28:12).

Summary conclusion

1. Both Micah and Isaiah stand in opposition to a group of נביאים (Mic 3:5ff.; 3:11; Isa 28:7ff.; indirectly in 3:2). With the *nebiim* others are closely linked: the כהנים (Mic 3:11; Isa 28:7) and also other leading circles (Mic 3:9ff.; Isa 3:2f.). Only Micah, however, explicitly connects the *nebiim* with Jerusalem.

2. Micah designates his prophetic opponents not only with the term נביאים; the words חזים and קסמים stand parallel with the נביאים in such a way as to indicate that Micah makes no distinction between these designations (3:6; in 3:11 the *nebiim* are said to "divine" (יקסמו). "Divination" itself is not viewed in a negative light. Isaiah, on the other hand, seems to link the קסמים with soothsaying and magical practices (3:2f.). Furthermore, Isaiah makes a distinction between the חזים and the נביאים which is unknown to Micah: Isaiah understands himself to belong to the חזים (30:10) but not the נביאים. Whereas for Isaiah the words חזים and ראים appear to be used synonymously, Micah does not use the word ראים.

3. Micah and Isaiah both have judgment speeches in which their prophetic opponents fall under accusation and announcement of doom (Mic 3:5ff.; 3:9ff.; Isa 28:7ff.). The reasons for the judgment are similar. Both speak of the debauched life of the נביאים who take great pleasure in alcohol (implied in Mic 2:11; Isa 28:7f.). Only Micah, however, indicts them for performing their official

---

[19] The rulers may be understood as royal advisers belonging to courtly wisdom circles, as the word נבחות suggests; see Wolff, as cited above in note 116; also Jensen, *tôrâ*, 115ff.

duties for financial gain (Mic 3:11). In both Micah and Isaiah, the נביאים are viewed as guilty of lies and deception (Mic 2:11; Isa 9:14, if considered to be genuine).

4. Both Micah and Isaiah cite the words of their prophetic opponents. In Micah the quotations, introduced by קרא (3:5b) or לאמר (3:11b; here, along with leaders and priests), either substantiate or add a further element to the accusation. In Isaiah, the opponents' words are not introduced by a formula and stand more independent of the accusation itself (Isa 28:9f.). The quotations indicate that Micah and Isaiah must have engaged in lively *disputations* with their prophetic opponents. Characteristic of these disputations are the rhetorical questions, introduced by הלוא in Mic 3:11 (cf. 2:6f., where a group of opponents, with prophets probably among them, have rhetorical, disputing questions attributed to them), and by את מי in Isa 28:9f. The disputing questions addressed to Micah and Isaiah indicate that their prophetic message was rejected by other groups of prophets.

5. A significant distinction becomes apparent with regard to the content of the words of the opponents. Micah's prophetic opponents are seen as preachers of שלום, i.e., they are salvation prophets (3:5b), who stand firmly rooted in the tradition of Zion's security and Yahweh's presence there (3:11b). There is, however, no hint in Isaiah that the נביאים with whom he disputes are connected with the Zion tradition; rather, they are probably to be linked with the political leaders who find security in political alliances. It is *Isaiah's* preaching of faith and trust in Yahweh which they reject. By contrast, the נביאים in Micah reject his preaching of doom (Mic 3:11b).

6. Both Micah and Isaiah proclaim a coming punishment for the *nebiim.* In Micah this is expressed in two ways. (1) The *nebiim* will have their revelations and therefore also their authority withdrawn (3:6f.). This judgment finds no correspondence in Isaiah. (2) The *nebiim,* along with other leading circles in Jerusalem, will be punished by the coming destruction of the city (3:12). Isaiah, too, announces an impending, destructive threat which will come with a foreign invasion (28:11-13).

7. Finally, not only did both prophets oppose other prophetic groups; they themselves were opposed and rejected. Because their messages were found unacceptable, attempts were made to silence them (Mic 2:6f.; Isa 30:10f.). Remarkably, they were opposed for different reasons: Micah, because he announced doom; Isaiah, because he counseled against political alliances and offered a different way to national security. This is not to say that Isaiah's preaching of disaster did not at times also provoke opposition. But the specific "Redeverbot" is linked to his political counsel of "rest and quietness."

4
Social Critique in Micah and Isaiah

> The most striking thing in a study of the canonical prophecy of the eighth century is the way in which it is directed at a whole series of serious social injustices which are evidently connected with the attitudes of a well-to-do middle class. There is talk of oppression and deprivation of rights, of corruption and indebtedness, of a social disorder which there seems neither the will nor the ability to right!

Thus S. Herrmann can write about the theme which is the center of attention in this chapter. As is well-known, Micah focused a sharp eye on the injustice and oppression which his contemporaries experienced. His sayings reveal not only that he spoke out vigorously *against* the responsible leaders of Jerusalem and Judah, but that he stood solidly *with* the weaker and poorer members of society in their oppressed situation. Two key words which recur several times in Micah's prophecy signal these two aspects of his social criticism: on the one hand, his accusation against the abuse and abhorrence of משפט (3:1, 9; cf. v. 8); and on the other, his solidarity with those whom he calls עמי (2:8, 9; 3:3, 5). It is our task in this chapter to explore the theme of social critique in the relevant texts in Micah and then, consistent with the previous chapters, examine similar material in Isaiah for purposes of drawing a careful comparison between these two eighth century contemporaries. The nature of the material to be studied here suggests that we divide this chapter in two parts. Part A deals with the social criticism in Micah and Isaiah in a general way; Part B has a somewhat narrower focus in that it looks at a particular example of oppression, namely, the expropriation of land by the wealthy and powerful. This division enables us first to gain a general impression of Micah's and Isaiah's critique and then compare especially two texts which exhibit a remarkable correspondence in form and content (Mic 2:1ff.; Isa 5:8ff.).

The comparison of Micah and Isaiah texts will be governed by lines of inquiry similar to the questions posed in the previous chapters:

(1) What are the form critical similarities and differences in those passages dealing with the theme of social critique?

---

[1] S. Hermann, *A History of Israel in OT Times* (1975) 235.

(2) Can one discern the older traditions which are taken up in these texts and how they are adapted?

(3) Which circles in the Israelite social structure are attacked by Micah and Isaiah, and what is the substance of their critique?

(4) What do Micah and Isaiah envision as the nature of divine judgment upon an Israelite society that is no longer a just society?

Recent studies of the prophets' social criticism have focused considerable attention upon the *origins* and *background* of this aspect of Israelite prophecy. K. Koch's article, "Die Entstehung der sozialen Kritik bei den Profeten," summarizes the different scholarly answers to this question under five categories:[2] (1) The prophets, as social critics, were preachers of divine law. (2) The prophets represent a general view of world morals and customs. (3) The prophets had an experience of the divine and of impending doom. (4) The prophets wanted to return to the "ideal time" of ancient Israel's societal orders. (5) The prophets—at least Amos and Isaiah—have roots in wisdom belonging to the pedagogy of the Israelite clans. With Koch's study we now have a sixth answer, which apparently locates the background of prophetic criticism in the unseverable relationship between the freedom of the individual peasant families and the faithfulness of Israel's God in leading and guiding them.[3] It is thus clear that at this point, a great lack of consensus exists on the question of roots and influence for prophetic social critique. It should be noted, however, that our purpose in this chapter is *not* to develop an answer to this problem. Nevertheless, our study of the given texts will inquire into what are their possible roots in the tradition.

A. INJUSTICE AND OPPRESSION

1. Micah

We begin with a text in which Micah utters a devastating critique of the injustice and oppression perpetuated by leaders and officials against the weaker members of Israelite society.

---

[2] In *PbTh,* 239ff. Some of the more important studies of prophetic social critique are the following: H. J. Kraus, "Die prophetische Botschaft gegen das soziale Unrecht Israels," *EvTh* 5 (1955) 295ff.; H. Donner, "Die soziale Botschaft der Propheten im Lichte der Gesellschaftsordnung in Israel," *OrAntiq* 2 (1963) 229ff.; O. H. Steck, "Prophetische Kritik der Gesellschaft," in *Christentum und Gesellschaft,* ed. W. Lohff, B. Lohse (1969) 46ff.; E. von Waldow, "Social Responsibility and Social Structure in Early Israel," *CBQ* 32 (1970) 182ff.; G. Wanke, "Zur Grundlage und Absicht der prophetischen Sozialkritik," *KuD* 18 (1972) 1ff.; F. Stolz, "Aspekte religiöser und sozialer Ordnung im alten Israel," *ZEE* 17 (1973) 145ff. O. Loretz, "Die prophetische Kritik des Rentenkapitalismus. Grundlagen-Probleme der Prophetenforschung," *Ugarit-Forschung* 7 (1975) 271ff., offers a brief review and summary of much of the recent material named above and criticizes the representative notion that prophetic opposition to social injustice is found *only* in Israelite prophetism. He argues that this phenomenon is found also in the history of ancient Near East, 273ff. S. Holm-Nielsen, "Die Sozial-kritik der Propheten," *Festschrift Carl Heinz Ratschow,* ed. O. Kaiser (1976) 7ff.

[3] "Die Entstehung," passim and esp. 256.

a. Mic 3:1-4

v. 1 And I said:[a]
    Hear now, O heads of Jacob
      and leaders of the house of Israel:
      Is it not for you to know justice?

v. 2 You who hate the good and love the evil;
    who[b] rip the skin from them
      and the flesh from their bones.

v. 3 ' 'c They eat the flesh of my people
    [and strip their skin off them][d]
      and break their bones.
    They chop them up as flesh[e] for the kettle,
      as meat for the cauldron.

v. 4 Then they will cry to Yahweh,
      but he will not answer them;
    he will hide his face [at that time][f]
      because their deeds are evil.

Textual notes:

a   *G* (cf. *S*) reads καὶ ἐρεῖ, which changes the first person style to the third person. Though some critics delete ואֹמַר as a gloss (e.g., Wellhausen), others find here the remnant of a first person report (e.g., Lescow, "Micha 1-5," 47ff.). Rudolph also deletes; see, however, Wolff, "Micha von Moresheth," *Suppl. VT,* Congress Vol. 1977 (1978) 413, who finds evidence here of Micah's own *literary* activity.

b   BHS suggests changing the participle to a finite form.

c   BHS deletes ואֹשֵׁר; Mays retains, citing 3:5.

d   Probably a gloss on v. 2b (cf. BHS; Rudolph). Some commentators rearrange the order of the verses (e.g., Mays: vv. 1, 2a, 3, 2b, 4).

e   Cf. BHS.

f   Likely a gloss according to most commentators (e.g., Smith; Budde, *ZAW* 38 [1919/20], 20).

(1) Form critically, this text gives the appearance of an easily analyzable unit. The summons to hear (cf. 3:9a), which is followed by the specific naming of the addressees, introduces the accusation (vv. 1b-3); the announcement of judgment, begun by אז ("then") concludes the unit. Thus we have a two-part prophetic judgment speech, without, however, the messenger formula (cf. 2:3) or even a לכן (cf. 3:12) to connect the two parts.[4]

Several elements in the text call for brief, further comment. Unlike 3:9, where a participial style follows the summons to hear, in v. 1b a rhetorical

---

[4] Cf. Westermann's similar analysis (*Basic Forms,* 174): introduction, v. 1a; accusation, vv. 1b-2a; development, v. 2b (v. 3 secondary); intervention of God, v. 4.

question, introduced by הלוֹא, commences the accusation.[5] This lends to the first
part of the accusation a disputational quality which may recall a passionate
debate between the prophet and the leaders on the subject of מֹשְׁפָט. The accusation continues in v. 2a, where, with a change to participial style, v. 1b is explicated
by the antithetical word pairs "hate/love—good/evil." With vv. 2b-3 the theme
of "no justice" is presented by the drastic image of physical torture and cannibalism; in v. 3 (if not in v. 2b) the style shifts from the direct address begun with
the vocatives in v. 1a to speaking about the addressees in the 3rd person plural
(similarly 3:9ff.) with verbs in the perfect.

In the light of 3:12, one might expect the announcement which follows in
v. 4 to describe some form of physical disaster or punishment. Instead, with three
verbal clauses in the imperfect, divine silence is the prophesied judgment. There
is no shift back to the direct address, as in 2:3ff.; 3:6; 3:12.

(2) Micah aims his social critique in this judgment speech at a definite
group: the רָאשִׁים (heads) and קְצִינִים (leaders). With these terms (cf. Mic 3:9),
Micah apparently takes up terminology that reaches back to premonarchical
times, when רֹאשׁ could designate a leader in a tribe or family who had both
military and judicial functions (cf. Num 25:4, 15; Deut 1:15). Though "heads"
can stand parallel with other similar terms (e.g., זְקֵנִים, Deut 5:23), here it is
paired with קְצִינִים (as in 3:9), a word used for a military leader in tribal times
(Jos 10:24; Jgs 11:6, 11, where רֹאשׁ is the synonym; cf. Mays). From the context
in Mic 3:1 and 9, it is clear that Micah refers to officials in Jerusalem whose
responsibility is to guarantee justice in the courts.[6]

(3) What are the main topics of Micah's criticism of these officials, and what
is the possible background in Israelite tradition? In Mic 3:1b-3 the accusation
is comprised of three different parts. Let us take each in turn.

(a) The accusation begins with a rhetorical question which has as its key
term the word הַמִּשְׁפָּט:

Is it not for you to know הַמִּשְׁפָּט? (v. 1b)

The formulation דַּעַת מִשְׁפָּט does not occur elsewhere in eighth century prophecy, although it is reminiscent of the phrase דַּעַת אֱלֹהִים in Hosea and finds an

---

[5] Cf. the similar formation of rhetorical questions framed by Micah's opponents in 2:7
and in 3:11bβγ. הלוֹא ". . . expresses the conviction that the contents of the statement are
well known to the hearer," Ges.-K. par. 150e. On the accusation formulated as a rhetorical
question, as in 3:1b, cf. Wolff, Ges. St., 12f.; also Westermann, Basic Forms, 142ff., and
the examples cited there. The "summons to hear" followed by a rhetorical question is not
unique to 3:1; cf. e.g., Isa 1:10f.; 7:13; 28:23; Joel 1:2; Job 13:6f.; see below, note 53, p. 116.

[6] It appears unlikely that one can make a distinction between "heads" and "leaders"
(thus Rudolph). These officials are probably royal appointees from Judean clans and
families (cf. among others, R. Knierim, "Exodus 18 und die Neuordnung der mosaischen
Gerichtsbarkeit," ZAW 17 [1961] 158f.). For a discussion of "heads" see J. R. Bartlett, "The
Use of the Word רֹאשׁ as a Title in the OT," VT 19 (1969) 1ff.

echo in Jeremiah.[7] It is to be noted that the significance of the term in Micah is underscored by the similar phrase in 3:9b, where the following words are addressed to the same group:

(you) who detest משפט and twist all that is הישרה

Although the heads and rulers do not practice justice, Micah himself claims to be filled with it (3:8, "I am filled with משפט").[8]

These three texts show emphatically that משפט is the key term in Micah's critique, which he especially links to the "heads" and "rulers." He requires that משפט be *known;* he accuses the leaders of "detesting" it and "twisting" it. But what is meant here by משפט? The word has been linked by some to covenant or amphictyonic law, which is seen as the background for Micah's accusations here.[9] However, the context of 3:1ff.; 3:9ff. (cf. 3:8) indicates that the prophet means *justice* as it is to be rightly administered by those responsible for the proper functioning of judicial procedures. While it is true that Pentateuchal texts such as Exod 18:13–27 and Deut 1:9–18 also speak about the need for righteous judges (cf. Mays), it appears more likely that Micah reflects some influence not by these traditions but by the traditions of the wise man when he speaks of משפט. Several considerations suggest this. Whereas the Pentateuchal traditions do not speak of knowledge or understanding of משפט, the wise men emphasized that:

Evil men do not understand משפט (Pr 28:5);

or they could say:

Then you will understand righteousness and משפט (Pr 2:9; cf. 1:2; Job 32:9)

To be sure, the verb בין is used instead of ידע, but the two terms can be synonymous and often stand parallel![10] The phrase "who detest justice" (המתעבים משפט) in 3:9b is not only similar to a text in Am 5:10, which reflects wisdom influence (cf. Wolff, BK XIV/2), but the parallel term "to twist the right" (הישרה יעקשו) is undoubtedly stamped by vocabulary that derives from the sapiential sphere. עקש (ni., pi.) and its noun forms appear to belong almost

---

[7] Cf. Hos 4:1; 6:6, and see Wolff, *Ges. St.,* 182ff.; Jer 5:4, "They do not *know* the way of Yahweh, the justice of their God"; cf. also 5:5; 8:7; 2 Kgs 17:26.

[8] The catch-word משפט in 3:8 would appear to link the verse closer to Micah's disputes with the heads and leaders (3:1ff., 9ff.) than with the *nebiim,* as its present position suggests.

[9] Thus, e.g., Sellin; Copass-Carlson, *A Study of the Prophet Micah* (1950) 112; Beyerlin, *Die Kulttraditionen,* 52ff.

[10] Cf. H. H. Schmid, art, בין *THAT* 1, 307.

exclusively to such tradition (cf. Pr 10:9; 28:18 [verbs]; 19:1; 22:5; 28:6; etc.), while
ישרה occurs hardly at all in the ancient legal traditions but is found frequently
in Proverbs and Psalms![11] Moreover, the formulation of 3:1, with its combination
of "summons to hear" followed by a disputing, rhetorical question introduced
by הלוא is a device of the wise man's disputation that Micah has apparently
borrowed (cf. esp. Isa 28:23ff. and see below, footnote 53, p. 116).

(b) Next, we note how the absence of "knowledge of justice" is elucidated
in the continuation of the accusation in v. 2a: these officials "hate the good and
love the evil." The two participial clauses contain two antithetical word-pairs
שנא/אהב and טוב/רעה. The motif is familiar from prophetic accusations (cf.
Am 5:10, 15; Isa 5:20) in contexts of social critique and lays strong claim to being
wisdom terminology at home in the pedagogical devices of the clan fathers![12] For
Micah, to know nothing of justice, to detest it and twist it (3:9b) is to "hate the
good and love the evil."

(c) The imagery changes in vv. 2b–3, which further illustrate Micah's charge
of injustice against the leaders. A series of phrases pictures their guilt in drastic
and powerful metaphor: they "rip the skin and eat the flesh" of those who are
called "my people" (עמי). These words portray extremely harmful action against
the neighbor. The word גזל, whose root meaning is "to snatch away violently,"[13]
is probably metaphorical for illegal deeds of oppression; it can be used of
robbery (Gen 31:31; Deut 28:31), but can stand parallel to עשק ("to oppress") as
in Mic 2:2 (cf. Deut 28:29). The legal tradition (Lev 5:23; 19:13), as well as the
wisdom tradition (Pr 22:22f.), speak against robbery and oppression. "To eat the
flesh" is not a reference to cannibalism but is a metaphor used elsewhere for
wicked actions against defenseless persons (cf. Ps 14:4; Pr 30:14; Hab 3:14).

Those who are the object of oppression and mistreatment from the leaders
are called עמי. The term is important in Micah and occurs in contexts of social
oppression also in 2:8, 9; 3:5. For a discussion of this, see Excursus III, below,
pp. 117ff.

(4) The announcement of judgment in v. 4 is not couched in the language
of divine intervention and disaster (cf. 1:9b, 12b; 2:3ff.; 3:12), but rather in terms
of the silence and the absence of God, which has a marked similarity to 3:7b.
The oppressors will "cry out (יזעקו) to Yahweh," a formulaic expression not
infrequent in the Deuteronomistic history (Jgs 3:9, 15; 6:6f.; 10:10, etc.) and
elsewhere (Hos 7:14; 8:2; Joel 1:14) which indicates a great need of divine help.
The word זעק (and its variant צעק) as a cry for divine assistance apparently

---

[11] Cf. Pr 2:7; 3:32; 8:9; 12:6; 14:12; etc.; Pss 17:2; 99:4. Later wisdom could also place
ישר parallel to משפט, Pr 1:3; 2:9; cf. Pss 17:2; 99:4; and see G. Liedke, art. ישר, *THAT*
1, 792f., who notes that ישר and its various forms are characteristic of Proverbs and
Psalms.

[12] Cf. Wolff, *Amos the Prophet* (1973) 67ff.; W. Whedbee, *Isaiah and Wisdom* (1971)
104f.

[13] Cf. J. Schüpphaus, art. גזל, *ThWAT* 1, 999ff.

belongs to the language of lament in the Psalms![14] The actual element of judgment is expressed by two parallel terms לא יענה and יסתר פניו, the latter being a fixed formula which belongs to OT prayer language![15] That Yahweh will not answer the prayers of disobedient people is also found in other prophetic announcements (1 Sam 8:18; Jer 11:11f.; cf. Jer 7:16; 14:12).

In Mic 3:1-4, then, we have a prophetic judgment speech addressed to officials and leaders who not only fail in their responsibilities to uphold משפט but who are guilty of violent acts of oppression. Those oppressed are called "my people," the weaker members of society with whom Micah identifies and sympathizes. It is clear that the prophet draws a sharp distinction between the oppressed and the oppressor, the latter incurring the judgment of Yahweh who will now hide his face in silence. In this example of prophetic social critique, it is apparent that Micah borrows heavily from language that is at home in the wisdom sphere.

b. Mic 3:9ff.

A form critical analysis of this text has already been presented above (pp. 48f.), where it was discussed in relation to the Zion tradition. What concerns us in this chapter are the elements of social critique in vv. 9ff.

Above we have noted the beginning accusation concerning the "detesting of משפט," etc. in v. 9b directed to the heads and rulers. Here, in contrast to 3:1ff., these leaders and their guilt are explicitly connected with Jerusalem, which for Micah is the seat of all corruption and wickedness. The accusing words in v. 10: "who build Zion with blood (דמים)" have been variously interpreted as using extortion to obtain means for erecting spendid buildings, or building Jerusalem with forced labor,[16] or the greed and confiscation of the property of innocent people who are then condemned to death![17] The word דמים no doubt emphasizes blood-guilt and violence (cf. Hos 4:2; Ezek 7:23; 22:1ff.; Nah 3:1; Hab 2:12)![18]

Following the charge of brutal oppression in v. 10, v. 11a further develops the opening accusation (v. 9b) by a series of three parallel clauses in the imperfect. Now the scope broadens to include prophet and priest alongside the ראשים. The thrice repeated motif in v. 11a is that of bribery, designated by three synonymous nouns כסף, מחיר, and שחד: ruler, priest and prophet pervert their office out of greed for money. The motif is familiar in other prophetic writings

---

[14] Cf. R. Albertz, art. צעק, *THAT* 2, 573f., who cites pertinent texts.

[15] Cf. L. Perlitt, "Die Verborgenheit Gottes," *PbTh*, 730. The motif of Yahweh's hiddenness is found in Isa 8:17 in Isaiah's lament, where the context is not a judgment speech. Yahweh's hiddenness in 8:17 is not from the rulers only but apparently all of Judah ("house of Jacob").

[16] E.g., Sellin; Mays.

[17] Cf. Smith.

[18] Cf. B. Kedar-Kopfstein, art. דם, *TDOT* 3, 241. עולה stands parallel to דמים and means "violence" (cf. Mays).

(cf. Isa 1:23; 5:23; Am 5:12; Ezek 22:12). Bribery (שֹׁחַד) is forbidden in ancient Israelite law (Exod 23:8; cf. Deut 16:19; 27:25). Given the wisdom influence we found reflected in 3:1ff. and v. 9b, a close connection with v. 11 and Pr 17:23 is not unthinkable ("A wicked man accepts a שֹׁחַד from the bosom to pervert the ways of מִשְׁפָּט"; cf. also Pr 6:35; 17:8; 21:14; Job 15:34; Ps 15:5).

Thus we see the social critique in 3:9ff. focuses on the hatred of justice, oppression, murder, and bribery, carefully linked to Jerusalem and ultimately requiring its downfall (v. 12).

2. Isaiah

In the following section we examine texts in Isaiah which relate to the theme of "social injustice and oppression." The primary aim here is to analyze passages which present us with material that is in some way comparable to the texts discussed above in Micah. Our best point of departure may be found in Isa 3:13–15.

a. Isa 3:13–15

v. 13 Yahweh presents himself to contend;
        he stands to speak justice over his people.[a]
v. 14 Yahweh enters into judgment
        with the elders of his people and their princes:
     "It is you who have devoured the vineyard,
        the spoil of the poor is in your houses.
v. 15 What do you mean by crushing my people
        by grinding the face of the poor?"
     [Says the Lord, Yahweh of hosts.][b]

Textual Notes:

a   G (S) presuppose עַמּוֹ. M has עַמִּים. Duhm follows M and understands "peoples" to be the Hebrew tribes; Gray sees the plural as a secondary interpretation which turns Israel's judgment into world judgment. The singular should probably be read, but not in the sense of Yahweh's bringing his people into the court of judgment (this he does to the rulers); rather, Yahweh comes to help "his people" (Fohrer), or acts as their advocate (cf. Limburg, "The Root רִיב in the Prophetic Lawsuit Speeches," *JBL* 88, [1969] 303).

b   Not in G, cf. BHS; Duhm deletes. But see Wildberger, who retains most of v. 15b.

This passage[19] is characterized by the words רִיב/רִין and belongs to the

---

[19] Although 3:12 is closely related to vv. 13ff., it is best understood as a fragment originally separate from these verses (thus Duhm; Kissane; Kaiser, et al.). Vv. 16f. begin a new unit, as is commonly recognized.

genre commonly called a "legal procedure" or Rechtsstreit.[20] The core of the saying is found in the Yahweh speech in vv. 14b-15a, which is an accusation preceded by the prophet's words of introduction in vv. 13-14a. The accusation begins with an emphatic וְאַתֶּם ("And you!") and is formulated as direct address, with the verb in the perfect.[21] The accusation is sharpened by a concluding rhetorical question begun by מַּלָּכֶם: "What do you mean," an abbreviated "Beschuldigungsformel" (v. 15a).[22] There is no explicit announcement of judgment (as in 1:2f.; 1:10-17), but it is perhaps implied (cf. Kaiser).

The passage shows interesting and numerous similarities to Mic 3:1ff. Both texts bring an indictment against responsible officials for their oppressive actions. The object of the leaders' mistreatment in both texts is עַמִּי, "my people," thereby drawing a sharp line of demarcation between oppressors and oppressed. Even the metaphorical language used in both is similar: cf. "they eat (אָכַל) the flesh" (Mic 3:3) with "you devour (בָעַר) the vineyard" (Isa 3:14b). Indeed, אָכַל and בָעַר stand parallel in Isa 10:17. Moreover גָזֵל in Mic 3:2b (also in 2:2) has a correspondence in גְּזֵלַת in Isa 3:14bβ,[23] and the violence implied in Mic 3:10 (דָּמִים) is not unlike what is meant by the word דכא in Isa 3:15; cf. Mic 3:3aβ, "they crush (פָצְחוּ) their bones" with Isa 3:15a, "you crush (תְדַכְּאוּ) my people and grind (תִּטְחֲנוּ) their faces." Form critically, the passages are not the same; the Micah text is a judgment speech (Gerichtswort) while the Isaiah text is a judicial proceeding (Rechtsstreit), the latter with no explicit announcement. In Micah, the accusation is formulated as prophetic speech, whereas in Isaiah, Yahweh presents the accusation. Yet the similar stylistic device of using a rhetorical question in the accusation (Mic 3:1b; Isa 3:15a) is to be noted. In both texts, the intention of such language is clear: the prophetic message is intolerant of violent oppression and unjust treatment of the weaker members of society by those who are supposed to be the responsible leaders.

But several noteworthy differences are immediately apparent. Whereas Micah calls the addressees רָאשִׁים and קְצִינִים, Isaiah speaks of זָקֵן (cf. 3:2, 5; 9:14) and שָׂרִים (cf. 1:23; 3:4; 30:4; 31:9). Micah never uses the word שָׂרִים or זָקֵן; although Isaiah can speak of the קְצִינִים (1:10), he never mentions the רָאשִׁים. Are these words generally synonymous, or can certain distinctions be made here? As far as זְקֵנִים and שָׂרִים are concerned, there is some disagreement. According to R. de Vaux, these two words are "almost identical and denote ruling classes of the monarchical period" who are administrative heads of families and men

---

[20] The literature on the רִיב form is extensive; for a recent discussion of Isaian texts, see K. Nielsen, "Das Bild des Gerichtes (Rib-Pattern) in Jes 1-12," VT 29 (1979) 317ff.

[21] H.-J. Boecker, Redeformen des Rechtslebens im AT, WMANT 14 (1964) 85, understands this as the speech of a plaintiff in the court, not the judge.

[22] Ibid., 86.

[23] In Isa 3:14bβ גָזֵל clearly refers to robbery; behind the metaphorical language in Mic 3:3, "to strip off (גָזֵל) the skin," we may discern both physical violence and robbery (cf. 2:2).

of position.[24] Yet one may ask whether זקנים does not refer more to those who are representative of the clan structure.[25] What Micah meant by ראשים may be the same as זקנים in Isaiah (the terms are parallel in Deut 5:23; Jos 23:2; 24:1; 1 Kgs 8:1). One distinction does seem apparent: Micah makes use of terminology derived from tribal structures (note that Micah says "Jacob; house of Israel"). Isaiah's use of שרים, on the other hand, reflects his close association with Jerusalem officials and the monarchy.[26] It seems most probable, however, that Micah and Isaiah mean to designate, more or less, the same circles of officials who in Jerusalem, but also in the provinces, are responsible for order and justice.

A further distinction emerges in the vocabulary of the accusations in Mic 3:1ff. and Isa 3:13ff. Both Micah and Isaiah speak of the oppressed as עמי. Isaiah, however, places parallel with this word the term עניים (3:15a; העני in 3:14b; cf. also 10:2; 14:32). עני(ים) is *never* used by Micah. Nor does Micah speak of oppression as דכא as in Isa 3:15a (cf. 19:10).[27] (The term is apparently unknown in the Pent. [exceptions, Num 11:8; Deut 23:2] and in the Deuteronomistic and Chronistic History Works). Isa 3:15a has been especially linked to Pr 22:22, "Do not rob the poor (דל) because he is poor, or crush (תדכא) the afflicted in the gate."[28] If Mic 3:1ff.; 3:9ff. and Isa 3:13ff. are influenced by elements of the wisdom tradition, one notes that, at least as far as these two texts are concerned, the vocabulary appropriated by each is different. We must see whether this observation is confirmed by other texts.

b. Isa 10:1ff.

In this woe-saying Isaiah again takes up the theme of social critique. The unit, vv. 1–3,[29] is commonly understood to belong with the series of woe-sayings in 5:8–24 (cf. Wildberger). The woe-cry (הוי) introduces the accusation; as is

---

[24] R. de Vaux, *Ancient Israel*, 69f.; 137f.

[25] Cf. Kaiser; Fohrer; Dietrich, *Jesaja*, 381; also see G. Macholz, "Zur Geschichte der Justizorganisation in Juda," *ZAW* 84 (1972) 314ff.

[26] According to Knierim, "Exodus 18," 158ff., the שרים are life-long, public officials directly responsible to the king; he thinks that the same can be said of ראשים, the latter being a sociological term, the former a political one.

[27] See especially M. Schwantes' study, *Das Recht der Armen* (1977) 111f., for a full discussion of דכא and Isa 3:13ff. as it relates to oppression of the poor.

[28] Thus especially Wildberger; agreement, but with caution, in Whedbee, *Isaiah and Wisdom*, 108f.; also Dietrich, *Jesaja*, 17, thinks Isaiah picks up not only Pr 22:22f., but also Exod 22:4 in 3:14b–15a. The connection with Exod 22:4 is doubtful, however, for the phrase "to devour the vineyard" is used in the literal sense, while Isaiah uses it metaphorically, as applying not to destruction of fields by animals but to social oppression. The close connection between Am 3:7 and Pr 22:22 has also been noted; cf. Wolff, *Amos the Prophet*, 71.

[29] The passage ends in v. 3. V. 4a is poorly transmitted and is difficult to translate; v. 4b is a secondary addition; cf. Fohrer; Wildberger.

typical of the form, the woe-cry is followed by a plural participle describing the actions which evoke the prophet's words of judgment.[30] The accusation is continued in v. 2; the announcement of judgment, introduced by the question מה־תעשו, follows in v. 3.

The addressees are not specifically named, but their actions are first described as "those who set forth iniquitous decrees, and who write troublesome requirements."[31] This undoubtedly refers to royal officials or judges who are responsible for the administration of justice, but who instead use their official position to promulgate statutes and ordinances which contribute to their own wealth.[32] This initial charge made by Isaiah becomes more specific in v. 2:

> They turn aside the needy from their legal rights
> and rob the poor of my people of justice.

As in Mic 3:1, 9, the important catchword משפט is used here, placed parallel with דין.[33] The similarity is obvious: in the Micah texts and in 10:1ff., responsible circles of leaders are guilty of twisting and manipulating משפט. The root גזל, which we noted in Mic 3:3 and in its noun form in Isa 3:14, occurs again here in v. 2: they *rob*, or snatch away, justice. The phrase may well be meant to allude to robbery itself, as in 3:14. Violent acts, in addition to the deprivation of legal rights, are meant by the word עמל in v. 1 (cf. Wildberger). Some critics think Isaiah in this accusation also has in mind the taking of property from the small land owners, appealing to 5:8.[34] But the focus of the text is not about depriving people of their land but their legal rights in court (cf. Am 5:15). This interpretation is supported by those mentioned here as the objects of such oppression: the poor, needy, widows, and orphans, who hardly can be thought of as landowners.

As in Mic 3:3, the עמי are named again as those who are the objects of mistreatment. But an interesting qualification is added here that distinguishes Isaiah's language about "my people" from Micah's: 10:2 speaks of the "poor of my people" (עניי עמי), indicating that here, at least, the "poor" are a group

---

[30] On the woe-saying in Micah and Isaiah, see below, pp. 122ff.

[31] For translation and text-criticism, see Wildberger.

[32] Cf. Gray; Fohrer; Whedbee, *Isaiah and Wisdom,* 107. Whereas Wildberger thinks these people write new laws (כתב), Gray suggests, more probably, that they do not make new laws but are administrators of the law who are manipulators of it, willing to take bribes.

[33] דין and שפט also parallel Isa 3:13; 1 Sam 24:26; in Isa 3:13, the two terms are used not in the sense of justice but refer to the process of judgment or vindication, with Yahweh as subject. On דין see G. Liedke, *THAT* 1, 445ff.

[34] Kaiser; Wildberger; Dietrich, *Jesaja,* 40. בז ("to plunder") might imply the taking away of property; together with שלל ("to spoil") it belongs in the sphere of war. However, the misdeeds against widows and orphans belong to the realm of their legal rights, as 1:17 (*defend* the fatherless, etc.) and 1:23 make clear.

within the larger segment of those known as "my people."[35] Moreover, Isaiah places the "poor of my people" parallel with דלים. Again, we note a characteristic difference between Isaiah and Micah: the latter knows only of the עמי as the oppressed class; he *never* mentions the עניים or the דלים. This would appear all the more significant in that Isaiah and Amos stand so close at this point: דלים in Am 2:7; 4:1; 5:11; 8:6; as in Isa 10:2, דלים stands parallel with עני in Am 2:7 (i.e., עניום) (further, see Excursus III below, pp. 117ff.).

In v. 2b, Isaiah refers to widows (אלמנות) and orphans (יתומים); as a specific class or group of the ill-treated, they are deprived of their legal rights, as in 1:17, 23. Neither Micah nor Amos includes widows and orphans in his purview.

The tradition historical roots behind Isa 10:1ff. appear to reach back both to the legal (cf. Exod 23:6; Deut 16:19; etc.) and to wisdom (Pr 17:23; 18:5) texts. Both Whedbee and Dietrich take the view that the wisdom tradition has been appropriated here;[36] Dietrich compares 10:1ff. with 3:13ff. as another example of Isaiah's combining laws from the book of the covenant (Exod 22:21) with sapiential admonition (Pr 22:22f.).[37]

Isa 10:1ff. and Mic 3:1ff., 9ff. apparently have in common an appropriation of wisdom elements; yet each has adapted this material in his own creative way. The distinction in the terminology for the oppressed group above all points to their individual use of the older tradition.

Finally, we may note the judgment spoken of in Isa 10:3, which expects, vaguely, a "day of punishment" (יום פקדה), described with partial help of theophany language ("storm from afar"), when these oppressors will be helpless. Their destruction is not explicitly stated, as in Mic 3:12, but they obviously do not escape divine punishment (cf. 3:4), which is probably to be related to the Assyrian menace.[38]

c. Isa 1:21ff.

The theme of משפט is taken up also in 1:21ff., a passage we have already discussed above in relation to the Zion tradition (above, chap. II, pp. 58ff.). Here our interest lies in the social criticism, which Isaiah connects particularly closely with Jerusalem. The lamentation (איכה) is over a city which in the past had been a city filled with משפט (v. 21).[39] The present lack of משפט is not due to the wickedness of its *inhabitants* but to its leaders: whereas Micah speaks of ראשים

[35] Cf. Schwantes, *Das Recht der Armen,* 105.
[36] Whedbee, *Isaiah and Wisdom,* 107f.; Dietrich, *Jesaja,* 18f.
[37] Dietrich, ibid.
[38] Cf. Dietrich, 45.
[39] It is interesting that what Isaiah says of Jerusalem in v. 21, namely, that it was once "full of justice," Micah, using the identical terminology, says of himself: "I am full of . . . משפט."

and קְצִינִים (3:1, 9), here Isaiah again mentions שָׂרִים (cf. 3:14), but adds to this the שֹׁפְטִים and יֹעֲצִים. The connection between these princes, judges, and counselors, and the lack of מִשְׁפָּט is clearly stated in v. 23: the princes are rebels (סֹרְרִים) and companions of thieves. The judges and counselors are corrupt, as v. 26 makes clear, for they need to be purified and restored. But the center of the accusation aims at problems of justice in two statements. (a) Just as Micah accuses the "heads" of judging for bribes (יִשְׁפֹּטוּ בְשֹׁחַד), so Isaiah claims that "everyone loves a bribe" (שֹׁחַד). In a similar accusation, Isaiah proclaims against those who "acquit the guilty for a שֹׁחַר" (5:23), thus depriving the innocent of his rights (צְדָקָה); cf. Am 5:12, which also speaks against bribery (he uses the word כֹּפֶר). (b) The lack of justice is further underscored by v. 23b: orphans and widows do not have their legal affairs properly taken care of (יָתוֹם לֹא יִשְׁפֹּטוּ). Except for the mention of orphans and widows (cf. 10:2), Isaiah's accusation, set forth in the context of a lament over Jerusalem, closely corresponds to what we have seen in Micah: leaders of Jerusalem are corrupt; they take bribes; weaker members of society suffer. A common tradition appears to be embraced by both prophets (rather than a dependence on each other), which may be traced to the teachings of the wise.[40] But Isaiah has given it a characteristic application: injustice resides in the capital city, embodied in the sinful actions of leaders (as in Mic 3:1ff. and 3:9ff.), but the city itself will be restored by purging it (*Läuterungsgericht*) of corrupt officials, whereas in Micah the city, together *with* its officials, is to be destroyed.

d. Isa 5:20, 22f.

The series of woe-sayings in Isaiah (5:8ff.; 5:18ff.) provide a number of parallels to Micah's social critique. Here we are interested only in 5:20, 22f. In Isa 5:23, which concludes the woe-series[41] begun in 5:18, the prophet again, as in 1:21ff., combines the motifs of "no justice" with "bribery" in his accusation: "those who acquit the guilty for a bribe" (שֹׁחַד) at the same time "deprive the innocent of his legal rights" (צִדְקַת צַדִּיקִים יָסִירוּ מִמֶּנּוּ). This corresponds very closely to Mic 3:9b and 11, where the same connection is expressed: the "heads detest justice" and "make judgments for bribes." Isaiah's word against drunkenness in the preceding verse (v. 22, cf. 5:11) has an analogue only in Micah's critique of the false "preachers" in 2:11, but a further parallel exists between Isa 5:20 and Mic 3:2a: "they hate the good (טוֹב) and love the evil (רָעָה Mic 3:2a) and "woe to those who call good evil and evil good (רַע טוֹב וּלְטוֹב רַע Isa 5:20).

---

[40] Cf. Wolff, *Amos the Prophet*, esp. 83; also Whedbee, *Isaiah and Wisdom*, passim. and esp. 102f. and cf. Pr 6:35; 17:8, 15, 23; 21:14; but the legal tradition also forbids bribery (Exod 23:8; Deut 16:19, etc.).

[41] The string of woe-sayings is usually regarded not as an original rhetorical unit, but owes its present arrangement to a literary ordering. V. 24 was added later to v. 23 (cf. Fohrer; Kaiser).

Although Isaiah in the woe-series in 5:18–23 does not designate a specific addressee (typical of the woe-form), there can be no doubt that he is speaking to the officials and the upper class. From these texts, we see once again the striking similarity of the accusations against the abuse of justice and the perverting of good into evil in Micah and Isaiah. And again, the dependence on a common tradition comes into view: the wisdom teachers in family and clan typically use the antithetic word pairs such as good-evil,[42] and the language of Isa 5:23 is very closely analogous to Pr 17:15 and 24:24.[43] Finally, we may draw attention to the absence of any announcement of judgment attached to the woe-sayings in Isa 5:20, 22f. Although the woe-saying itself can in fact occur with or without an announcement,[44] its absence in these verses connects them with Isa 3:13ff., also where there is no announcement, and poses an interesting contrast to Micah's expectation of doom for officials (3:4) and the city (3:12). This difference must be further explored in succeeding paragraphs.

e. Isa 5:1–7

The "Song of the Vineyard" in Isa 5:1–7 requires our attention in that it takes up the motif of משפט in v. 7. One of the most esthetically pleasing of Isaiah's sayings, its precise form critical category has been much discussed, despite the fact that the prophet announces that he will "sing a song" (שירה).[45] The "song" beings in v. 1b; its subject is a "vineyard" (כרם) which has been well-tended and cultivated, lacking nothing (v. 2). The speaker changes in vv. 3ff., when the friend or the "beloved"[46] now addresses the audience, the song having ended in v. 2. The new speaker is obviously Yahweh, who addresses the "inhabitants of Jerusalem and the men of Judah," calling on them to make a judgment (שפטו) about the vineyard. The ostensible problem is that the vineyard has not produced precious grapes but "wild grapes" (באשים). This failure of the vineyard is given particular emphasis by the twice-repeated phrase יעש באשים (vv. 2b, 4b), which in both instances comes last in the sentence. Wild grapes bring destruction, announced in vv. 5b–6, where the repeated first person of Yahweh underscores

---

[42] See esp. Wolff, *Amos the Prophet,* 67ff., and Whedbee, *Isaiah and Wisdom,* 103ff.

[43] Whedbee, ibid., 101ff.

[44] In Isa 5:8–10, an announcement follows the woe-cry of accusation (on which, see below, pp. 127ff.). Isa 5:11f., 18ff., according to Fohrer, present a woe-series without an announcement. Concerning the woe-sayings in Amos on this particular point, cf. Wolff, *Amos* (Hermeneia), 245: "The pedagogical woe-sayings, whose existence within oral clan wisdom must be postulated, contained no elaborated element of threat," but "the prophet was free to expand the basic form of the woe-cry through addition of an announcement of judgment." The same thing applies to Isaiah.

[45] For a review of the scholarly discussions of the genre of Isa 5:1–7, see J. T. Willis, "The Genre of Isaiah 5:1–7," *JBL* 96 (1977) 337ff. Willis argues that the passage is best classified as a parable, which he calls a "parabolic song of a disappointed husbandman."

[46] On the phrase שירת דודי, see Wildberger's discussion of the problems of its interpretation.

the divine wrath which is provoked: "I will remove its hedge, and it shall be devoured,[47] . . . it shall be trampled down. I will make it a waste. . . ."

After the accusation (vv. 2b, 4b) and announcement of judgment (vv. 5b, 6), a concluding verse, introduced by כי, interprets the metaphor of the vineyard: the כרם is in fact the very ones addressed by the owner of the vineyard (Yahweh) in v. 3; however, in v. 7 the "inhabitants of Jerusalem, men of Judah" are now called "house of Israel, men of Judah." Furthermore the "grape-wild grape" imagery is interpreted: the much sought-after grape is משפט and צדקה which Yahweh looks for; instead he finds only משפח and צעקה, commonly rendered "bloodshed"[48] and "cry." This would indicate, also in the light of 10:1ff., 1:21ff., and 5:23, that what has been "looked for" (קוה), emphasized by its repeated occurrence (vv. 2, 4, 7), is the practice of *justice* among the people of Yahweh. This lack of משפט places v. 7 in the closest proximity with Micah's social critique, as we have observed before. But two things are noteworthy by way of contrast: (1) Isaiah can accuse not only the officials and rulers of the lack of justice in the land but the entire nation, Jerusalem *and* Judah (vv. 3, 7). According to what we have seen in Micah, it is Jerusalem that is the residence of those who practice oppression; but Judah, those outside Jerusalem whom Micah can call עמי, are not guilty of injustice but are the objects of it. Here we therefore see that Isaiah's social critique can encompass the whole land, as the words of v. 3 and v. 7 make clear. (2) The word-pair משפט/צדקה, which also belongs to Amos' social critique (5:7, 24; 6:12), is *not* used by Micah, who speaks rather of משפט and הישרה.

This distinction is not insignificant for our investigation, for it indicates that, in terms of the diction used within the context of social critique, Isaiah and Amos stand closer together than Micah and Isaiah. This is also, then, a further example of the difference in Micah's and Isaiah's appropriation of a common background in the tradition.[49]

f. Isa 1:10ff.

In this text,[50] commonly assigned to Isaiah's earliest period, there are two elements which are of particular interest to our question: the addressees, and the

---

[47] The imagery of "devouring the vineyard" obviously recalls Isa 3:14, but the use of the imagery differs: in 3:14 it is the leaders who have devoured the vineyard by their unjust treatment of the poor; in Isa 5:5, Yahweh's punishment is described as a destruction and devouring of the vineyard.

[48] משפח is a hapax legomenon whose meaning is uncertain. Duhm translates "Blutregiment," implying "Blutvergiessen." Fohrer and Wildberger translate, appropriate to the context, "Rechtsbruch"; see the discussion in Wildberger.

[49] That the word-pair "justice and righteousness" derives from clan wisdom's concern for the proper administration of justice has been shown by Wolff, *Amos the Prophet,* 59ff.; cf. Pr 16:8; 21:3; also 1:3; 2:9.

[50] The unit begins in v. 10 with the "Lehreröffnungsformel," v. 17 concludes the passage (Gray; Fohrer; Wildberger) rather than vv. 18–20 (Procksch; Kissane; Kaiser).

משפט motif in v. 17. The passage itself is thought to be a prophetic adaptation or imitation of "priestly torah,"[51] which in vv. 11-15 presents a striking polemic against cultic practices. Yahweh speaks here in the first person, emphatically rejecting the "sacrifices, burnt offerings, blood of bulls, solemn assemblies," and the like. Such a cultic polemic has close parallels in Am 4:4-5; 5:5-6, 14f.; 5:21-25.[52]

The unit is introduced with a two-part "summons to hear instruction" (שמעו/האזינו)[53] with a corresponding double vocative designating the addressees: "rulers of Sodom" (קציני סדם) and "people of Gomorrah" (עם עמרה). The reference to Sodom and Gomorrah (cf. 1:9; 3:9; BHS and others read סדם instead of זרים in 1:7) may imply by association that Jerusalem, too, is a thoroughly wicked place and also that the city will meet the same kind of destruction which befell Sodom and Gomorrah.[54] With the word קצינים (also in 3:6f.; 22:3) Isaiah uses a term which we found in Mic 3:1, 9. It would appear, then, that both prophets could speak of the leaders of the city of Jerusalem with common terminology.[55] One may ask, however, whether Micah and Isaiah use the term in different ways. In Isa 1:10, "leaders of Sodom" seems to imply that the קצינים are city magistrates only,[56] those who exercise judicial functions and are responsible for justice. Mic 3:1, 9, on the other hand, speak of "leaders of the house of Israel," a designation that goes beyond Jerusalem and encompasses the whole of Judah. But it is questionable whether such a distinction can be drawn, for in Isa 3:7, the prophet speaks of the קציני עם, which must mean the leaders of the entire people, as v. 8 indicates (Jerusalem and Judah). In any case, we do observe in Isa 1:10 the parallel placement of "people" and "leaders." Both are objects of the cultic critique in vv. 11-15 and of the admonitions in vv. 16-17.

---

[51] Cf. J. Begrich, "Die priesterliche Tora," *Ges. St.,* ThB 21 (1964) 243ff.; Wildberger.

[52] For an analysis of the structure of Isa 1:10-17, see Fey, *Amos und Jesaja,* WMANT 12 (1963) 68ff., who attempts to relate this text to the comparable Amos passages.

[53] As in Mic 3:1, a summons to hear is followed by a rhetorical question. J. Jensen, *The Use of tôrâ by Isaiah,* 72, argues that the pattern of "call to attention" followed by rhetorical questions is a characteristic wisdom device, referring to Isa 28:23f.; Job 13:6; 21:2; 34:16; 37:14. Jensen also argues that the word תורה in Isa 1:10, as well as the entire passage, is to be seen against the background of wisdom (73-83).

[54] For a discussion of this, see J. Vollmer, *Geschichtliche Rückblicke,* 161f., who emphasizes—correctly—that the exhortations in vv. 16f. would be meaningless if the comparison of Jerusalem with Sodom and Gomorrah already meant unavoidable destruction of the capital.

[55] Jensen, *The Use of tôrâ by Isaiah,* 71f., makes a case for understanding קצין in Micah and Isaiah in terms of wisdom. He notes that the term occurs only 13 times in the OT and that nine of these are in wisdom (Pr 6:7; 25:15; [Sir 48:15]) or prophetic texts (Isa 1:10; 3:6f. [twice]; 22:3; Mic 3:1, 9); the other texts are Jos 10:24; Jgs 11:6, 11; Dan 11:18. Jensen thinks that both Micah and Isaiah are making use of wisdom language with respect to the word קצין and in their critique of social injustice.

[56] Cf. Kaiser; Wildberger.

This differentiates Isaiah from Micah in a significant way, for Micah never understands עַם to be those who stand together *with* the leading circles. He knows only of leaders versus the people (always called "my people"); or, those who oppose and oppress "my people" can be called "this people" (2:11, on this, see Excursus III below).

After a polemic against the cult in vv. 11-16a, the prophet focuses on the theme of social justice. As in Mic 3:1ff., the catch word מִשְׁפָּט is combined with the antithetic word-pair "good-evil" (cf. Isa 5:20 + 23). And just as in Mic 3:1ff., the קְצִינִים are addressed — those who above all should be concerned for מִשְׁפָּט. But the distinction between Mic 3:1ff. and Isa 1:16b-17 is to be noted. Instead of an accusation against the leaders (and people) for perverting justice, culminating in an announcement of doom (Mic 3:1ff., 3:9ff.; Isa 10:1ff.), here Isaiah issues an *admonition,* which implies that repentance can be achieved and old abuses corrected.[57] The heart of the admonition is in v. 17 in the words "seek justice and make the violent keep straight"[58] (דִּרְשׁוּ מִשְׁפָּט אַשְּׁרוּ חָמוֹץ). The word אַשֵּׁר is understood by Wildberger in analogy to its usage in 3:12 and 9:15, where it means to "lead"; he thus translates "lead well those who are oppressed."[59] As in 1:23; 10:2, the admonition includes a concern for the orphans and widows (v. 17b). Here the words שָׁפַט and רִיב give concrete examples of what it means to "seek justice."

Thus unlike Micah, Isaiah could address the issue of the failure of מִשְׁפָּט among his people, not only with threat of punishment (10:1ff.) but with a prophetic *admonition* to improve the lot of the underprivileged and their needs for justice.

Before summarizing the results of Part A, the term עַמִּי in Micah and Isaiah is to be dealt with in an Excursus.

EXCURSUS III

עַמִּי IN MICAH AND ISAIAH

The importance of Micah's use of the term עַמִּי "my people" is evident by the number of times it is used: it occurs no less than six times in chaps. 1-3 (1:9; 2:4, 8, 9; 3:3, 5).[60] Though Micah nowhere speaks of "the people" (הָעָם), he does once refer to those he calls הָעָם הַזֶּה (2:11, BHS proposes לְעָם). We may note

---

[57] Fohrer; Wildberger.

[58] Gray understands אַשֵּׁר to mean "to go straight on" (Pr 9:6) and, in the light of the pi. in Isa 3:12; 9:15, translates "cause to go straight on" or "keep straight the violent" (חָמוֹץ). Donner, "Die soziale Botschaft," 237, note 20, understands אַשֵּׁר as "vorwärts schreiten" and suggests as a translation: "help forward (אַשְּׁרוּ) those who are oppressed with respect to the law" (חָמוֹץ).

[59] Thus Wildberger.

[60] The word עַמִּי in 2:4 occurs in a later addition to the verse; see below, textual note f, p. 122; also in Mic 6:3, 5, 16, which are later passages and thus beyond the scope of the discussion here. In Mic 6:16, read עַמִּים, which is presupposed by G; cf. BHS and Mays.

the following characteristics of the usage of עמי in Micah: (1) The word occurs only in the context of prophetic, not divine, speech; "my" refers to Micah himself, who thereby expresses his solidarity, even a lamenting kind of sympathy, for "his people." (2) Except for 1:9[61] the word occurs only in accusations addressed to leading circles — rulers, wealthy, prophets — who oppress "my people." Thus it can be seen that Micah draws a sharp distinction between two groups: the oppressors and the oppressed. (3) The עמי are nowhere viewed as standing under the judgment of Yahweh. Whereas the rulers, etc., are closely identified with Jerusalem and its destruction (3:9ff.), the עמי are apparently for Micah the true people of Yahweh, those who dwell in the towns and land of Judah.[62]

Isaiah uses the word עמי a total of eight times (1:3; 3:12, twice; 3:15; 5:13; 10:2; 22:4; 32:13);[63] in addition we find (ה)עם (1:4, 10; 3:5, 7; 6:5, 10; 7:8, etc.); also עמו (3:13 *G*; 3:14; 5:25; 14:32). Important for our purposes here is particularly the phrase העם הזה (6:9f., twice; 8:6, 11, 12; 9:15; 28:11, 14; 29:13).

A comparison of the עמי passages in Isaiah with those in Micah results in the following observations: (1) Whereas עמי stands only in the contexts of prophetic speech in Micah, it occurs frequently in *divine speech* in Isaiah;[64] "my people" means "Yahweh's people." In the prophet's mouth this becomes עמו. (2) Like Micah, Isaiah can name the עמי in the context of an accusation directed toward the leading circles who are the oppressors (3:15; 10:2; cf. the lament in 3:12). (3) Unlike Micah, Isaiah can speak of the עמי as the *object* of an accusation (1:3; cf. 1:4, 10; 9:12, where (ה)עם is used) or in an announcement of judgment (5:13; עמו in 5:25; העם in 3:5; cf. 7:17).

Two further distinctions emerge in such a comparison. In the first place, Micah apparently knows only of two groups within Jerusalem and Judah, the oppressors and the oppressed. Except for 2:8 (נשי עמי), no further division within the group עמי is found. Isaiah, however, thinks of a group within "my people" who are the עניים: cf. עני עמי in 10:2; עניי עמי in 14:32 (*genitivus partitivus*, cf. זקני עמו in 3:14 and Meyer, par. 97.4b). For Isaiah, therefore, the עניים can appear not merely as "identical with the people, but [as] a part of the larger political whole" known as "my people."[65] This leads to a second related distinction: whereas Micah never places any other group designation parallel with עמי, Isaiah, in texts where "my people" are objects of oppression, places

---

[61] 1:9 speaks not simply of "my people" but of the "gate of my people"; on this phrase, see above, p. 45.

[62] Cf. Mays: "Micah used the term ["my people"] for the population of Judah when he speaks of their suffering under the oppressors in Jerusalem or from Assyrian invaders," commenting on 1:9.

[63] Isa 32:18 is regarded as secondary by most critics; see Hoffmann, *Die Intention*, 16f. for a review of critical opinions on these texts.

[64] According to Fey, *Amos und Jesaja*, 62, note 3, all of the Isaiah texts containing "my people" except 22:4 are spoken by Yahweh; similarly Hoffmann, *Die Intention*, 18, note 62, but with more caution. From a form critical viewpoint, in 10:2 and 5:13 — the former a part of the accusation in a woe-saying, the latter an announcement — the prophet rather than Yahweh is to be seen as the speaker.

[65] Schwantes, *Das Recht der Armen*, 105.

parallel with the עמי the terms עניים in 3:15 and דלים in 10:2. For Isaiah, therefore, the עמי appears at times almost to be equivalent to the דלים or the עניים.[66] Micah *never* uses these words, which might suggest that for him the עמי is the functional equivalent of the "poor, oppressed," etc.[67]

For Micah, the opposite of "my people" can be expressed by the phrase העם הזה (2:11), which is part of the irony and sarcasm expressed by 2:11. The preceding context indicates that those referred to as "this people" are Micah's opponents against whom he speaks in vv. 8f., those who exploit "the women of my people"; "this people" thus stands in direct antithesis to "my people." Isaiah not infrequently speaks of "this people" (passages listed above), a phrase which Duhm has called Isaiah's "eigentümliche verächtliche Bezeichnung Israels."[68] For Isaiah, a more complex relationship exists in his use of the two expressions "my people" and "this people." According to Hoffmann, the distinction between the two terms is a chronological one: during his first period of activity Isaiah speaks of "my people," who then in a second or later period become "this people."[69] Important for our purposes is to note the following: for Isaiah "this people" is usually comprehensive, denoting all the people of Jerusalem and Judah (except 9:15, which refers to the Northern Kingdom); cf. especially 6:9ff.: the judgment on "this people" extends to "cities, houses, land, the whole country"; also 8:6, 11, 12; 28:11; 29:13f. Whereas Micah uses the phrase "this people" to refer to his opponents, those who oppress "my people," Isaiah hereby designates as "this people" all those who are *no longer* recognized by him (and Yahweh) as "my people."

We may summarize the foregoing in several brief statements: (1) Although Micah and Isaiah both speak of "my people" and "this people," there a significant divergences in the meaning and function of the terms. (2) In Micah, "my people" are those with whom the prophet identifies himself, his landsmen *in Judah* who bear the brunt of oppression of the Jerusalem leaders, wealthy, etc., and who are never said to stand under the judgment of Yahweh. (3) In Isaiah, "my people" can designate those in Judah *and in Jerusalem* who indeed stand under oppression of the leading circles, but also those who stand under divine condemnation; this is evident when Isaiah thinks no longer in terms of "my people" but of "this people." For Isaiah, the leaders, the peasants, in short,

[66] Cf. Wildberger on Isa 3:13–15, who notes that Isaiah almost comes to an identification of the Gottesvolk with the דלים (*sic!* he means the עניים, 3:15).

[67] With respect to the use of these different terms to designate the "poor" etc., it is to be noted that Isaiah and Amos are much closer together than are Micah and Isaiah. Cf. Am 2:6, 7; 4:1; 5:12; 8:4, 6, with Isa 3:14f.; 10:2; 11:4; 14:30, 32. (Cf. Am 7:8, 15; 8:2; 9:10[14]; each of these texts presents Yahweh as saying "my people"; in the first three, the words are "my people, Israel," indicating that Amos, like Isaiah, uses "my people" to refer to the entire group that he addresses, in this case, the Northern Kingdom.)

[68] Duhm, 68. For a general discussion of this interpretation, see Hoffmann, *Die Intention*, 17, and the literature cited.

[69] Hoffmann, 16ff. Fey, *Amos und Jesaja*, 63, understands Isaiah's use of "my people" and "this people" not in terms of their use in different periods of the prophet's activity, but rather in the light of Isaiah's various assessments of the people as standing under Yahweh's protection or his judgment.

everyone, becomes "this people" who are about to meet disaster.[70] (4) Finally, whereas Micah's usage of the expression "my people" expresses *his* closeness and sympathy, indeed, his lamenting for them, much like the vocative "O my brother" in the mourning songs, in Isaiah the expression appears to be rooted in covenant conceptions which emphasize that the people are "Yahweh's people" (cf. Hos 1:9; 2:1, 3; 2:25; 4:6, 8, 12; 6:11).

We may briefly summarize our conclusions for Part A.

1. Micah's proclamation against the corruption of the leaders and their oppression knows only one *form.* The prophetic *judgment speech,* with accusation and announcement, is in each instance addressed to a very specific audience: the ראשים and the קצינים (3:1-4; 3:9-12). The closest parallel in form in Isaian texts on the theme of social critique is the woe-saying in 10:1-3; but also the "Song of the Vineyard" in 5:1-7 includes accusation and announcement. The remaining Isaian texts, however, are remarkable in that they do not contain the accusation-announcement pattern: 3:13-15; 1:10 (11-15), 16f.; although 1:21-26 does have both elements of the prophetic judgment speech, it concludes with a note of *restoration,* not ultimate destruction. What is important here is that the forms used to express this theme indicate a characteristic difference in the way each prophet conceived of his social critique. Micah has only one expectation: judgment. Isaiah can expect judgment, but also the possibility of repentance, and even a restored order in Jerusalem.

2. The predominant *motif* in the accusations of both prophets is expressed in the term משפט. Both accused the responsible leaders of far-reaching abuses of משפט: they "detest justice and twist what is straight" (Mic 3:9b), they "do not know justice" (Mic 3:1b); indeed, they "rob the poor of justice" (Isa 10:2) and "deprive the innocent of his legal rights" (צדקה 5:23). In vain, Yahweh "looked for justice" (5:7), admonished that the leaders and people "seek justice" (1:17), and even promised that the fallen city, in whom there is no longer any justice (1:21), will again be filled with righteousness and "faithfulness." Clearly, both are doing battle for the cause of justice for the weak and oppressed. Both explicate the lack of justice with similar language: it negates the "good" and promotes the "evil" (Mic 3:3; Isa 5:20; cf. 1:16b-17a); both indict the practice of bribery (Mic 3:11; Isa 1:23; 5:23); speak against robbery (Mic 3:3; on 2:2, see below; Isa 3:14; 10:2); and accuse of physical abuse (Mic 3:2b-3; 3:10; Isa 3:15). The legal procedure as such is specifically indicated by the use of the verb שפט (Mic 3:11; Isa 1:17, 23). Interestingly, Micah does not know the word-pair משפט/צדקה although both Isaiah (5:7; צדק in 1:21) and Amos (5:7, 24; 6:12) use these terms in their social critique.

---

[70] Although it would go beyond the scope of our discussion to deal with the concept of "remnant" here (for a recent discussion of the remnant concept in Isaiah, see G. Hasel, *The Remnant* [1972] 216ff.), it could be asked whether for Micah "my people" are not a kind of "remnant" left after destruction befalls Jerusalem and its wicked officialdom.

3. Both prophets make a strict division between leaders who oppress and those who are oppressed, but the terms for each differ to some degree. Whereas Micah refers to the leading circles only as ראשים and קצינים, the latter term being shared by Isaiah (1:10; also 3:6f.; 22:3), Isaiah has a richer vocabulary for designating the leading circles: זקנים and שרים (3:14); שפטים and יעצים (1:26). That Micah and Isaiah originated from and later moved about in different circles undoubtedly accounts for this distinction. On the use of עמי in both prophets and the vocabulary attached to this term in Isaiah, see Excursus III above.

4. The remarkable similarities in thought, vocabulary, and intention in the social critique in these two prophets seem best accounted for by their adaptation and dependence on a common heritage. We found satisfactory evidence that the wisdom heritage plays a significant role in these prophetic passages; it must be emphasized, however, that it has not been our purpose more carefully to define "wisdom" here as to, say, the possible differences between court and clan wisdom. The occasional use of form-elements, such as the "summons to hear" followed by rhetorical questions, further suggests their dependence on wisdom tradition (see footnote 53, p. 116).

B. EXPROPRIATION OF THE LAND

In two remarkably similar passages Micah (2:1-5) and Isaiah (5:8-10) turn their critique of society upon a specific problem which provides yet another example of the absence of משפט in Jerusalem and Judah: the building of large estates (Latifundia) and the amassing of wealth at the expense of the landed peasants. To these two texts we now turn our attention.

1. Micah 2:1-5

v. 1   Woe to those who plan iniquity
        and those who work at evil[a] in their beds.
    In the light of the morning they do it,
        because the power is in their hands.

v. 2   They covet fields and seize them,
        houses and take them.
    They oppress a man and his house,
        a man and his inheritance.

v. 3   Therefore thus says Yahweh:
        "Behold, I am planning evil [against this family.][b]
    You shall not withdraw your necks from it,
        nor shall you walk upright." [For it is an evil time.][c]

v. 4   In that day a taunt-song shall be raised over you;
        a lament shall be sung,[d] saying:[e]
    "We are utterly ruined.
    [The property of my people is measured.
    There is no one to return it again.][f]

> Our fields are divided up."g
>
> v. 5   Therefore, youh shall have no one
>   to cast the measuring line by lot in the assembly of Yahweh.

Textual notes:

a   The difficulty of "working evil" in the bed has often drawn comment; some delete as a gloss; cf. Willi-Plein, *Vorformen,* 75. Rudolph, however, reads פעל as the second object of חשב.

b   A later insertion; see especially Jeremias, "Deutung," 334.

c   Also an addition, ibid., 335.

d   נהיה is probably due to dittography; BHS; Mays.

e   Read ואמר instead of אמר; cf. BHS, Mays; differently Rudolph.

f   Jeremias, "Deutung," 334, argues convincingly that this lament is a later insertion: the subject changes; the insertion destroys the word plays, changes the meter, and borrows vocabulary from the surrounding context. See p. 334, note 21 for the text of the insertion.

g   Read the pu. form: *G;* BHS; Mays.

h   Read לכם; cf. BHS, et al.

     a. This prophetic accusation (vv. 1–2) and announcement of judgment (vv. 3–5) is introduced by הוי.[71] Typical of the form-element whereby the "woe" is followed by participles, there is no addressee named here (unlike the "summons to hear" followed by vocatives in 3:1, 9). Rather, the addressees are immediately described according to their actions: "they plan evil," etc. V. 2 continues the initial indictment by making it more explicit with concrete examples. The complex announcement is introduced by the messenger formula preceded by לכן (לכן also occurs in 3:6; 3:12, introducing an announcement, but without the messenger formula). First Yahweh speaks, using terminology picked up from v. 1 (חשב רע); the style is that of direct address. The announcement is interrupted by a quotation (introduced by ואמר, see above, textual note e), a משל, put into the mouth of those accused;[72] the quotation apparently received a later expansion (see above, textual note f). Interestingly, the quotation is not a response to the words of Yahweh in v. 3 so much as an anticipation of v. 5, for not until then is the punishment connected with the division of the land and the subsequent loss of that land for the accused. The announcement in v. 5

---

[71] There is no need in this context to rehearse the discussion concerning the roots of the prophetic woe-saying. See the summaries of previous research, with bibliography, in Wolff, BK XIV/2. H.-J. Krause, "hôj als profetische Leichenklage über das eigene Volk," *ZAW* 85 (1973) 15ff. also reviews the history of research. Above all, see Hardmeier, *Texttheorie,* 154ff.

[72] It is interesting to note that in this passage a quotation is used to expand the *announcement,* whereas in 3:5 and 3:11, as well as in many other examples of prophetic speech, a quotation expands the accusation.

(introduced by a second לכן) is now the voice of the prophet (Yahweh in the 3rd pers.). Just as v. 2 makes more specific the accusation in v. 1, so v. 5 makes more definite and concrete the announcement in v. 3.

b. The general formulation of the accusation in v. 1 (planning-carrying out evil) is made more specific and concrete in v. 2. Constructed of two parallel lines with an obvious chiastic structure (fields-house, v. 2a; house-inheritance, v. 2b), v. 2 continues the style of the accusation in v. 1 by describing in the third person the actions which evoke the prophet's הוי. It is clear from the verbs גזל and עשק that the text belongs to the sphere of prophetic social critique (cf. Mic 3:2; Isa 3:14; 10:2).[73] The first verb, חמד ("to covet") appears to recall the words of the Decalog in Exod 20:17 ("Thou shall not covet they neighbors house . . ."; cf. Deut 5:21). Beyerlin[74] concludes that Mic 2:2 is, point for point, to be seen exclusively against the background of amphictyonic law. That there is some difficulty in this view may be seen from several factors. (1) The terms גזל and עשק are well attested in the wisdom of Proverbs (גזל, Pr 22:22; 28:24; עשק, Pr 14:31; 22:16; 28:3, 17) and therefore do not belong exclusively to cultic legal sentences. (2) As A. Alt has pointed out in his important study of Mic 2:1–5, this text reflects the ancient orders concerning the regulation of land tenure and the property rights of a landed peasantry.[75] Micah is thus protesting against the powerful and wealthy — no doubt officials connected with the royal administration in Jerusalem — who are building Latifundia (large estates) by expropriating land from the small land owners. This concentration of more and more land in the hands of a few struck at the heart of ancient Israel's *Bodenrecht.* It is this which informs Micah's accusation rather than cultic law. (3) Furthermore, it is significant that Micah levels his critique of the *Grossgrundbesitzer* with the help of language which is originally at home in the "settlement" tradition: he speaks of נחלה (v. 2), חלק (v. 4), חבל and גורל (v. 5).[76] The word נחלה designates the "inheritance" or land appointed by "lot" (גורל), which could also be known as "portion" (חלק). This land, apportioned to tribe or family, could be inherited or bequeathed, or in case of indebtedness, lost as payment for debt.[77] But its

---

[73] The phrase "to oppress (עשק) a man and his household" in v. 2b stands closely parallel in thought to Isa 3:15, "you crush (דכא) my people."

[74] Beyerlin, *Die Kulttraditionen,* 57, also Rudolph; Allen. On חמד, cf. Gerstenberger, art. חמד *THAT* 1, 579ff.

[75] Alt, "Micha 2:1–5 ΓΗΣ ΑΝΑΔΑΣΜΟΣ in Juda," *KS* 3, 374 and passim. He thinks the formulation in v. 2, "Ein Mann — ein Haus — ein Erbanteil an Grund und Boden" is originally much older than Micah and taken over by him, thus "Der Anteil des Königtums an der sozialen Entwicklung in den Reichen Israel und Juda," *KS* 3, 349. See especially this article for Alt's view that the Canaanite officialdom brought about the later changes in Israelite society and economy; further bibliography in note 2 above, p. 102.

[76] See above all von Rad, "The Promised Land and Yahweh's Land in the Hexateuch," in *The Problem of the Hexateuch and other essays* (1966) 79ff., for the important texts citing occurrence of these four terms in the Hexateuch and Judges.

[77] On land allotment in general, see Elliger, "Allotment," *IDB* 1, 85. For נחלה, see Wanke, art. נחלה *THAT* 2, 55f.

genuine owner remained Yahweh ("The land is mine; you are strangers and sojourners with me," Lev 25:23), which according to von Rad is the theological notion which stands behind all Israelite regulations regarding land tenure.[78] (4) Such ancient norms, it should finally be noted, were given expression in Egyptian as well as Israelite wisdom. Greed and seizure of property is an age-old concern in all agricultural societies. Here we need only cite the following suggestive texts: ". . . supplant no man of the property of his father";[79] "Be not greedy after a cubit of land";[80] "Do not remove an ancient landmark or enter the fields of the fatherless."[81] In v. 2 we see a combination of several elements which are rooted in different spheres of tradition: ancient Israelite *Bodenrecht* is given expression in terminology originally at home in the Settlement tradition; the wisdom tradition's opposition to amassing wealth and acquiring land; the Decalog's prohibition against חמד.

    c. Though the precise literary connection between 2:8-10 and 2:1-5 remains unclear and disputed,[82] it is clear that the substance of vv. 8-10 relates to the accusation in v. 2. Despite a very corrupt text, vv. 8-10 have to do with oppression and mistreatment of עמי. In vv. 8-9 Micah accuses an unspecified group, apparently the large estate owners, but probably included here would also be the general upper class and officials of Jerusalem:

v. 8   ^aBut you! Against^a my people
        you arise^b as an enemy.
    ^cFrom the peaceful
        you strip their cloak,^c
    ^dtaking away security,
        plotting war.^d
v. 9   You drive the women of my people
        from their^e pleasant homes;
    from their^e children you take
        their^e dignity forever.

Textual notes:

a-a   Read ואתם לעמי; cf. BHS; Mays. Sellin reads לא עמי, which is not likely
        and misunderstands Micah's use of the term עמי.
b   Read תקומו; cf. Wellhausen; Robinson; BHS.
c-c   Read מעל שלמים אדרת; cf. BHS. Rudolph offers a complex and
        apparently unnecessary emendation.

---

[78] Von Rad, *OTT* 1, 299f.
[79] Egyptian *Instructions, ANET,* 415.
[80] Ibid., 422.
[81] Pr 23:10; also Pr 22:16, 18; and see Whedbee, *Isaiah,* 93ff.
[82] See above, note 99, p. 91.

d - d This translation follows Mays, which is dependent on the reconstruction מעביוים בטח הושבים מלחמה; otherwise, BHS. Any reconstruction here remains problematic and uncertain.

e The 3rd pers. fem. plur. suff. should probably be read; cf. BHS; Mays.

Vv. 8 and 9 are closely linked to 3:1ff. by the words עמי and פשט; but they also fit closely with 2:2. Thus v. 9 is linked to v. 2 by the word בית: v. 2 speaks of "taking away בתים"; v. 9 puts it equally as drastically: "the women are driven from their pleasant houses" (מבית).[83] The result of this is expressed in v. 9b: the children are deprived of their fathers' farms[84] with possibly no future but slavery and servitude.[85] That women and children are mentioned here could mean that their husbands have become enslaved for their debts or that the women and children are widows and orphans. Beside the accusation of taking their houses (and land) in v. 9, Micah also refers to taking away the "cloak" (אדרת v. 8), i.e., the outer and more expensive garment is seized as security for debt, which is forbidden in Exod 22:26, 27.[86]

After Micah's accusation in vv. 8-9, those addressed by Micah, the estate owners, now speak to the נשי עמי (v. 9)[87] issuing a threatening command (imperatives): "Arise and go" (קומו ולכו). The women may no longer remain on their land, "for it is no place to rest" (v. 10a). The function of v. 10a is not only to elucidate the thought in v. 2 but to give a precise illustration of v. 9aα: "You drive out (תגרשון) the women of my people." After this quotation of his opponents' words, Micah continues to speak in v. 10b, which, however, is notoriously corrupt (Wellhausen leaves it untranslated in his commentary). The generally accepted reconstruction of the verse by Ehrlich[88] may be translated:

> For the gain of the slightest thing
> you pledge with a ruinous pledge.

This is then a further prophetic accusation against those who seize the land from the farmers who, having fallen into debts, are unable to make their payments.[89]

---

[83] Wellhausen's proposal to read מבני instead of מבית in the light of 1:16 (also Marti) is questionable; see Smith for reasons against this interpretation.

[84] Cf. Allen.

[85] Mays. But it is not entirely clear that selling children into slavery is meant by v. 9b. Ehrlich, *Randglossen* 5, is perhaps correct in stating that v. 9b is not about selling the family into slavery because of debts, but about the family's poverty, which compels it to exchange its comfortable house for a miserable shack and its children's good clothes (הדר) for rags.

[86] Cf. Smith.

[87] Thus Duhm, "Anmerkungen," 86; Sellin, et al.

[88] Ehrlich, *Randglossen* 5, 278, followed by Sellin; Robinson; et al. Read מאומה instead of טמאה and read תחבלו חבל.

[89] Thus Mays; otherwise Rudolph.

Jeremias[90] has argued that v. 10b in its present form ("Because of uncleanness you shall be destroyed by a ruinous destruction") is a later, intentional reinterpretation of Micah's accusation, changing it into a judgment of all of Israel.

Thus vv. 8–10 complement v. 2 by picking up the motif of expropriation of land (cf. v. 9 with v. 2abβ) as well as the motif of oppression and mistreatment of the weaker members of society (cf. v. 8 with v. 2bα).

d. How does Micah understand the judgment of Yahweh on the accused? In vv. 3–5 the coming judgment is presented in terms of three elements: (1) A Yahweh-speech in v. 3 speaks of disaster (רעה; cf. 3:11bγ) only in general terms; whether v. 3b refers to a yoke or noose around the neck and precisely what this means is unclear.[91] (2) The formula "in that day" (v. 4) introduces a quotation of those who will experience the coming רעה. Designated as a משל and a נהי[92] which lament the punishment (v. 4, see above, textual note f),[93] the thrust of the quotation resides in the words שדינו יחלק; שדינו picks up שדות in v. 2aα and יחלק anticipates משליך חבל בגורל in v. 5. (3) In the conclusion (v. 5) to the announcement (and the unit), begun by a second לכן,[94] the prophet directly addresses the large estate owners and enlarges upon the quotation put into their mouths: not only are the lands they have accumulated to be divided up (cf. v. 4bβ), but in this new distribution of the land no one will allot to them any portion of it (v. 5).

It was A. Alt who first clearly understood the meaning and significance of this passage. He correctly saw that the announcement of doom is directed *only* to the *Grossgrundbesitzer*, not all of Judah; that a future exists for the Judean people in the land, who will experience a new, equitable division of this land. This will re-establish the old orders of land tenure, while the heart of an essentially Canaanite system represented in Jerusalem's officials will be totally destroyed (3:12).[95]

[90] Jeremias, "Die Deutung," 340.

[91] The figure of a yoke as punishment is common to OT prophecy (Isa 9:3; 10:27; Jer 27:8, etc.; cf. Smith). Sellin thinks Micah refers not to a yoke but to a sling which snatches away those caught in it. The metaphor, at any rate, need not be interpreted as deportation; cf. Alt, *KS* 3, 376.

[92] On משל as a taunt song, cf. Isa 14:4; Hab 2:6–8; Ezek 12:22–23; 18:2–3 and J. Crenshaw, "Wisdom," in *Old Testament Form Criticism*, ed. John Hayes, 229ff. On נהי as an "Untergangslied," see Hardmeier, *Texttheorie*, 333f., who compares Mic 2:4 with Jer 9:18.

[93] שדד should be translated as "ruined" rather than "destroyed," for the context speaks not of the destruction of the estate owners but of their loss of the land, i.e., their financial ruin.

[94] Nowack and Marti saw in v. 5 a later addition because of the second לכן (cf. v. 3) and the content of the verse. There are, however, no convincing grounds on which to contest its genuineness; cf. Sellin; Rudolph; Mays.

[95] Alt's interpretation of this has been criticized on two fronts: Koch ("Die Entstehung der sozialen Kritik bei den Propheten," 242) points out correctly that there is no data to show that the Jerusalem officials intended to replace the ancient Israelite land laws with

Our analysis in previous chapters of 3:1-4; 3:9-12; 1:8-16 confirms Alt's conclusions on several points: Micah never announces Yahweh's judgment on all of Judah; the goal of disaster is always a group or a city (cf. 1:16); he makes a strict distinction between the people of Judah, whom he calls עַמִּי and the officials and upperclass in Jerusalem.

In this woe-saying, we have a text which is closely related to 3:1-4 and 3:9-12: those who oppress others for gain and profit violate Yahweh's requirement of what is just. The oppression in 2:1ff., however, is specifically connected with the building of large estates by the wealthy at the expense of the land-holding peasantry. The judgment for such deeds results not in destruction (3:12) or Yahweh's silence (3:4) but the loss of this land (v. 4) when it is redistributed to its original and rightful stewards (v. 5).

2. Isaiah 5:8-10

Although the tradition provides us with only one woe-saying from Micah, quite a variety of such prophetic words are attributed to Isaiah. According to Janzen's study of the prophetic woe-sayings in Isaiah, such passages belong in three groups: a series of woes in 5:8-24; a second series in chaps. 28-31, and then scattered occurrences in 1:4; 1:24; 10:1; 17:12; 18:1.[96] Our interest here focuses chiefly on Isa 5:8-10 as it compares with Mic 2:1-5. The text may be translated as follows:

v. 8   Woe to those who add house to house
      and join field to field,
  until there is no more room,
      and you dwell alone in the midst of the land.
v. 9   Yahweh of hosts has sworn[a] in my hearing:
  "Surely great houses shall be desolate,
      large and beautiful, without inhabitants.
v. 10 For ten acres of vineyard shall yield just one[b] bath,
      and a field sown with an homer of seed shall yield merely an
  ephah."

Canaanite laws. Loretz, "Die prophetische Kritik," attempts to demonstrate that Israel's social problems, and the prophets' reaction to them, are not to be understood against the background of the relationship of Israelite royal domain and the royal officials to Israel's ancient legal orders. Rather, he contends, the situation in Israel parallels that of their environment in the ancient Near East and thus does not reflect something unique in Israel (pp. 271ff.).

[96] W. Janzen, *Mourning Cry and Woe Oracle*, BZAW 125 (1972) 49. The shape of the woe series in 5:8-24 suggests that Isaiah himself did not order this material as it now stands (thus Duhm).

Textual notes:

a   The sentence needs a verb; "to swear" is perhaps to be added in light of
    אם לא in v. 9b; cf. 14:24 and see BHS; Wildberger.

b   Read אחד; cf. BHS.

    a. Even a superficial comparison of form and content reveals a number of striking congruities between Mic 2:1-5 and Isa 5:8-10. Both are examples of a prophetic הוי saying in which a plural participle(s) follows the woe cry in order to begin the accusation;[97] a finite verb or verbs continue the participle(s) (Mic 2:1f.; Isa 5:8). Both conclude with an announcement of judgment (Mic 2:3b-5; Isa 5:9b-10), which is introduced by either a "messenger formula" (Mic 2:3a, begun by לכן) or a "swear formula" (Isa 5:9a, see textual note a, above) in which Yahweh (or Yahweh Sabaoth) is presented as the speaker of the following announcement. Interestingly, such a formula introducing the announcement is *not* found in other comparable examples of the woe-saying, i.e., those with an announcement.[98]

    But noteworthy variations within the similar form are to be observed. The accusation in Mic 2:1-2 is somewhat more elaborate; Micah, before naming the deeds of guilt in v. 2 in the series of perfect verbs, refers to the "planning" and the "power" to carry out the plans, and also to the time of the execution of these plans "in the morning" (v. 1). By comparison, Isaiah's accusation is simpler in content and structure, although he not only mentions the deeds of guilt (5:8a) but what the effect of these deeds will be (v. 8b). Likewise in the announcement, certain variations are to be seen. In Mic 2:3b-5 the announcement is, again, more elaborate, with three different elements: (1) a Yahweh speech, vv. 3aβ-4aα$_{1.2}$; (2) a quotation put into the mouth of the accused, v. 4aα$_3$, bβ; (3) a concluding announcement spoken by the prophet, v. 5 (Yahweh referred to in the third person). By contrast, the announcement in Isa 5:9b-10 is briefer in scope, consisting only of two synthetically parallel lines. Furthermore, one notes that there is a directness and a personal quality in Micah's announcement: not only is he telling about the coming punishment of *persons* themselves, but the style is in direct address. Isaiah's announcement (5:9b-10) talks not about persons but houses, fields, and crops, with no direct address; its style therefore is impersonal.

    b. The content of the two texts is also in many respects similar. The accusations make use of the same vocabulary: Micah and Isaiah are concerned with "fields" and "houses"; cf. "they covet שדות" (Mic 2:2aα) with "they add שדה בשדה" (Isa 5:8aβ), and "they take away בתים; they oppress a man and

[97] Other examples: Isa 5:11, 18, 20; 10:1; Am 5:18; Jer 23:1; etc. See the complete statistical details of the woe passages in Wolff, *Joel and Amos* (Hermeneia) 242f., note 108.

[98] Form critically, the announcement is a variable that occurs in some woe passages (e.g., Isa 5:13f., 24; 28:2-4; 30:3-5; 31:2-3; Hab 2:16; cf. E, Gerstenberger, "The Woe Oracles of the Prophets," *JBL* 81 [1962] 253) but not in others (e.g., Isa 5:18f.; Am 5:7-10).

"ביתו" (Mic 2:aβbα) with ". . . who join בית בבית" (Isa 5:8aα). That these words refer to the Latifundia of the wealthy and upper classes is quite clear. Whether the method of acquiring land and houses is simply by buying them up,[99] or by taking them in payment for debt, or by some unlawful means, is not at first clear; nor is there the express mention of greed, though this is surely implied. What is noticeable, however, is that Micah's language emphasizes the overpowering oppression and ill-treatment of those who lose their house and land; passionately he accuses the estate owners of coveting, robbing, taking, oppressing (2:2), of driving out the women from their homes (vv. 9a, 10a). This does not seem to be the language of a business transaction; and, although Isaiah speaks in a milder vein (they "join" and "add" houses and fields), he no doubt refers to the same circumstances. In addition to the differences here in the way the two prophets describe the actions connected with the expropriation of property of the less powerful members of Judean society, it is to be noted that whereas both speak of בית and שדה, only Micah uses language associated with the ancient distribution of the land when he speaks of נחלה and גורל. Such language finds no echo in Isaiah, who speaks more generally of the ארץ (v. 8b).[100] This is perhaps suggestive of the differences in their background and respective roots in tradition: they are referring to the same problem in their society, but Micah, who comes from the provinces, speaks the language of one acquainted with the land and its ancient traditions of land distribution.

c. Are these texts, in terms of their overall similarities, related to each other in a particular way? Weiser suggests that Micah knew Isaiah and possibly "borrowed" from his contemporary.[101] In Fohrer's opinion, Micah must have been familiar with the preaching of Isaiah and therefore was "influenced" by him.[102] These views, however, help very little in that it is not clear what "borrowing" and "influence" precisely mean. Moreover, it is much more probable that the simliarities are to be accounted for not by dependence of one prophet upon the other, but rather by dependence on a common tradition or traditions.[103]

However, it is not an easy task to determine the form and tradition historical roots of either text. There is disagreement among critics on the background and provenance of the prophetic woe-sayings[104] as well as on the tradition historical

---

[99] Cf. J. Bardtke, "Die Latifundien in Juda während der zweiten Hälfte des achten Jahrhunderts v. Chr. (Zum Verständnis von Jes 5,8–10)," *FS A. Dupont-Sommer* (1971) 238.

[100] Of the 8th century prophets, such language is peculiar to Micah; but cf. Jer 3:19; 10:16; 12:14; etc.; Ezek 25:15; 36:12; etc.

[101] Weiser, *ATD* 1, 24.

[102] Fohrer, *Introduction to the OT,* 444.

[103] The same has been shown to be true regarding the relationship of Isaiah to Amos, cf. Wolff's (*Amos the Prophet,* 80ff.) critique of Fey's thesis that Isaiah exhibits a kind of literary dependence upon Amos; see also Whedbee, *Isaiah and Wisdom,* passim.

[104] For a review and critique of the various positions, see Hardmeier, *Texttheorie,* 166ff., 376ff., who locates the background of the prophetic woe cry in the death laments.

roots of the accusations in Mic 2:2 and Isa 5:8. What is there in ancient Israelite material which could inform us on the Israelite customs or laws regulating land tenure? With Alt, it has become customary to speak of the "althergebrachte (or kleinbäuerliche) Gesellschafts- und Wirtschaftsordnung" in ancient Israel which generally governed the use of the land![105] It seems beyond doubt that Micah and Isaiah in these texts under consideration reflect such older rules and customs. If, however, one asks through what means they would have known of such an "Ordnung," two answers have been proposed. The one wishes to see here in both prophets a reflection of covenantal law. Thus as we have already noted above (p. 123), Beyerlin understands Mic 2:1-5 in the light of covenant law and finds, among others, a parallel between Mic 2:2 and Deut 27:17 concerning the protection of a person's land![106] Somewhat similarly, Kaiser suggests that Lev 25:8ff. provides the background of Isaiah's accusation![107] The second answer attempts to connect the Micah and Isaiah texts not with a legal code per se but with a broader prohibition against "the unlawful seizure of property" which "violates age-old ethical rules indigenous to any sedentary society."[108] Such an understanding is traced by Whedbee,[109] for example, to biblical and non-biblical wisdom. There is much to be said for this view, particularly if one traces the prophetic woe-cry to Israelite clan wisdom![110] The texts cited by Whedbee do prohibit greed for land, seizing houses, disturbing boundaries, entering the fields of the fatherless, and so on. Whedbee's argumentation makes it seem probable that both Mic 2:1-5 and Isa 5:8-10 reflect the very same concerns as he finds in wisdom material. On the other hand, a genuinely close correspondence between the Proverbs he cites (22:16; 23:10; 22:28) and the vocabulary of our two texts is in fact wanting. The reference to "removing ancient landmarks" (Pr 22:28; 23:10), for example, is not the *specific* concern of our two prophets (but cf. Hos 5:10), although the general concern expressed in these wisdom texts is the sphere within which Mic 2:1-5 and Isa 5:8-10 are possibly to be located. Perhaps the most that can be said is that Micah and Isaiah do in fact reflect in these two sayings a knowledge of the "ancient social and economic orders" which governed land use; that a close correspondence between these texts and covenant law is by no means evident; that quite possibly the wisdom tradition may be posited as the background of their concern with the oppression of the peasant by the taking

---

[105] Alt, "Der Anteil," 348f.; idem, "Micha 2:1-5," 374 and passim; Donner, "Die soziale Botschaft," 235, 241; Wanke, "Grundlage," 10f.

[106] Beyerlin, *Kulttraditionen,* 57ff.

[107] Kaiser, *ATD* 17, on Isa 5:8; cf. Wildberger.

[108] Whedbee, *Isaiah,* 94; see his critique of the views which relate these texts to covenant law, 93f.

[109] Whedbee, 94f., cites the following wisdom texts: Egyptian *Instructions, ANET* 415, 422, 423; Pr 22:16, 28; 23:10; Job 20:19; 22:8.

[110] The close connection between prophetic woe sayings and clan wisdom is observed by Gerstenberger, "The Woe-Oracles of the Prophets," *JBL* 81 (1962) 249ff.; Wolff, *Joel and Amos* (Hermeneia), 243ff.

of his house and land. This interpretation gains support from our discussion of the other texts in Micah and Isaiah on the theme of social critique (above, Part A), where we drew attention to certain wisdom elements that appear here.

d. In the accusations, both Micah and Isaiah expect punishment to come upon the land barons. What Micah speaks of as רעה which Yahweh himself is to bring (2:3aβb), Isaiah describes in terms of שמה ("desolation") of the beautiful houses (5:9b). It is possible that both have a political enemy in mind; nevertheless, only Micah mentions Yahweh as the agent of the coming disaster (as also in 1:6, 9, 12b; cf. 3:4, 7). The significant difference, however, lies in the nature of the punishment on the estate owners. For Micah, they will be deprived of the land they have expropriated (punishment fits the crime), as v. 4bβ indicates. Moreover, when the land, having been taken from them, is redistributed, they will be excluded from the sacral assembly which "throws the measuring line" to reapportion the land (v. 5). Micah's expectation, therefore, is not that a foreign enemy will have control of the Judean provinces, for the peasants will continue to farm the lands. For Isaiah, on the other hand, the impending doom for the estate owners suggests that a more drastic disaster is to come. Houses will be made "desolate" (שמה; cf. especially 6:11; also 1:7), with no one to live in them (5:9b). In the light of Isa 1:7, "desolation" means more than simply that the houses will become empty; this implies the destructive power of a raging enemy force, no doubt the Assyrians![111] Here Isaiah goes quite beyond Micah, for Isaiah proclaims a ravaging of the land and its houses which destroys. A different image is used in 5:10; land which has been taken in violation of the old orders will produce only meager crops. V. 10 probably refers not to the devastation of crops by an invading army but to a crop failure due to poor natural conditions![112]

Thus, although the formulation of the accusations in Mic 2:1f. and Isa 5:8 are very familiar, the announcements of doom have quite different expectations about the future; for Micah the Judean peasants will again care for the land; for Isaiah the land will be devastated, the inhabitants removed, with the implication that a foreign power will gain political control. Yet a further distinction may be observed in the two announcements: whereas Micah's announcement moves in the sphere of tradition relating to land tenure, Isaiah's announcement apparently takes up covenant threats of devastation and harvest failure![113]

SUMMARY CONCLUSION

Whereas Part A examined texts on the general theme of social oppression (see pp. 120f. for conclusions to Part A), Part B focused on two texts which are remarkable for their similarity in form and content (see subsections a-d, pp. 128ff. for

---

[111] Cf. Dietrich, *Jesaja*, 47f., who emphasizes that here in Isaiah's social critique an element of external political matters intrudes. Wildberger thinks that the tradition historical background of v. 9b (and also v. 10) is the *Bundestradition* (Deut 28:37; 2 Kgs 22:19; etc.).

[112] Cf. Wildberger; Dietrich, *Jesaja*, 47; cf. also Am 5:11.

[113] Cf. Wildberger.

conclusions to Part B). Here it suffices to make only general observations. We noted in Part A that Micah expects a destructive punishment upon those who oppress their neighbors, whereas Isaiah speaks not only of punishment but also of restoration, and with his admonition, the possibility of "turning." A curious reversal is to be noted in Part B, for here we find (Mic 2:1ff.) that Micah does not speak of an explicit "doom" or destruction of the greedy land barons, but merely of a future exclusion from any ownership of the land. By contrast, Isaiah expects a severe punishment of the land barons, who will be destroyed, with their homes and land devastated. Furthermore, it may be noted that whereas the texts in Part A have to do with leaders who are explicitly identified as such (rulers, elders, heads, etc.) and are more or less closely connected with Jerusalem, the texts in Part B neither identify those who are accused, nor link them to the capital city. This may suggest that the prophets' words about dispossession of the land were not spoken in Jerusalem but in the provinces.

Conclusions

A. RETROSPECT

This study began with the broad question of the relationship between the prophecy of Micah and Isaiah. Recognizing that they were contemporaries, active in Jerusalem, and witness to some of the same political events and crises, it is not without some justification that scholars have often supposed, but never investigated critically, that Micah and Isaiah exhibit many similarities in their prophetic messages. While rejecting such general categories as "kinship," "teacher-disciple," and the like, this study has attempted to approach the question by examining the forms, traditions, and themes present in Micah's proclamation and comparing them with Isaiah. The nature of the undertaking has been to inquire into the similarities and differences in these areas, with a view toward establishing, if possible, wherein lies Micah's own uniqueness and particularity. In general it may be said that no evidence of what might be called "influence" has been discovered. In those cases where a decided similarity has been found, the evidence points rather in the direction of dependence upon common tradition or common speech forms which were available to them. But what, by way of summary, may now be said as to our final conclusions? There is no need to restate in detail the conclusions of the individual chapters, or to rehearse the details of the various textual analyses within these chapters. However, let us now attempt a final general summary of the study's main conclusions.

1. Micah is familiar with the ancient Israelite theophany tradition which is rooted in the victory hymns of premonarchic Israel, as was Isaiah. Micah's use of the traditional material, as compared with Isaiah, exhibits several characteristic differences. Micah incorporates the two-part theophany *Gattung* into a prophetic judgment speech which serves the function of illustrating and strengthening divine judgment on Israel, specifically, Samaria. Furthermore, the theophany tradition in Micah, in contrast to Isaiah, is given a radical reversal: Yahweh comes, no longer to save his people, but to bring his just judgment. Our study of the theophany material illustrates how both prophets, in adapting older traditional material, put it to different use as regards the form as well as the function of the tradition.

2. Micah is concerned with the city of Jerusalem and the Zion tradition, like his contemporary Isaiah. Although both prophets share the view that the city's leadership is corrupt and that Jerusalem stands under Yahweh's wrath, a number of elements which are characteristic of Micah distinguish him from Isaiah. The city must not only fall, but will be annihilated. The motivation for this resides solely in a corrupt leadership. It is the city and her leaders which incur divine

wrath; not once does Micah place Judah alongside Jerusalem in his accusations of guilt. According to Micah, there is no hope for the city's survival; especially is there no refuge to be found in Zion because of an alleged divine presence there: Zion is not inviolable, and any trust in the old Zion dogma is understood by Micah as a false faith. The polemic against, and rejection of, the Zion tradition is unequivocal. Regarding prophetic speech forms, only Micah has a typical prophetic judgment saying (accusation-announcement) in which Zion's punishment is proclaimed. On the other hand, in both Micah and Isaiah, elements of the dirge are incorporated into their announcements of impending threat to Jerusalem.

3. Micah stands in vocal opposition to a group of נביאים, whom he sees closely connected with priests as well as other leaders; the same obtains for Isaiah. Our study has indicated that various lines of correspondence in the general conflict which Micah and Isaiah have with such prophetic opponents exist. Yet various contrasts between Micah and Isaiah emerge which help establish Micah's own perspective on this theme of prophetic conflict. There is a difference, for example, in terminological usage of the two prophets. Interestingly, Micah thinks of the נביאים, חזים, and the קסמים as more or less equivalent, and accuses them of abusing their office, whereas Isaiah distinguishes between the נביאים and the חזים, regarding himself as belonging to the latter. Unlike Isaiah, Micah's conflict with the prophets links them closely with the Zion tradition and the city's security. On the basis of this tradition, the prophets reject Micah's proclamation of doom, whereas Isaiah's opponents reject not his message of doom but his offer of salvation through trust. Furthermore, only Micah both links the prophets closely to Jerusalem ("her prophets") and thinks of them as "salvation prophets" (they preach *shalom*). Form critically, the sayings in both Micah and Isaiah exhibit elements of the disputation in which they cite the words of their prophetic opponents, indicative of their intense debates with them. Yet, only Micah has a judgment speech which focuses exclusively on the prophetic opponents and announces their downfall. For Isaiah, the prophets never stand alone as the sole object of his attack. Finally, both Micah and Isaiah were themselves opposed by other groups, apparently the leaders, who not only rejected their prophetic message but attempted to silence them. Again, Micah was opposed for his message of judgment; Isaiah for his words which urged trust in Yahweh as the path to security.

4. Micah's social critique bears a considerable amount of similarity to that of Isaiah. Both cry out against the oppression of weak members of society, against abuse of privilege among leaders who conduct their official duties for financial gain, against the expropriation of land and houses of the peasants. In both we noted that משפט is the overarching concern in their social critique, and that there is a common dependence upon some elements drawn from the wisdom tradition. But Micah's own characteristic viewpoint is apparent in several ways. His sayings concerning social injustice issue forth *only* in words of accusation and judgment. Unlike Isaiah, Micah allows no room for an admonition to do

justice; nor is there any hint or suggestion that Micah calls for repentance. For him the social sins of the leaders result in the destruction of Jerusalem which is total; the leaders are not to be "purified" along with the city and restored, as in Isaiah. But those outside Jerusalem in the small towns and in the land of Judah are not included in the capital's destruction. Indeed, Micah's view of the future concerns not Jerusalem but the land, for the Judean peasants will have their expropriated land restored to them; hence it is with them, whom Micah calls "my people," that any future existence is to be found.

B. PROSPECT

Although we have attempted here to emphasize those elements which illustrate the contrasts in the message of Micah and Isaiah, it appears that, fairly early in the tradition and redaction of their sayings, their prophecy was understood as standing in the closest possible relationship. As a result the two books apparently underwent a common redaction process. Indeed, B. Childs has argued (*Intro. to the OT,* 434ff.) that the traditions of Micah were handed on and shaped by a circle of redactors who preserved and edited the Isaiah corpus. Evidence for a common redaction is to be found in such similar elements, Childs notes, as the formula "in that day," used as a major redactional device (Mic 4:6; 5:9; 7:12; Isa 7:18ff.; 22:8ff.); the very rare expression "from now and ever more" (Mic 4:7; Isa 9:6; 59:21); the expression "for the mouth of Yahweh has spoken" (Mic 4:4; Isa 1:20; 40:5; 58:14); the expression "he (Yahweh) will reign in Mount Zion" (Mic 4:7; Isa 23:23 – only here in the OT). Childs locates the redactional group responsible for shaping the books of Micah and Isaiah in Jerusalem, from the beginning of the seventh century throughout the early post-exilic period. Thus the question of the similarity and commonality of Micah and Isaiah can be continued in a study of their redaction.

On the other hand, the dissimilarity of Micah and Isaiah may be perceived in a different realm of subsequent tradition. Jeremiah seems to follow in the tradition of Micah in a number of respects, whereas his prophetic opponent, Hananiah, as has sometimes been observed, stands more in the tradition of Isaiah, with respect to the future of Zion, at least. Without attempting to do more than suggest possibilities, we may note the following points of contact and similarity between the prophecy of Micah and Jeremiah. (1) Micah is named and quoted in Jer 26:18, his prophecy (Mic 3:12) having been remembered by the "elders." Like Micah, Jeremiah has prophesied the destruction of Jerusalem (e.g., 9:11). (2) Micah, who was the first classical prophet to do battle with the shalom prophets and to describe their work in terms of שֶׁקֶר, is followed by Jeremiah, who elaborates on the theme at some length (e.g., 6:14; 8:11; 14:13ff.; 23:23, etc.). (3) The false security expressed by Micah's opponents in the face of announcements of doom (cf. 3:11) is taken up as a theme against which Jeremiah often preached (e.g., 5:12; 8:19). This suggests that the question of the continuity and similarity between Micah and Jeremiah could shed further light on our understanding of the prophets' connection with tradition and with each other.

Bibliography

Albertz, R., art. צעק, *THAT* 2, 568ff.

Albright, W. F., "The Chronology of the Divided Monarchy of Israel," *BASOR* 100 (1945) 16ff.

Allen, L. C., *The Books of Joel, Obadiah, Jonah and Micah*, NICOT (1976).

Alt, A., "Der Anteil des Königstums an der sozialen Entwicklung in den Reichen Israel und Juda," *Kleine Schriften zur Geschichte des Volkes Israel* 3, ed. M. Noth (1959) 348ff.

———. "Der Staatstadt Samaria," *Kleine Schriften* 3 (1959) 258ff.

———. "Micha 2,1-5 ΓΗΣ ΑΝΑΔΑΣΜΟΣ in Juda," *Kleine Schriften* 3 (1959) 373ff.

———. "The Origins of Israelite Law," *Essays on Old Testament History and Religion* (1966) 79ff.

Anderson, G. W., *A Critical Introduction to the Old Testament* (1959).

Bach, R., *Die Aufforderungen zur Flucht und zum Kampf im alttestamentlichen Prophetenspruch*, WMANT 9 (1962).

Baltzer, D., *Ezechiel und Deuterojesaja. Berührungen in der Heilserwartungen der beiden grossen Exilspropheten*, BZAW 121 (1971).

Bardtke, H., "Die Latifundien in Juda während der zweiten Hälfte des achten Jahrhunderts von Chr.," *Hommages à André Dupont-Sommer* (1971) 235ff.

Barr, J., "Theophany and Anthropomorphism in the Old Testament," *Congress Volume*, Suppl VT 7 (1962) 31ff.

Barth, C., "Die Antwort Israels," *Probleme biblischer Theologie*, ed. H. W. Wolff (1971) 44ff.

Bartlett, J. R., "The Use of the Word ראש as a Title in the Old Testament," *VT* 19 (1969) 1ff.

Bauer, W., Arndt, W. F., Gingrich, F. W., *Greek-English Lexicon of the New Testament* (1957).

Begrich, J., "Die priesterliche Tora," *Gesammelte Studien zum Alten Testament*, ThB 21 (1964) 232ff.

———. "Jesaja 14,28-32," *Gesammelte Studien*, ThB 21 (1964) 121ff.

———. *Studien zu Deuterojesaja*, ThB 20 (²1969).

137

Beyerlin, W., *Die Kulttraditionen Israels in der Verkündigung des Propheten Michas,* FRLANT 72 (1959).

———. *Herkunft und Geschichte der ältesten Sinaitraditionen* (1961).

Boecker, H.-J., *Redeformen des Rechtslebens im Alten Testament,* WMANT 14 (1964).

Braun, H., art. πλανάω, *TDNT* 6, 233ff.

Bruno, A., *Micha und der Herrscher aus der Vorzeit* (1923).

Budde, K., "Das Rätsel von Micah 1," *ZAW* 37 (1917/18) 77ff.

———. "Micha 2 und 3," *ZAW* 38 (1919/20) 2ff.

Carley, K., *Ezekiel Among the Prophets,* StBTh 2nd Series 31 (1975).

Caspari, W., *Die israelitischen Propheten* (1914).

Cheyne, T. K., *Introduction to the Book of Isaiah* (1895).

Childs, B., *The Book of Exodus,* OTL (1974).

———. *Introduction to the Old Testament as Scripture* (1979).

———. *Isaiah and the Assyrian Crisis,* StBTh 2nd Series 3 (1967).

Clements, R. E., *Prophecy and Tradition* (1975).

Crenshaw, J., "Amos and the Theophany Tradition," *ZAW* 80 (1968) 203ff.

———. *Prophetic Conflict: Its Effect Upon Israelite Religion,* BZAW 124 (1971).

———. "Wedōrēk 'al-bāmŏtê 'āreṣ," *CBQ* 34 (1972) 37ff.

———. "Wisdom," *Old Testament Form Criticism,* ed. J. Hayes (1974) 225ff.

Christensen, D. L., "The March of Conquest in Isaiah 10:27c–34," *VT* 26 (1976) 385ff.

Copass, B. A. and Carlson, E. L., *A Study of the Prophet Micah* (1950).

Cross, F. M., *Canaanite Myth and Hebrew Epic: Essays in the History of the Relgion of Israel* (1973).

———. "The Council of Yahweh in Second Isaiah," *JNES* 12 (1953) 274ff.

Davis, G. H., "Theophany," *IDB* 4 (1962) 619f.

Dietrich, W., *Jesaja und die Politik,* BEvTh 74 (1976).

Donner, H., "Die soziale Botschaft der Propheten im Lichte der Gesellschafts-ordnung in Israel," *OrAntiq* 2 (1963) 229ff.

———. *Israel unter den Völkern. Die Stellung der klassischen Propheten des 8. Jahrhunderts v. Chr. zur Aussenpolitik der Könige von Israel und Juda,* Suppl VT 11 (1964).

Driver, S. R., *Introduction to the Literature of the Old Testament* (1913; ⁷1963).

Duhm, B., "Anmerkungen zu den zwölf Propheten," *ZAW* 31 (1911) 81ff.

———. *Das Buch Jesaia,* HKAT 3,1 (1892; ⁵1968).

——. *Israels Propheten* (²1922).

Ehrlich, A., *Randglossen zur hebräischen Bibel* 5 (1912; ²1968).

Ehrman, A., "A Note on Mic 2:7," *VT* 20 (1970) 68f.

Eichrodt, W., *Der Heilige in Israel: Jesaja 1-12 übersetzt und erklärt* (1960).

Eisenbeis, W., *Die Wurzel šlm im Alten Testament*, BZAW 113 (1969).

Eissfeldt, O., *The Old Testament: An Introduction* (1965).

Elliger, K., "Allotment," *IDB* 1, 85f.

——. *Deuterojesaja in seinem Verhältnis zu Tritojesaja*, BWANT 4, 11 (1933).

——. "Die Heimat des Propheten Micha," *Kleine Schriften zum Alten Testament*, ThB 32 (1966) 9ff.

Engell, I., *The Call of Isaiah* (1949).

Ewald, H. G. A., *Die Propheten des Alten Bundes* 1 (²1867-68).

Fey, R., *Amos und Jesaja: Abhängigkeit und Eigenständigkeit*, WMANT 12 (1963).

Fichtner, J., *Obadja, Jona, Micha* (1957).

Fischer, J., *Das Buch Jesaias* 1 HS (1937).

Fohrer, G., art. Σιών, *TNDT* 7, 292ff.

——. *Das Buch Jesaja*, ZBK, vol. 1 (²1960); vol. 2 (²1962).

——. *Introduction to the Old Testament* (1968).

——. "Micha 1," *Das Ferne und nahe Wort: Festschrift L. Rost*, BZAW 105 (1967) 65ff.

——. "Remarks on Modern Interpretation of the Prophets," *JBL* 80 (1961) 313ff.

Fritz, V., "Das Wort gegen Samaria Mi 1,2-7," *ZAW* 86 (1974) 316ff.

Gerlemann, G., art. דם, *THAT* 1, 448ff.

Gerstenberger, E., art. חמד, *THAT* 1, 579ff.

——. "Psalms," *Form Criticism of the Old Testament*, ed. J. Hayes (1974).

——. "The Woe-Oracles of the Prophets," *JBL* 81 (1962) 249ff.

Gottwald, N., *All the Kingdoms of the Earth* (1964).

Gray, G. B., *A Critical and Exegetical Commentary on the Book of Isaiah 1-27*, ICC (1913).

——. "Theophany," *Encyclopaedia Biblica* 4 (1899-1903) 5033ff.

Gray, J., *I and II Kings*, OTL (³1977).

Gressmann, H., *Der Messias*, FRLANT 43 (1929).

Grether, O. *Hebräische Grammatik für den akademischen Unterricht* (²1955).

Gross, K., *Die literarische Verwandtschaft Jeremias mit Hosea*, Diss. Berlin (1930).

Guillaume, A., *Prophecy and Divination Among Hebrews and Other Semites* (1938).

Gunkel, H., "Theophanie," *RGG²* 5, 1130ff.

Gunkel, H., and Begrich, J., *Einleitung in die Psalmen* (²1966).

Habel, N., "The Form and Significance of the Call Narratives," *ZAW* 77 (1965) 310ff.

Hallo, W. W., "Isaiah 28:9-13 and the Ugaritic Abecedaries," *JBL* 77 (1958) 324ff.

Hardmeier, C., *Texttheorie und biblische Exegese. Zur rhetorische Funktion der Trauermetaphorik in der Prophetie*, BEvTh 79 (1978).

Harvey, J., "Le 'Rib-Pattern'," *Biblica* 43 (1962) 172ff.

Hasel, G., *The Remnant* (1972).

Hayes, J. H., "The Tradition of Zion's Inviolability," *JBL* 82 (1963) 419ff.

Hempel, J., *Althebräische Literatur* (1930).

———. "Theophanie," *RGG³* 6, 841ff.

Herbert, A. S., *Isaiah Chapters 1-39*, The Cambridge Bible Commentary (1973).

Hermisson, H.-J., "Zukunftserwartung und Gegenwartskritik in der Verkündigung Jesajas," *EvTh* 33 (1973) 54ff.

Herrmann, S., *A History of Israel in Old Testament Times* (1975).

Hoffmann, H. W., *Die Intention der Verkündigung Jesajas*, BZAW 136 (1974).

Holladay, W. L., "Form and Word-play in David's Lament over Saul and Jonathan," *VT* 20 (1970) 152ff.

Holm-Nielsen, S., "Die Sozialkritik der Propheten," *Festschrift Carl Heinz Ratschow*, ed. O. Kaiser (1976) 7ff.

Hossfeld, F. L. and Meyer, I., *Prophet gegen Prophet. Eine Analyse der alttestamentlichen Texte zum Thema: Wahre und falsche Propheten*, BibB 9 (1973).

Huber, F., *Jahwe, Juda und die anderen Völker beim Propheten Jesaja*, BZAW 137 (1976).

Huffmon, H., "The Covenant Lawsuit in the Prophets," *JBL* 78 (1959) 285ff.

Jahnow, H., *Das hebräische Leichenlied im Rahmen der Völkerdichtung*, BZAW 36 (1923).

Janzen, W., *Mourning Cry and Woe Oracle*, BZAW 125 (1972).

Jenni, E., art. בוא, *THAT* 1, 264ff.

———. "Kommen im theologischen Sprachgebrauch des AT," *Wort-Gebot-Glaube. Festschrift Walter Eichrodt*, AThANT 59 (1970) 251ff.

Jensen, J., *The Use of tôrâ by Isaiah*, CBQ Mon. Series 3 (1973).

Jepsen, A., "Gottesmann und Prophet. Anmerkungen zum Kapitel 1. Könige 13," *Probleme biblischer Theologie,* ed. H. W. Wolff (1971) 177ff.

———. "Kleine Beiträge zum Zwölfprophetenbuch," *ZAW* 56 (1936) 96ff.

———. *Nabi* (1934).

Jepsen, A. and Hanhart, R., *Untersuchungen zur israelitisch-jüdischen Chronologie,* BZAW 88 (1964).

Jeremias, J., art. נביא, *THAT* 2, 7ff.

———. "Die Deutung der Gerichtsworte Michas in der Exilszeit," *ZAW* 83 (1971) 330ff.

———. "Die Vollmacht des Propheten im Alten Testament," *EvTh* 31 (1971) 305ff.

———. *Kultprophetie und Gerichtsverkündigung in der späten Königszeit Israels,* WMANT 35 (1970).

———. "Lade und Zion," *Probleme biblischer Theologie,* ed. H. W. Wolff (1971) 183ff.

———. *Theophanie. Die Geschichte einer alttestamentlichen Gattung,* WMANT 10 (1965).

Johnson, A. R., *The Cultic Prophet in Ancient Israel* (²1962).

———. *Sacral Kingship in ancient Israel* (1967).

Jones, K., "Winged Serpents in Isaiah's Inaugural Vision," *JBL* 76 (1967) 410ff.

Kaiser, O., *Isaiah 1-12: A Commentary,* OTL (1972).

———. *Isaiah 13-39: A Commentary,* OTL (1976).

———. *Einleitung in das Alte Testament* (1969).

vander Kam, J., "The Theophany of Enoch I 3b-7, 9," *VT* 23 (1973) 129ff.

Kedar-Kopfstein, B., art. דם *TDOT* 3, 234ff.

Keil, C. F., *Biblischer Commentar über die zwölf kleinen Propheten,* BC 3,4 (³1888).

Keller, C. A., "Das quietistische Element in der Botschaft des Jesaja," *ThZ* 11 (1955) 81ff.

King, P. J., "Micah," *Jerome Biblical Commentary* (1968) 283.

Kissane, E., *The Book of Isaiah I-XXXIX* (1960).

Klopfenstein, M. A., art. שקר, *THAT* 2, 1010ff.

Knierim, R., art. חטא, *THAT* 1, 541ff.

———. "Exodus 18 und die Neuordnung der mosaischen Gerichtsbarkeit," *ZAW* 13 (1961) 146ff.

———. "The Vocation of Isaiah," *VT* 18 (1968) 47ff.

Koch, K., "Die Entstehung der sozialen Kritik bei den Profeten," *Probleme biblischer Theologie,* ed. H. W. Wolff (1971) 236ff.

————. *The Growth of the Biblical Tradition* (1969).

Köbert, R., "môrad (Mi 1,4) 'Tränke'," *Biblica* 39 (1958) 82f.

Koehler, L., "*Sîg, sîgîm* = Beiglätte," *ThZ* 3 (1947) 232ff.

Kostlin, F., *Jesaia und Jeremia* (1879).

Kraus, H.-J., "Die prophetische Botschaft gegen das soziale Unrecht Israels," *EvTh* 15 (1955) 295ff.

————. *Klagelieder,* BK XX (³1968).

————. *Prophetic und Politik,* Theol. Ex. Heute NF 36 (1952).

Krause, H.-J., "hôj als profetische Leichenklage über das eigene Volk im 8. Jahrhundert," *ZAW* 85 (1973) 15ff.

Küchler, F., *Die Stellung des Propheten Jesaja zur Politik seiner Zeit* (1906).

Kühlewein, J., art. זנה, *THAT* 1, 518ff.

Kuntz, J. K., *The Self-Revelation of God* (1967).

Lambuschagne, C. J., art. קרא, *THAT* 2, 666ff.

Lescow, Th., "Jesajas Denkschrift aus der Zeit des syrisch-ephraimitischen Krieges," *ZAW* 85 (1973) 315ff.

————. "Redaktionsgeschichtliche Analyse von Micha 1–5," *ZAW* 84 (1972) 46ff.

Liedke, G., art. רם, *THAT* 1, 448ff.

Lindblom, J., *Micha literarisch untersucht* (1929).

————. *Prophecy in Ancient Israel* (1962).

————. "Theophanies in Holy Places in Hebrew Religion," *HUCA* 32 (1961) 91ff.

Lippl, J., Theiss, J., Junker, H., *Die Zwölf Kleinen Propheten,* HS VIII, vol. 1 (1937); vol. 2 (1938).

Long, B., "The Effect of Divination upon Israelite Literature," *JBL* 92 (1973) 489ff.

Loretz, O., "Die prophetische Kritik des Rentenkapitalismus. Grundlagen-Probleme der Prophetenforschung," *Ugarit-Forschung* 7 (1975) 271ff.

Lutz, H.-M., *Jahwe, Jerusalem und die Völker,* WMANT 27 (1968).

Maag, V., "Malkût JHWH," Suppl VT 7 (1960) 129ff.

Macholz, G., "Zur Geschichte der Justizorganisation in Juda," *ZAW* 84 (1972) 314ff.

Marsh, J., *Amos and Micah,* Torch Bible Commentaries (⁴1967).

Marti, K., *Das Buch Jesaja,* KHC (1900).

————. *Das Dodekapropheton,* KHC (1904).

Mays, J. L., *Micah, A Commentary,* OTL (1976).

McKenzie, D., "Judicial Procedure at the Town Gate," *VT* 14 (1964) 100ff.

Melugin, R., "Deutero-Isaiah and Form Criticism," *VT* 21 (1971) 326ff.

Mendelsohn, I., "Divination," *IDB* 1, 856ff.

Milgrom, J., "Did Isaiah Prophesy during the Reign of Uzziah?" *VT* 14 (1964) 164ff.

Miller, J. W., *Das Verhältnis Jeremia und Ezechiel sprachlich und theologisch Untersucht* (1955).

Mitton, C. L., "Peace in the OT," *IDB* 3, 704ff.

Morgenstern, J., "Biblical Theophanies," *ZA* 25 (1911) 139ff; *ZA* 28 (1913) 15f.

Mowinckel, S., *Le Décalogue Études d'Histoire et de Philosophie Religieuses...* (1924).

Müller, H. P., "Die kultische Darstellung der Theophanie," *VT* 14 (1964) 183ff.

Münderlein, G., *Kriterien wahrer und falscher Prophetie. Enstehung und Bedeutung im Alten Testament,* Europäische Hochschulschriften XXIII, Bd. 33 (1974).

Muilenburg, J., "The Speech of Theophany," *Harvard Divinity Bulletin* 28 (1964) 34ff.

Nielsen, K., "Das Bild des Gerichtes (Rib-Pattern) in Jes. 1–12," *VT* 29 (1979) 309ff.

Noth, M., *Exodus,* OTL (1962).

——. *Überlieferungsgeschichte des Pentateuchs* (1948).

Nowack, W., *Die kleinen Propheten übersetzt und erklärt,* HK 3, 4 (1897, ³1922).

Osswald, E., *Falsche Prophetie im Alten Testament* (1962).

Overholt, T., *The Threat of Falsehood,* StBTh 2nd Series 16 (1970).

Pedersen, J., *Israel* III–IV (1940).

Perlitt, L., *Bundestheologie im Alten Testament,* WMANT 36 (1969).

——. "Die Vorborgenheit Gottes," *Probleme biblischer Theologie,* ed. H. W. Wolff (1971) 367ff.

Pfeiffer, G., "Entwöhnung und Entwöhnungsfest im Alten Testament. Der Schlüssel zu Jesaja 28,7–13," *ZAW* 84 (1972) 341ff.

Plöger, O., "Priester und Prophet," *ZAW* 63 (1951) 157ff.

Porteous, N., "Jerusalem-Zion: The Growth of a Symbol," *Festschrift W. Rudolph: Verbannung und Heimkehr* (1961) 235ff.

Preuss, H. D., art. בוא, *ThWAT* 1, 536ff.

——. "...ich will mit der sein," *ZAW* 80 (1968) 139ff.

Pritchard, J., *Ancient Near Eastern Texts Relating to the Old Testament* (³1969).

Procksch, O., *Die kleinen prophetischen Schriften vor dem Exil,* Erläuterungen zum Alten Testament 3 (1910).

——. *Geschichtsbetrachtung und geschichtliche Überlieferung bei den vorexilischen Propheten* (1902).

——. *Jesaia* 1, KAT 9 (1930).

——. *Theologie des Alten Testaments* (1950).

Quell, G., art. ἁμαρτία, *TDNT* 1, 267ff.

——. *Wahre und falsche Propheten. Versuch einer Interpretation* (1952).

von Rad, G., art. εἰρήνη, *TDNT* 3, 402ff.

——. *Das formgeschichtliche Problem des Hexateuchs,* BWANT 4, 26 (1938).

——. *Der Heilige Krieg im alten Israel* (⁴1965).

——. "Die falschen Propheten," *Gesammelte Studien zum Alten Testament* 2, ThB 48 (1973) 212ff.

——. *Old Testament Theology,* vol. 1 (1962); vol. 2 (1965).

——. "The Promised Land and Yahweh's Land in the Hexateuch," *The Problem of the Hexateuch and other essays* (1966).

Rast, W., *Tradition History and the Old Testament* (1972).

Rendtorff, R., art. προφήτης, *TDNT* 6, 796ff.

Riessler, P., *Die kleinen Propheten oder das Zwölfprophetenbuch* (1911).

Roberts, J. J. M., "The Davidic Origins of the Zion Tradition," *JBL* 92 (1973) 329ff.

——. "Zion Tradition," *IDBSup* 985ff.

Robinson, Th. and Horst, F., *Die Zwölf Kleinen Propheten,* HAT 1, 14 (³1964).

Rohland, E., *Die Bedeutung der Erwählungstraditionen Israels für die Eschatologie der alttestamentlichen Propheten,* Diss. Heidelberg (1956).

Rost, L., *Israel bei den Propheten,* BWANT 4, 19 (1937).

Rudolph, W., *Micha-Nahum-Habakuk-Zephanja,* KAT 13, 3 (1975).

Saebø, M., "Formsgeschichtliche Erwägungen zu Jes. 7:3–9," *StTh* 14, 1 (1960) 54ff.

Sanders, J., "Hermeneutics in True and False Prophecy," *Canon and Authority,* eds. B. Long; G. Coats (1977).

Sawyer, J. F. A., art. תעה, *THAT* 2, 1055ff.

Scharbert, J., "Das Verbum PQD in der Theologie des AT," *BZ* 4 (1960) 209ff.

Schlesinger, K., "Zur Wortfolge im hebräische Verbalsatz," *VT* 3 (1953) 386ff.

Schmid, H. H., art. בין, *THAT* 1, 305ff.

——. *Gerechtigkeit als Weltordnung,* BHTh 40 (1968).

——. šalôm, "Frieden" im Alten Orient und im Alten Testament (1971).

Schmidt, H., *Die grossen Propheten,* SAT 2, 2 (²1923).

Schmidt, J. M., "Gedanken zum Verstockungsauftrag Jesajas," *VT* 21 (1971) 68ff.

——. "Probleme der Prophetenforschung," *VuF* 17 (972) 39ff.

Schmidt, W. H., "Die Einheit der Verkündigung des Jesajas. Versuch einer Zusammenschau," *EvTh* 37 (1977) 260ff.

——. "מִשְׁכָּן als Ausdruck Jerusalemer Kultsprache," *ZAW* 75 (1963) 91ff.

Schmitt, R., *Zelt und Lade als Thema alttestamentlischer Wissenschaft* (1972).

Schnutenhaus, "Das Kommen und Erscheinen Gottes im AT," *ZAW* 76 (1964) 1ff.

Schreiner, J., *Sion-Jerusalem, Jahwes Königssitz. Theologie der heiligen Stadt im Alten Testament* (1963).

Schüpphaus, J., art. גּוֹל, *ThWAT* 1, 999ff.

Schwantes, M., *Das Recht der Armen,* BET 4 (1977).

Scott, R. B. Y., "The Book of Isaiah," *IB* 5 (1956).

Seebass, H., "Micha ben Jimla," *KuD* 19 (1973) 109ff.

Sellin, E., *Das Zwölfprophetenbuch,* KAT 12, 1 (².³1929-30).

van Selms, A., "Isaiah 28:9-13: An Attempt to Give a New Interpretation," *ZAW* 85 (1973) 332ff.

Smith, J. M. P., *A Critical and Exegetical Commentary on the Books of Micah, Zephaniah, and Nahum,* ICC (1911, reprinted 1965).

von Soden, W., *Grundriss der Akkadischen Grammatik,* AnOr 33 (1952).

Soggin, J. A., "Der prophetische Gedanke über den Heiligen Krieg, als Gericht gegen Israel," *VT* 10 (1960) 79ff.

Stade, G., "Bemerkungen über das Buch Micha," *ZAW* 1 (1881) 161ff.

——. "Mi 1,2-4 und 7,7-20, ein Psalm," *ZAW* 23 (1903) 163ff.

——. "Mi 2,4," *ZAW* 6 (1886) 122f.

——. "Streiflichter auf die Entstehung der jetzigen Gestalt der alttestamentlichen Prophetenschriften (Micha 1,2-4 & 7,7-20)," *ZAW* 23 (1903) 163ff.

——. "Weitere Bemerkungen zu Mi 4. 5," *ZAW* 3 (1883) 1ff.

Stählin, G., art. κοπετός, *ThW* 3, 835ff.

Staerk, W., *Das assyrische Weltreich im Urteil der Propheten* (1908).

Steck, O. H., "Bemerkungen zu Jesaja 6," *BZ* NF 16 (1972) 188ff.

——. *Friedensvorstellungen im alten Jerusalem,* ThSt 111 (1972).

——. *Israel und das gewaltsame Geschick der Propheten,* WMANT 23 (1967).

——. "Prophetische Kritik der Gesellschaft," *Christentum und Gesellschaft,* eds. W. Lohff; B. Lohse (1969) 46ff.

Stolz, F., "Aspekte religiöser und sozialer Ordnung im alten Israel," *ZEE* 17 (1973) 145ff.

———. "Der Streit um die Wirklichkeit in der Südreichsprophetie des 8. Jahrhunderts," *WuD* 12 (1973) 9ff.

———. *Strukturen und Figuren im Kult von Jerusalem,* BZAW 118 (1970).

de Vaux, R., *Ancient Israel: Its Life and Institutions* (1961).

Vetter, D., art. חזה, *THAT* 1, 533ff.

Vollmer, J., *Geschichtliche Rückblicke und Motive in der Prophetie des Amos, Hosea und Jesaja,* BZAW 119 (1971).

Vriezen, Th., "Essentials of the Theology of Isaiah," *Israel's Prophetic Heritage: Essays in honor of J. Muilenburg,* eds. B. W. Anderson and W. Harrelson (1962) 128ff.

von Waldow, E., "Social Responsibility and Social Structure in Early Israel," *CBQ* 32 (1970) 182ff.

———. "Theophanie," *VuF* 4 (1969) 69ff.

Wanke, G., art, נחלה, *THAT* 2, 55ff.

———. *Die Zionstheologie der Korachiten in ihrem traditionsgeschichtlichen Zusammenhang,* BZAW 97 (1966).

———. "Zur Grundlage und Absicht prophetischer Sozialkritik," *KuD* 18 (1972) 1ff.

Warmuth, G., *Das Mahnwort. Seine Bedeutung für die Verkündigung der vorexilischen Propheten Amos, Hosea, Micha, Jesaja und Jeremia,* BET 1 (1976).

Weiser, A., *Das Buch der zwölf Kleinen Propheten* 1, ATD 24 (⁵1967).

———. Einleitung in das Alte Testament (⁵1963).

———. "Zur Frage nach den Beziehungen der Psalmen zum Kult. Die Darstellung der Theophanie in den Psalmen und im Festkult," *Festschrift A. Bertholet* (1950).

Wellhausen, J., *Die Composition des Hexateuchs und der historischen Bücher des Alten Testaments* (²1899).

———. *Die Kleinen Propheten übersetzt und erklärt,* Skizzen und Vorarbeiten 5 (³1898, reprinted 1963).

Westermann, C., *Basic Forms of Prophetic Speech* (1967).

———. "Der Friede im Alten Testament," *Gesammelte Studien* 2, ThB 55 (1974).

———. *The Praise of God in the Psalms* (1965).

———. "Sprache und Struktur der Prophetic Deuterojesajas," *Forschung am Alten Testament, Gesammelte Studien,* ThB 24 (1964) 92ff.

———. "Struktur und Geschichte der Klage im Alten Testament," *Gesammelte Studien,* ThB 24 (1964) 266ff.

Westermann, C. and Albertz, R., art. גלה, *THAT* 1, 418ff.

Whedbee, J. W., *Isaiah and Wisdom* (1971).

Wildberger, H., "Die Völkerwallfahrt zum Zion, Jes. II 1-5," *VT* 7 (1957) 62ff.

——. *Jesaja*, BK X/1 (1972).

Willi-Plein, I., *Vorformen der Schriftexegese innerhalb des Alten Testaments. Untersuchungen zum literarischen Werden der auf Amos, Hosea und Micha zurückgehenden Bücher im hebräischen Zwölfprophetenbuch*, BZAW 123 (1971).

Willis, J. T., "The Genre of Isaiah 5:1-7," *JBL* 96 (1977) 337ff.

——. "The Meaning and Authenticity of Mic. 5:9-14," *ZAW* 81 (1969) 353ff.

——. "Micah 2:6-8 and the 'People of God'," *BZ* NF 14 (1970) 72ff.

——. "Some Suggestions on the Interpretation of Micah 1:2," *VT* 18 (1968) 372ff.

Wolfe, R. E., "The Book of Micah," *IB* 6 (1956).

Wolff, H. W., *Amos' geistige Heimat*, WMANT 18 (1964).

——. *Amos the Prophet: The Man and His Background* (1973).

——. "Das Zitat im Prophetenspruch," *Gesammelte Studien zum Alten Testament*, ThB 22 (1964; ²1973) 36ff.

——. "Der Aufruf zur Volksklage," *Gesammelte Studien*, 392ff.

——. "Die Begründungen der prophetischen Heils- und Unheilssprüche," *Gesammelte Studien*, 9ff.

——. *Dodekapropheton 1. Hosea*, BK XIV/1 (²1965).

——. *Dodekapropheton 2. Joel und Amos*, BK XIV/2 (1969).

——. *Frieden ohne Ende*, BibSt 35 (1960).

——. "Hauptprobleme alttestamentlicher Prophetie," *Gesammelte Studien*, 206ff.

——. *Hosea: A Commentary on the Book of the Prophet Hosea*, Hermeneia (1974).

——. "Hoseas geistige Heimat," *Gesammelte Studien*, 232ff.

——. *Joel and Amos: A Commentary on the Books of the Prophets Joel and Amos*, Hermeneia (1977).

——. *Mit Micha reden* (1978).

——. "Wie Verstand Micha von Moreschet sein prophetisches Amt?" *Congress Volume*, Suppl VT, 1977 (1978).

——. " 'Wissen um Gott' als Urform der Theologie," *Gesammelte Studien*, 182ff.

van der Woude, A. S. "Micah in Dispute with the Pseudo-Prophets," *VT* 19 (1969) 244ff.

———. "Micah II 7a und der Bund Jahwes mit Israel," *VT* 18 (1968) 388ff.

Wright, G. E. "The Lawsuit of God: A Form-Critical Study of Deuteronomy 32," *Essays in honor of James Muilenburg*, eds. B. W. Anderson and W. Harrelson (1962) 26ff.

Würthwein, E., "Der Ursprung der prophetischen Gerichtsrede," *ZThK* 49 (1952) 1ff.

———. "Elijah at Horeb: Reflections on 1 Kings 19:9-18," *Proclamation and Presence* (1970) 152ff.

———. "Zur Komposition von I Reg. 22:1-38," *Das ferne und nahe Wort,* BZAW 105 (1967) 245ff.

Zimmerli, W., *Ezechiel,* BK XIII/1 (1969).

———. "Prophetic Proclamation and Reinterpretation," *Tradition and Theology in the Old Testament,* ed. D. Knight (1977).

Abbreviations

Commentaries are cited in full the first time; thereafter only by author's name. If no biblical text is noted, the reference is to the passage under discussion. Other works are cited by shortened title after the first full citation.

ANET	*Ancient Near Eastern Texts* (³1969), ed. J. B. Prichard
AnOr	Analecta Orientalia
AThANT	Abhandlungen zur Theologie des Alten und Neuen Testaments
ATD	Das Alte Testament Deutsch
BASOR	*Bulletin of the American Schools of Oriental Research*
BC	Biblischer Commentar über das Alte Testament
BDB	F. Brown, S. R. Driver, C. A. Briggs, *Hebrew and English Lexicon of the Old Testament*
BET	Beiträge zur biblischen Exegese und Theologie
BEvTh	Beiträge zur Evangelischen Theologie
BHS	Biblia Hebraica Stuttgartensia
BHTh	Beiträge zur historischen Theologie
Bib	*Biblica*
BibB	Biblische Beiträge
BibSt	Biblische Studien (Neukirchen)
BiOr	*Bibliotheca Orientalia*
BK	Biblischer Kommentar
BWANT	Beiträge zur Wissenschaft vom Alten und Neuen Testament
BZ	*Biblische Zeitschrift*
BZAW	Beihefte zur Zeitschrift für die alttestamentliche Wissenschaft
CBQ	*Catholic Biblical Quarterly*
CBQ Mon. Series	Catholic Biblical Quarterly Monograph Series
CTA	Corpus de tablettes en cunéiformes alphabétiques, A. Herdner
esp.	Especially
EvTh	*Evanglische Theologie*
FRLANT	Forschungen zur Religion und Literatur des Alten und Neuen Testaments
G	Septuagint

Ges.-K.	*Gesenius' Hebrew Grammar,* ed. E. Kautzsch, tr. and rev., A. E. Cowley (²1910)
HAT	Handbuch zum Alten Testament
HS	Die Heilige Schrift des Alten Testaments, eds. F. Feldmann and H. Herkenne
HUCA	*Hebrew Union College Annual*
IB	*The Interpreter's Bible*
ibid.	Ibidem, in the same place or source
ICC	International Critical Commentary
IDB	*Interpreter's Dictionary of the Bible,* ed. G. A. Buttrick
IDBSup	*Supplementary volume to IDB*
JBL	*Journal of Biblical Literature*
JNES	*Journal of Near Eastern Studies*
KAT	Kommentar zum Alten Testament
KBL	L. Koehler and W. Baumgartner, *Lexicon in Veteris Testamenti Libros* (1953; ³1967ff.)
KuD	*Kerygma und Dogma*
KHC	Kurzer Hand-Commentar zum Alten Testament
KS	*Kleine Schriften*
M	Masoretic Text
Meyer	R. Meyer, *Hebräische Grammatik* 2 (²1955)
NICOT	New International Commentary on the Old Testament
OrAntiq	*Oriens Antiquus*
OTL	Old Testament Library
par.	paragraph
Q	Qere
PbTh	*Probleme biblischer Theologie. Gerhard von Rad zum 70. Geburtstag,* ed. H. W. Wolff
RGG³	*Religion in Geschichte und Gegenwart* (³1957–1965)
S	Peshitta
SAT	Die Schriften des Alten Testaments
StTh	*Studia Theologica*
Suppl VT	Supplements to Vetus Testamentum
StBTh	Studies in Biblical Theology
T	Targum
ThB	Theologische Bücherei
TDNT	*Theological Dictionary of the New Testament,* ed. G. Kittel and G. Friedrich
TDOT	*Theological Dictionary of the Old Testament,* ed. G. J. Botterweck and H. Ringgren
THAT	*Theologisches Handwörterbuch zum Alten Testament,* ed. E. Jenni and C. Westermann
ThSt	*Theologische Studien* (Zürich)

ThW	*Theologisches Wörterbuch zum Neuen Testament*, ed. G. Kittel and G. Friedrich
ThWAT	*Theologisches Wörterbuch zum Alten Testament*, ed. G. J. Botterweck and H. Ringgren
ThZ	*Theologische Zeitschrift*
V	Vulgate
VT	*Vetus Testamentum*
VuF	*Verkündigung und Forschung*
WMANT	Wissenschaftliche Monographien zum Alten und Neuen Testament
WuD	*Wort und Dienst*
ZA	*Zeitschrift für Assyriologie*
ZAW	*Zeitschrift für die alttestamentliche Wissenschaft*
ZBK	Zürcher Bibelkommentare
ZEE	*Zeitschrift für evangelische Ethik*
ZThK	*Zeitschrift für Theologie und Kirche*

Index

1. TEXTS

2. SUBJECTS